HEARTS

BROKEN

For Karen,
So happy
you were
here!
Love,
Michele

by

MICHELE PIRAINO

HEARTS BROKEN by MICHELE PIRAINO

First Edition, 2017 Published in the United States of America

ISBN

480-560-4933 Arizona 585-342-0795 New York

mkd@bootstrappublising.net www.Bootstrappublishing.net

For my sister, Dede,

who has always been my faithful

cheerleader.

"All great artists draw from the same

the human heart, which tells us that we are

more alike than we are unalike."

-Maya Angelou

PROLOGUE

I don't know if you believe in heaven and the afterlife, but I have found them to be so. My name is Erica McIntyre. I gave birth to my Martina shortly after I died from a pulmonary embolism. Can you believe it? My daughter is one of the few babies who have survived a post-mortem C-section. She is perfect... at least Dwight and I think so. Dwight is her father. We met in high school, when we were juniors, on the very first day of school. My own father died that day after a heart attack. Dwight was the first and only love of my life. He was shot, the victim of a random act of violence, only a few months before I died. Now I know the answer to Eric Clapton's question in his song "Tears in Heaven." Dwight and I are together again, and it is the same for us in heaven. Oh, did I tell you that Dwight is African-American? I was a privileged white girl living in the suburbs. My father was a doctor. Dwight was poor and lived in the inner city. His father was in prison. Needless to say, our relationship was complicated.

My daughter is now Martina Dee Williams. She is being raised by my mother and her new husband, Brad. My mother used to be what you would call a WASP... you know, a White, Anglo-Saxon Protestant. Brad has really changed her. She is now a wonderful mother to her biracial granddaughter and goes to mass every Sunday. Brad is a gifted neurosurgeon, as was my dad. I think he's a really good guy. He never had any children of his own. He convinced my mom that they should adopt Martina and make their arrangement permanent. My mom, Beverly, was not too sure about starting motherhood all over again at the age of forty-five. For a while, it looked like Dwight's mom, Ruby, would raise Martina. She is ten years younger than my mother. Brad really adores my Martina. It is obvious how much he loves her and how much he loves my mom.

It is September first. Today is Martina's third birthday. My mom, being my mom, who can be kind of strict, told her that she could invite three friends to her party. Next year when she turns four, she will be allowed to invite four friends, and so on. This has always been her rule. Brad hired professional puppeteers, and there is a puppet show going on in the backyard. There is also a popcorn machine like the kind you see at a carnival. Mom made candied apples. The little girls are giggling and having such a good time. My daughter has quite an eclectic group of friends. These are little girls who are in her preschool class.

Lucy is the granddaughter of my mother's friend Pam. My mom used to own a boutique clothing store in the village. Pam was the manager, and later Mom sold her the business. Lucy has two dads, one being Pam's son, Kyle. He is married to his partner, Mark. They had Lucy with the help of a surrogate. She is an adorable little girl with red hair and freckles. She is out-going and laughs so easily. She is very much like her father, Mark. Mark is a pastry chef with a big ego and an outrageous personality. Of course, he made Martina's cake, which itself is a puppet theater. The little girls are enchanted with the cake, and when no one was looking, Lucy took her finger and sampled the frosting.

Martina's friend Ivy is new to her school. She and her father and older sister just moved here from Philadelphia. Her father, Spencer, is a young widower. He is only thirty-seven. He took a job at the University of Rochester Medical Center. He is a pediatrician. Ivy's mother was killed by a drunk driver when Ivy was only two and her sister, Haley, was five. Ivy is quiet and shy. I think she is a little scared of the puppets. She always has one eye out looking for her daddy. She seems like kind of a sad little girl. My Martina is very protective of her and makes sure she always sits next to her.

Martina's third guest is Scarlett. Scarlett is a beautiful child with curly black hair and brilliant blue eyes that always seem to sparkle. You almost don't notice that she is missing most of her right arm. Apparently, she was born with a problem called ABS, which is amniotic band syndrome. When she was developing in her mother's uterus, a heavy band of amniotic tissue amputated her arm below the elbow. Scarlett is adept at doing things with her left arm. Of course, Martina is always looking out for her, too. It appears that it is only Lucy that Martina doesn't worry herself about. Like Martina, Lucy can take care of herself. I think Lucy is probably her best friend.

Martina's family and her friends' families are anything but ordinary.

Chapter 1

Beverly and Brad

Brad finished reading Martina her favorite bedtime story and kissed her good night. "Did you enjoy your party, sweet pea?"

"Oh, I did, Daddy, thank you so much. The puppets were so funny and the cake that Lucy's daddy made was so yummy! I love you, Daddy, you are the best ever." Brad kissed her and turned on her night light. He loved Martina with every ounce of his being. He almost never thought about the fact that she wasn't his in any biological sense.

Brad was a little worried about his wife, though. She didn't seem herself today. Maybe it was because the day Martina was born would always be the day that Erica had died. It was more than that. She didn't look like she felt well. She was making tea in the kitchen. Brad wrapped his arms around her and kissed the back of her neck. "This was a really fun day," he said.

"I know, but I'm exhausted." When she turned around, there were tears in her eyes.

"This has to be such a difficult day for you...probably bittersweet. Am I right?"

"It's more than that. You aren't going to believe this, but I am worried that maybe I could be pregnant."

"Oh, Beverly, you know that's highly unlikely. You're forty-eight years old!"

"Right, but it's not impossible. Up until two months ago, my periods were regular. I have skipped two now. At first I thought it was probably a menopause thing. Menopause was bound to happen sooner or later. But I've been so tired, and today I started feeling the nausea. I threw up twice making those damned candied apples."

"Just take the test, or go see your doctor on Monday." Brad held her and stroked her hair. "I know a pregnancy could come with all kinds of problems, but just maybe it would be okay."

Beverly was becoming unglued. "Brad, listen to this loud and clear: I don't want to have a baby now!" She slammed the door of the kitchen cupboard. "I probably took out the diaphragm too early. Hell, there were times we couldn't wait for me to put it in. What is the matter with us?"

Beverly hated that her doctor would no longer prescribe birth control pills for her. After Erica's death, her doctor had made her have testing to determine if she had the same problem that had put Erica at risk for developing a blood clot. The test showed that she, too, had the gene mutation Factor V Leiden. He had said that she should definitely not take a pill containing estrogen, but new studies have indicated that even progestin only pills could slightly increase her risk for a clot. Considering her age, he didn't think birth control pills were a wise choice at all. He had suggested a copper IUD, which was non-hormonal, or a barrier method. Beverly had heard too many bad stories about IUDs from her friends who had them. She just preferred not to have one. She'd thought a diaphragm would be okay. She had used one before, early in her marriage to Tom.

Now Brad was at a loss for words. He was trying to suppress the flicker of joy that he felt. He didn't want to say the wrong thing, so he said, "Honey, let's just go to bed."

The next morning, he awoke to the sound of Beverly vomiting in the bathroom. He could also hear her sobbing. He went in and held her hair back, then put a cold washcloth on her forehead. Martina wandered into their room. "What's wrong with Mommy?"

"Mommy's tummy is upset. Come on downstairs and I will make you some breakfast." He made them scrambled eggs and toast and later turned on *Sesame Street* for Martina. When he went back upstairs, Beverly was back in bed.

He kissed her forehead. "After I shower, I'll get Martina dressed and take her to church. I'll stop at the drugstore on the way home and pick up that test." Beverly just nodded. She couldn't believe this could be happening.

She took a shower and went downstairs. She put water on for tea. She remembered that ginger tea and toast had always helped to settle Erica's stomach when she was pregnant. *What a mess the month of September has become... first Tom's death, then Erica's, Martina's birthday, and now this?* She didn't want to get ahead of herself, but she knew it was probably so. Her life had been filled with so many improbabilities that had become reality.

Brad came home as she was finishing her tea. "Where's Martina?" she asked.

"We saw Helen at church, and she asked if it was okay if Martina went over to her house for lunch. I thought it was a good idea." Brad really liked Helen, Beverly's former mother-in law. She was an extraordinary lady. He was still amazed

13

that she'd been able to successfully perform CPR on Erica until the EMTs had come. If it weren't for Helen, his Martina would not be here. "Hey, I've got the test. I think you should take it."

Beverly grabbed the bag and headed for the bathroom. The pink line was unmistakable. Beverly's hands were shaking as she looked at the stick. She brought it out to show Brad.

He kissed her. "Beverly, I can't deny it. I'm kind of excited." "Well, I'm not. I feel awful, and I'm scared. Besides, being a mother to Martina is all I can handle now. I'm a grandmother, for Christ's sake. In two years, I will be fifty! This, to me, is not good news."

Brad held her. "It's a beautiful day. Let's take a walk."

"Brad, you know how much I love you and Martina, but this now is all too much. I just don't think I can do it. I really don't want to do it."

"But that's what you thought when Martina was born, but look, she has brought so much joy into our lives. You are a wonderful mother to her."

"Brad, this is different. I can do something about this."

"You want to terminate the pregnancy?" Brad looked devastated, the hurt on his face unmistakable.

Beverly couldn't help it. Terminating the pregnancy was truly what she wanted, but she felt awful about what it might do to Brad. All of a sudden, a big wave of nausea hit, and she vomited behind some bushes.

They walked the rest of the way home in silence. Beverly went to their room to lie down, and Brad went to pick up his little girl and take her to the park. Martina was excited to see that her friend Ivy was also at the park. She ran to the climbing gym to play with her. Brad chatted with her father, Spencer. He was also a doctor at the medical center, and their paths crossed from time to time. Brad thought Spencer was a nice guy but kind of intense. He had heard that he was a recent widower.

Chapter 2

Spencer

A year ago, Spencer had thought he had it all. He'd had an incredibly beautiful wife and two adorable little girls, Haley and Ivy, who were ages five and two. He'd been in private practice with three other pediatricians whom he highly respected. He and Anna, his wife of only seven years, had just finished renovating their home in Conshohocken, a suburb of Philadelphia. Conshohocken was historically a mill town. It was an up-and-coming neighborhood for commercial and residential real estate development. Spencer and Anna had bought a historic brick house, originally built in 1860. Anna was an interior designer. She'd designed and coordinated work on the renovation with a spectacular result. She was able to do much of her work from home, which was just the way she liked it, because being a mother was everything to her.

At the end of August last year, she'd been driving home from meeting a client and was broadsided on the driver's side of her car by a drunk driver merging onto the Schuylkill Expressway. He walked away from the accident, but Anna was killed instantly. The guy's blood alcohol level was .16, twice the legal limit. He had also been smoking marijuana. It was this scumbag's third offense. He'd been driving with a suspended license and taken his mother's car because his own had a mandatory ignition interlock. His mother had sat in court and wept for her son. She'd said that he had emotional problems because he had been bullied in school as a child. She'd said he was a "good boy with a kind heart." He'd still been charged with vehicular homicide and sentenced to ten years in jail.

Spencer felt physically ill whenever he thought about the guy. His mother had come to Anna's funeral.

Anna and Spencer were both from the Philadelphia area. She'd had a much more affluent childhood. Her father was a bank president. Spencer's father was a history teacher and taught in a center city Philadelphia high school. Anna had attended the prestigious Fashion Institute of Technology (FIT) in New York City for her degree in interior design. Spencer had gone to Drexel University in Philadelphia for his undergraduate degree and stayed on for medical school. He'd done his pediatric residency at the University of Rochester Medical Center. He'd opted for the schools that could give him the best scholarships.

Spencer had met Anna in Cape May, N.J. Cape May was a popular vacation spot on the Jersey shore for people living in Philadelphia. Many had vacation homes there. They'd met at a wedding. Anna was a childhood friend of the bride's, and Spencer had gone to Drexel with the groom. It'd been a perfect day for a wedding. It was mid-September... blue sky, sunny, light ocean breeze, and temperature a perfect eighty degrees. Spencer had gone stag, as he was currently unattached. He'd been too busy in the fourth year of his residency to care about women. He'd dated casually but had not had a serious relationship since his senior year as an undergrad, and that had ended badly. Anna had been there with a date. Spencer thought the guy was really a jerk. An hour into the reception, and the guy was already pretty intoxicated. Spencer had been seated at the same table as Anna and her date. He couldn't take his eyes off her, and her date didn't even seem to notice. She was absolutely beautiful. Her hair was chestnut brown and her eyes were hazel. It was her smile. That's what had attracted him most. But of course, she had an incredible body, and she'd looked too good to be true in the strapless yellow dress she was wearing. Anna's date had been up and down to the bar most of dinner. When the band started up after dinner, he was mostly on the dance floor, and not necessarily with Anna.

Spencer was at the bar and saw her walk up to order a drink. "Let me get that for you. It's Anna, right?"

"Right, it's Anna… Anna Nichols." He shook her hand and she flashed him that beautiful smile.

"Spencer Harris… I guess we never got around to introductions at the table. What are you drinking? Is it vodka and tonic?"

"Yes, please. I think my date is AWOL again."

Spencer was feeling a little bold. "Pretty lady, if you were my date, it would never happen." Spencer could see that her eyes lit up when he said it, and she flashed him the smile again. "Is he your boyfriend?" He regretted the question as soon as he asked it. "Oh, God, you don't have to answer that."

"No, that's okay, he's just my date. Jeremy is someone I grew up with. He has always been a clown. The bride was also one of my best friends growing up. She told me Jeremy didn't have a date, either, so she suggested we come together. He's actually pretty harmless. He just likes to party. I don't have a boyfriend." They continued to chat at the bar, getting acquainted. Spencer found her easy to talk to. She seemed very down to earth. Anna lived in the city of Philadelphia with a roommate she'd met in college. They were trying to start their own interior design business. Until it became profitable, she was also working at Pottery Barn. She was staying at her parents' beach house in Cape May this weekend. She asked him a lot about his pediatric residency, his family, and life growing up in Philadelphia. Spencer could easily figure out that she had had a much more affluent upbringing.

The band was awesome and the dance floor was always full. One of Spencer's favorite songs started, "When a Man Loves a Woman," and he took Anna's hand and led her out onto the dance floor. The singer was a big black guy who sounded just like Percy Sledge. Being that it was a slow song, he got to hold her close. Her hair was soft and smelled terrific. They stayed on the dance floor until the band finished its set. Jeremy wandered over as they were walking back to the bar.

"Dude, are you moving in on my date?" He put his arm around Anna.

"We were just dancing, Jeremy, as I noticed you have been dancing, but not with me most of the night."

A dark look came over Jeremy's face. He glared at Spencer. "I think we should talk about this outside," he said.

Spencer smiled at Anna and shrugged. He followed him out.

As soon as they walked out the door, he punched Spencer in the face. He hit him square on the cheekbone. "Just leave Anna alone," he said. "I don't know who the fuck you think you are!" Spencer was taken completely by surprise. He'd thought the guy was goofy but not a fighter.

When Jeremy walked back in, Anna could see him rubbing his fist. "What did you do?" she gasped.

"I just taught him some manners." He was clearly at that point of intoxication when a person couldn't reason with him. Anna walked out to check on Spencer. It was easy to see that for sure he would have a shiner in the morning.

"I'll get some ice," she said.   The wedding was at an old Victorian mansion.   Anna brought out the ice, and they sat on a bench in the garden and talked some more. She asked him if he was going back to Rochester the next day. He said that he was planning on leaving by early afternoon.

"Can I take you to breakfast?" Spencer asked.

"I'd like that," she said.   She gave him the address of her parents' house.   Spencer leaned over and kissed her.   She for sure was kissing him back.   They walked a little in the garden, and he kissed her again.

"I really enjoyed meeting you, Anna. Will you get home okay?"

"Some of my high school friends are going out after the wedding.   I'll be fine.   I go way back with some of these people."

"Okay then, I'll see you tomorrow.   Is ten o'clock okay?"   She kissed him on his uninjured cheek and walked away.   She turned around and smiled.

I'm in love, he thought.

Anna and Spencer had a very casual breakfast the next morning and later took a walk on the beach.   Spencer hated that he might not ever see Anna again. They exchanged phone numbers and email addresses, and he walked her home.   He kissed her and asked if maybe they could get together over Thanksgiving weekend.   Spencer knew that he was not on call the entire weekend, and that he was planning on going to Philadelphia to stay with his dad.   His father was a widower who'd never remarried.   His mother had died from breast cancer when Spencer was in high school.   Spencer was the youngest of three boys. His older brothers were married with kids. One of his brothers lived in Philadelphia, the other in Baltimore. They would all be together for Thanksgiving.

They had met up the following Thanksgiving weekend on Friday night. Anna's roommate had been out of town, and she'd had the place to herself. Spencer had taken her to dinner and gone back to her apartment. They'd had their clothes off in no time and hadn't left her apartment until Sunday morning. Spencer had known he should be spending time with his dad, but he just couldn't tear himself away from Anna. So was the beginning of their whirlwind romance.

They'd visited each other as much as they could on weekends either in Rochester or Philadelphia. They'd been engaged by May and married in September, a year after they'd met. Their wedding had been in Cape May. Anna had insisted on booking the same band for the wedding so that "When a Man Loves a Woman" could be their wedding song. Anna's parents had money. The wedding had been at Congress Hall, a prestigious seaside resort. It was a historic landmark. She was an incredibly beautiful bride. Their lives together had been a fairy tale but one with an abrupt and sad ending when Anna died in the car wreck.

Spencer had tried so hard after Anna died, but he just couldn't seem to climb out of that dark hole of grief and depression and function as a doctor and single father of two little girls. He couldn't get it together. Anna had done everything. Spencer's life didn't work without her. He was struggling. His kids were struggling. When Anna had been alive, their housekeeper, Flora, had come to clean once a week. She was a sweet and capable woman in her late fifties. Spencer had convinced her to take on the role of nanny. She'd come first thing in the morning and got Haley on the bus for kindergarten and stayed to care for Ivy until Spencer got home from work. Ivy had been only two and wasn't old enough for preschool. Haley was an outgoing little girl. She continued to talk about her mother all the time but seemed to accept the fact that she had died. Spencer had her seeing a psychologist, and he thought it was helping her to adjust. Ivy just cried a lot. She'd become very withdrawn. Flora had tried very hard, but she couldn't seem to reach her. Spencer knew that Ivy was lagging behind in her speech and her socialization.

Ivy would brighten up a little when her daddy got home, but most of the time Spencer did not have the emotional energy to deal with her. Some days Ivy had cried so hard when he was ready to leave for work that he couldn't bear to leave her. The partners in his pediatric practice had always covered him without question, but he'd known he wasn't pulling his share. He'd felt guilty about neglecting work, then guilty about neglecting his kids, and he was just so damned lonely. He was busy but never had time for himself. Anna was everywhere, but his house wasn't a home without her.

His father had been a big support to him. He was an exceptional grandfather. He could even coax Ivy out of her shell. Everyone had tried to help. There was sometimes too much help. Anna's mother had something to say about everything. She was forever criticizing Flora. Flora was doing her best, but she wasn't Anna. Spencer thought that his mother-in-law had been a little jealous about the role that Flora was playing in his daughters' lives. Anna had two sisters, and like Spencer, she was the youngest. Anna's sisters were great and always there for him, but they were busy with their own kids. Spencer's brothers were great at getting him out for some kind of sporting event or a beer, but they didn't get it.

He'd gotten an email from a friend in his residency program and learned that the University of Rochester was recruiting a physician to take on the role of medical director in their ambulatory pediatric practice. The role included supervision of the residents. Spencer had always liked Rochester and thought it was a nice place to raise a family. The university was expanding its pediatric department. They were pushing to make it a free-standing children's hospital. Maybe this was what he needed to jump-start his life. Maybe he could start his new life if he wasn't surrounded by the painful memories of the past.

He'd asked one of his sisters-in-law to take the girls so that he could fly to Rochester for an interview. He'd been hired. His job would start in July, when the new interns arrived. He'd gone back to look at houses and bought a great house in one of Rochester's suburbs, a quaint village along the Erie Canal. He'd interviewed nannies. This nanny was younger, so maybe she would have more energy for dealing with Ivy. He'd really thought the move would be good for him and the girls. Haley had been a little reluctant about moving, but she was an accepting and easygoing child. She'd been excited that she would have a new house, a new room, and a new school. Ivy hadn't seemed to care. Spencer's father had been very supportive but Anna's mother not at all. Spencer knew how much she loved the girls, but her constant interference had been making his life more difficult. The process had been stressful, but Spencer had sold his house and made the move. It had gone more smoothly than he'd anticipated. He was beginning to feel settled in. He really missed his family and their support, but he was meeting some really nice people.

Chapter 3

Kyle and Mark

Lucy asked one of her daddies to get down on the floor with her to play Barbies. That would have to be Kyle, because Mark was on the couch with a heating pad on his back. He had just taken a Vicodin. This was the case more and more. Mark had developed chronic back pain. His MRI showed that he had spinal stenosis. Constantly being on his feet at the bakery didn't help. The days that he worked on a particularly big project, like an elaborate wedding cake, he came home in excruciating pain. Mark had always been such a fun and easygoing guy, but the pain was changing his personality. He was having problems with depression. Mark's problems were putting a strain on his marriage. Mark was fifty-one... fifteen years older than Kyle. Their age difference had never seemed to matter, but now Kyle was wondering if they could continue to make their marriage work.

They had been friends for a long time before they'd started dating. He had never known anyone like Mark. Kyle had struggled with his sexuality until late in his twenties. He'd met Mark and was finally able to figure it out. Mark was kind and smart and so much fun to be around. He was good-looking, in a sexy-older-guy kind of way. Kyle had fallen very much in love with him. Mark had wanted to marry Kyle before he got away. They had been so happy, and Mark was anxious to start a family. He'd convinced Kyle that he'd waited a long time to find the love of his life, and if he wanted to be a father, he should get to it. He wasn't getting any younger. Mark could talk Kyle into anything. Kyle wanted children, too. Kyle's mother had always been so supportive. They could give her the grandchild she so desperately wanted.

Kyle and Mark had found a surrogate who'd agreed to not only donate her womb but also her egg. It kept things simple, because it only involved an intrauterine insemination when she was ovulating. It, however, was very costly. They had put an ad in a few college newspapers. Melanie had been a senior at Syracuse University. She was already deeply in debt with her undergraduate education. She'd wanted to go to law school. When she'd seen the ad, she'd known this was her ticket. She really liked Kyle and Mark, and they liked her. She was healthy, intelligent, and had above-average looks. She wasn't currently involved in a relationship, and she was estranged from her family. Her parents were divorced and had gone their separate ways when Melanie had gone to college. Melanie had felt abandoned by them. Their divorce had cost them so much money that they wouldn't or couldn't help their daughter with college. She'd had to rely on scholarships and student loans.

Melanie had wanted to take some time off to study for the LSATs. She could study and work part time while she was pregnant. Hopefully the insemination would work, and she could start law school in another year. Melanie was liberal-minded. This seemed like a good plan, and she could also help a couple who really wanted a child when the deck was stacked against them. She thought Kyle and Mark would be wonderful parents. She felt good about her decision. She was always a champion for the underdog.

Melanie had become pregnant after the first insemination. They'd used a combination of Mark's and Kyle's sperm. Melanie had had a completely normal pregnancy and uncomplicated delivery. Kyle and Mark had legally adopted

Lucy, and it was decided that Melanie would no longer be involved in Lucy's life. The three of them had agreed that would be the best for all concerned. Kyle and Mark felt blessed to have Lucy. She brought so much joy to their lives. Kyle had always harbored a secret fear that somehow he and Mark could lose Lucy. Now Kyle was worried about Mark and his marriage.

Chapter 4

Ruby and Mario

Sometimes Ruby couldn't believe her good fortune. She still mourned for her son, Dwight, and she always would, but she had a new life. She had Mario, who was a wonderful husband and father to her girls. She had a new stepson, Anthony, who was a good-natured, sweet boy, and she had new life stirring inside of her. Mario and Ruby had just left the doctor's office after having her eighteen-week ultrasound. She was having another set of twins, this time a boy and a girl. They got into the car and Ruby was still crying her tears of joy. "Oh, sweet Jesus… Mario, can you believe this?" He kissed her. "Baby, it's all good." They had known about the twin pregnancy since her first trimester ultrasound five weeks ago, but they didn't want to say anything to anyone until they knew that everything looked okay. Ruby was anxious about the pregnancy, although she was feeling great and everything was going well.

Mario was a registered nurse. He worked in the OR. He had a leadership position and made fairly good money, but he wanted more… not only more money but more for his career. He had been thinking of about going back to school to become a certified nurse anesthetist. When he'd found out about Ruby's pregnancy, he'd really wanted to move forward with his plan. They would have five children. He could significantly increase his earning power. He read that he could make more than one hundred fifty thousand dollars a year. If he continued to work full time, he knew the university would pay for his education. There was a program at the State

University of Buffalo. He'd applied and was accepted. He'd just started classes. He was able to arrange his schedule so that he would be free for his classes. The trade-off was he had to work a lot of weekends. Ruby was so proud of Mario and was supportive. She knew they would need the money.

Ruby was still working. She told Mario that she had worked too hard to finish school and become an RN to stop now. They needed the money, and she wanted to be able to take more time after the babies were born. Ruby planned to work as far into the pregnancy as her doctor would allow. She'd gone to thirty-six weeks with the girls and hoped to do as well this time. She was, however, twelve years older. She was thirty-nine. She was happy that one of the babies was a boy. She missed having a son. She wondered what Dwight would have said about all this. He would be twenty-one now. Ruby could almost hear him say, "Ma, it will be all right, now." Ruby looked wistfully out the car window as Mario drove them home from her appointment. He could see that she was crying again, but he could tell they weren't tears of joy this time. Since she'd become pregnant, Ruby had become emotionally labile. She'd been so strong after Dwight was shot, but now she was grieving again. "Oh, God, I miss my baby," she said.

Ruby wanted to have Beverly and Brad come over for a barbeque to celebrate Martina's birthday. She'd had to work the day of the little birthday party that Beverly had for Martina's preschool friends, and she wasn't able to go. The twins had gone to help out, and they'd filled Ruby in on all the details. It sounded over the top. Brad spoiled Martina even more than Beverly did. Ruby liked Brad, though. She would never forget all the nice things that he'd done for Dwight, and if her son wasn't here to raise his daughter, she was happy that a fine man like Brad had stepped in to be her daddy. Beverly and Brad didn't know about Ruby's pregnancy yet.

It was a lovely evening. Ruby put out a feast. They had barbequed chicken, corn bread, potato salad, and grilled vegetables. Ruby made a peach cobbler for dessert. She brought it out with three candles, and they all sang "Happy Birthday" again. Whenever Martina was around, everyone had a good time. She was such a happy child. Her antics were priceless.

Ruby noticed that Beverly didn't eat much, and she wasn't drinking. Normally she would have been on at least her third glass of Chardonnay by now. She looked tired. Ruby knew that September was an incredibly hard month for her, because it was the month that she'd lost her husband and then her daughter a year later. Ruby thought that probably Beverly wasn't herself tonight because of all that.

Mario tapped his glass with a knife and said he had an announcement to make. "Ruby and I have some news that we can't keep secret anymore. We are expecting twins…a boy and a girl. The babies are due on February fourth."

Beverly smiled, but she also cried. Brad got up to shake Mario's hand and give Ruby a hug. Ruby's girls, Danielle and Denise, had been told the night before. They sat there with big smiles on their faces. Danielle said, "Miss Martina, you are going to have another auntie and uncle very soon!" Of course, she didn't understand the "auntie and uncle" part, so Denise said, "Grandma Ruby is having a baby, no, two babies!"

Ruby had always been "Grandma Ruby" and Beverly was "Mommy." They all knew that now that Martina was three, they would probably have to start explaining their unique family configuration.

"Hooray!" She jumped up and down, clapping her hands. She climbed up on Ruby's lap to give her a hug and a kiss. Mario grabbed Martina and twirled her in the air.

Brad raised his glass. "To Ruby and Mario... Congratulations, this is wonderful news!" Beverly finally composed herself enough so that she could hug Ruby. "Oh, Ruby, I am so happy for you." She kissed Mario on the cheek and gave each of the girls a hug. That's all she could manage, because she was feeling a little nauseous all of a sudden. Brad knew it was time to go home.

Brad had to pull over on the way home, and Beverly vomited into a plastic grocery bag that Brad brought in the car. Beverly said, "I noticed that Ruby has put on weight, but I had no idea that she was pregnant. Oh, God, twins. I hope everything will be okay."

Brad smiled. "There must be something in the water boosting the fertility of grandmothers."

"Not funny, Brad!" Beverly started crying again.

"Daddy, why are you making Mommy cry when she doesn't feel good? Say that you are sorry!"

"I'm sorry," he said contritely

When they got home, Brad put Martina to bed. "Daddy, take Mommy to the doctor tomorrow. Her tummy is still sick."

He kissed her good night. "I will, sweet pea, don't worry."

Beverly went right to bed. Brad went back downstairs and poured himself a glass of Scotch. As happy and hopeful as he was about Beverly's pregnancy, he was also extremely worried.

Chapter 5

Brad took the morning off. He knew he needed to go with Beverly to her doctor's appointment. Her ob-gyn doc was an older man. Brad was surprised he wasn't retired already. Dr. Renaldi was well respected in the medical community. He was a perinatologist, and once the chairman of the ob-gyn department at the University of Rochester before he'd stepped back down into private practice. He had delivered both of Beverly's children. Brad knew she was fond of him and trusted him completely. He was a charming man, short in stature, with white hair and twinkly eyes.

Brad and Beverly sat across from him at his desk. He shook both of their hands and smiled. "Well, this is surprising news," he said. "I guess that diaphragm didn't work out too well for you."

"I have to be honest, I wasn't really careful about always using it. I kind of thought the chances of me becoming pregnant at age forty-eight were pretty slim," Beverly said.

"More important is how you two feel about this news. Beverly, you first, what are you thinking?"

"I am shocked, and to be completely honest, not happy to be pregnant at this time in my life. I'm afraid, too. What if something is wrong with our baby? I remember how stressful it was when our Johnny was born with his heart defect. I have buried two children. I know that, at my age, there is a good chance that the baby could have some kind of birth defect. I am worried about my own health. I have a three-year-old at home. I don't know how I can be pregnant and take care of

Martina, too. I just don't have the energy…physically or emotionally." Dr. Renaldi passed her the box of tissues.

"And you, Brad, what's on your mind?"

Brad took hold of Beverly's hand. "I can't deny that I'm excited about the possibility of having a biological child of my own, but please understand, I love our Martina like she was my biological daughter. But of course, I'm worried about Beverly. I want her to remain in good health, and in this matter, her feelings trump mine."

"Well, let's first see if this is a viable pregnancy." Dr. Renaldi led them into another exam room to perform an ultrasound. Beverly couldn't help but think that it wasn't that long ago that she'd been in this very room with Erica when she had her ultrasound for Martina. It was all so overwhelming. Brad could see that she was trembling. He held her hand as the doctor put the ultrasound gel on her abdomen. "Beverly, there is cardiac activity, and the fetal heart rate is about 160 beats per minute. I would say that the fetus has a gestational age of eight weeks and four days. Your due date is April eleventh. I'll give you two a moment, and then you can join me back in my office."

Beverly was crying. "Oh, Brad, what are we going to do? Grab that basin for me. I think I'm going to be sick." Brad did his best to comfort her, but he had his own feelings to deal with. He'd thought that, considering Beverly's age, they would probably see an empty gestational sac. Not so; there was a fetus with cardiac activity. They had some tough decisions to make.

They sat with Dr. Renaldi as he explained their options. Beverly was still trembling and sat with a basin on her lap.

"Beverly, it is understandable if you decide that terminating this pregnancy is better for your emotional health. Pregnancy at your age also puts your physical health at risk. However, you have no current medical problems, other than the Factor V Leiden blood-clotting risk. For that problem, you would have to take daily injections of a medication to prevent clotting. You have a healthy weight and normal blood pressure, which is favorable, because women over thirty-five, and especially over forty, have a higher chance of developing pre-eclampsia and gestational diabetes. At age forty-eight, there is a high rate of miscarriage... over sixty percent."

"Of course, there are fetal concerns, as well, because your eggs are older and of poorer quality. You have a much higher risk of carrying a fetus with a genetic problem or birth defect. Probably most people think about Down's syndrome, but there are many other problems associated with chromosome abnormalities. I won't dwell on that, because you already said that you were aware of that. I can give you percentages if you want, or show you some graphs, but that might just complicate your decision-making. You can be on the good side of bad numbers or the bad side of good numbers."

Brad listened carefully so that he could hear it the way it was explained to Beverly. As soon as Beverly had told him about the possibility of pregnancy, he had done an extensive search of information on his own. It had been a long time since his obstetrics rotation in medical school. He'd never realized how fascinating maternal-fetal medicine could be. So many advancements had been made, and yes, older women were having successful pregnancies all the time.

"What you might want to do is a procedure called a CVS, which is a chorionic villus sampling. We can do it in about two weeks. It only takes a few minutes, and we can do the procedure right here in the office. With ultrasound guidance, we pass a needle through your abdomen and then through your uterus and collect cells from the placenta. This can also be done by putting a catheter through your cervix. The genetic material is studied for abnormal chromosomes or genetic diseases. It cannot detect all birth defects. Results take about two weeks. The risks are pregnancy loss, infection, and bleeding. If you know that the fetus has normal chromosomes, it might make your decision easier. If you do decide to terminate the pregnancy, it will involve a surgical procedure because you will be greater than eight weeks' gestation. I know this is a difficult and complicated decision. Take your time making it. In the meantime, I am going to give you a prescription for Phenergan, which is a medication that can help to control your nausea. Try to rest and drink all the water you can. If you can keep a prenatal vitamin down, that would be helpful. Now you and Brad can call me anytime for any problems or further questions." He shook their hands and went on to his next patient.

They talked a little on the ride home. "Oh, Brad, this is such a tough decision. I hate that we have to make it."

"Beverly, it's really your decision. I love you and I will support you unconditionally, regardless of what you decide. I have a few hours before I have to be back at the hospital, and you said that Pam is picking up Lucy and Martina at school for a playdate. Let's go and talk while the information is still fresh in our minds. It's a beautiful morning. We can find a quiet bench along the canal. I can run into Wegmans and get that prescription filled."

Beverly waited in the car. Wouldn't you know it, she saw a young man collecting carts in the parking lot. He had Down's syndrome. Then she recognized him. His mother had brought him to Dwight's wake. Dwight's boss had spoken of him in his eulogy at the funeral. Dwight had been a friend and mentor to him. She remembered that his name was Gary. *Oh, God, will my child have Down's syndrome or something much worse?* She also knew that people born with Down's syndrome sometimes had heart defects. Then she thought about her son, Johnny, and losing him because of his heart defect... Tetralogy of Fallot. She realized that even if this baby was normal, she would be sixty-six when he or she graduated from high school. *How normal is that for a kid?*

Brad came back with the prescription, a box of saltines, an herbal iced tea for her, and a coffee for him. Beverly knew she was lucky to have such a loving and thoughtful husband. She did love him, but she wasn't sure she wanted to have his baby, not at this time in her life anyway.

Beverly sat down on the bench and took the anti-nausea pill. She told Brad about seeing Gary and how ironic it was that she saw him that very morning. He reached out to hold her. "Oh, honey, I'm sorry. That must have been difficult for you." She tried to tell him everything that was on her mind. The Phenergan was working and had helped to compose her. She was able to talk without becoming too emotional. Then she knew there was something she needed to tell Brad. It was something big that she had never shared with him. Beverly needed to tell him about the abortion that she'd had in college.

"Brad, I have an ugly secret that I've told to only a few people, but now I know I need to tell you. When I was a freshman in college, I went to a mixer at a fraternity house. I had too much to drink. I was flirting with this one guy all night. He seemed like a nice guy. He asked me to go up to his room, and I went. I wouldn't say he forced himself on me, but he was aggressive and persistent. The next day, I woke up with a wicked hangover and a lot of regrets. When I saw him on campus after that night, he barely acknowledged me. A month later, I found out I was pregnant. I went to Planned Parenthood and spoke to a counselor. She said that I needed to forgive myself, and that one mistake didn't have to ruin my life. I had an abortion. At the time, it seemed like the right thing to do. Whenever I think about it, though, I always feel a little guilt and remorse." She looked into Brad's eyes but couldn't read him.

"Thank you for sharing that." It was all he said. Brad knew that his wife was a complicated woman, but this took him by surprise. Now he was painfully aware that she really might decide to terminate their pregnancy.

"Brad, I love you, and I hope you know ten years ago, I would have wanted to have your baby. I just don't know if I can do it now."

"Okay," he said. "You still have time to think before you make a final decision. I mean what I said to Dr. Renaldi. It has to be your decision."

That night, Beverly was actually able to prepare and eat a normal meal. She gave Martina a bath, read her a story, and put her to bed. Maybe the medication was helping her to feel better. Maybe it was because everything was out in the open now, and she and Brad had had such a good conversation. When she got into bed, she reached out for Brad. They made love... something they hadn't done for a few weeks. She fell asleep his arms.

Just before dawn, Beverly startled and awoke. Her heart was racing. She'd had a horrible dream. In her dream, she heard

Martina calling out to her. "Mommy, come outside and meet my new friend." Martina and a little boy were riding their tricycles in the driveway as Brad sat in a lawn chair and watched them. From behind, the little boy looked like Johnny, but after he turned around, she could see that he had Down's syndrome. When he smiled, there was a dusky blue color around his mouth. Then she noticed that someone had written with sidewalk chalk on the driveway. It said "BABY KILLER".

Brad was already in the shower. The dream was too disturbing to even talk about. She remembered how Erica had loved to write with chalk on the driveway. Once when she was really angry with Beverly, she'd written, *I hate you Mommy.* Beverly had never forgotten it. Erica had become angry with Beverly when she'd suggested to her that she might want to have an abortion. Erica had said that she would never kill a baby. She also remembered how frightening it was when Johnny would be playing and became short of breath. His color would turn that dusky blue. Erica would say he was turning into a smurf. *God, what an ugly dream!*

Brad walked out of the bathroom with a towel around him. He came over and kissed her. "Brad, I am going to call Dr. Renaldi this morning and schedule the CVS." He kissed her again. "I'm glad," he said.

Chapter 6

Spencer was trying to finish up in clinic so he could get home. Tonight, was the family picnic at Ivy's preschool. One of the residents was holding him up, because he had a patient who wouldn't hold still so that she could be examined. Spencer didn't think this particular resident would ever make it in pediatric medicine. He was impatient and became easily frustrated, but in fairness, it was only his first year. Sometimes Spencer wondered who was most difficult... the patients, their parents, or his residents. He was so ready to get out of there. He hated going to these events as a single parent. Anna was always so good at these things. She would have made some incredible dish to pass. Spencer knew he had to stop at Wegmans and pick up something.

Lizzie had the kids dressed and ready to go. So far, she was working out pretty well. She had graduated from college last year with her degree in elementary education. She was unable to land a teaching job, so she'd decided to start work on her master's degree and take a job as a nanny. The girls seemed to like her, and she seemed to have a good way with Ivy. She really didn't cook, though. Spencer was hoping to have someone who would get dinner started before he came home. He was working on his own culinary skills. He left a list for the housekeeper who came once a week. She did the shopping, and he did his best with the cooking. His dad was a great cook. He needed his dad to teach him how to prepare some simple meals. Right now, his repertoire was boxed mac and cheese, hot dogs, hamburgers, chicken fingers, and grilled cheese. They ordered pizza a lot. Sometimes they did breakfast for dinner. He made the kids pancakes or scrambled eggs. On the nights he came home really tired, they just had cereal. *Anna would not be happy.* He knew he had to get more fruits and veggies into the kids' diets.

Spencer had met some of the other parents already. He really liked Brad Williams. He thought that he was very down-to-earth…not at all arrogant like some surgeons could be. He did a fair amount of pediatric neurosurgery. He knew that Brad and his wife were older than the other parents. He had heard that Martina was actually his wife's granddaughter, and Martina was biracial. He didn't know the whole story.

One of Ivy's friends had a really pretty mommy. Her little girl, Scarlett, was adorable. Spencer was in awe of how well this little girl functioned with only one arm. The other children just seemed to accept her the way she was. Scarlett strongly resembled her mother. She, too, had curly black hair and bright blue eyes. Scarlett's mother was petite. She had a nice smile. That was always the first thing he noticed about a woman. Tonight, she smiled at him. She was by herself. He didn't notice a ring on her finger. She came over to introduce herself. "You're Ivy's daddy, right? I'm Bridget O'Connell, Scarlett's mom." Spencer shook her hand. "Spencer Harris… It's nice to meet you."

"I know you are the new medical director in the peds clinic. I've heard some really good things about you. I'm a nurse in the NICU."

"Well, I'm glad we finally met, then," Spencer said. He thought that maybe she was hitting on him a little. He kind of liked it. He wondered if she was single…no ring and no partner with her tonight. Maybe she'd forgotten to put her ring back on after work. Wearing rings was frowned upon for NICU nurses because of the infectious disease risk, and preemies had such tender, fragile skin. Maybe her partner or husband couldn't make it tonight.

Brad Williams walked over. "I'm glad you two finally met," he said. "Bridget is a fine nurse. She's taken excellent care of some of my tiniest patients." Bridget smiled and asked if Beverly had come tonight.

"No, she hated to miss it, but she wasn't feeling well. She made some incredible brownies for tonight. Make sure you get one." His daughter, Martina, ran up to him and pulled his hand. "Daddy, my friends and I need someone to give us a push."

"He's a nice guy," Spencer said.

"He really is. I know you lost your wife not that long ago and you moved here from Philadelphia. Scarlett and I thought maybe you and Ivy could come over for dinner some night. It's probably difficult being a single father in a new town. Maybe you could use a break."

"That's really nice. We'd like that, but actually I have two daughters. Ivy's sister, Haley, is six.

"I would love to have all of you. Would this Saturday work? I'm off this weekend."

"Okay, that works for us, too. Is your address in the school directory?"

"It is. Do you want to come around five? The kids can play a little while before dinner."

"Thank you. I will see you then." The line was forming for dinner. Bridget and Spencer went to round up their kids to help them serve up their plates.

41

Ivy wanted to eat with Martina, so Spencer and the girls went to sit with her and Brad. Spencer and Brad talked. Spencer still wasn't certain that Bridget was single. For all he knew, he could show up for dinner, and her husband would also be there. He thought that maybe Brad might know. He decided to ask him.

"I don't know for sure," he said, "but I bet my wife knows." Spencer told Brad about the dinner invitation and how he kind of hoped that she was unattached. Brad smiled. "I'll ask Beverly and send you an email. She really is nice and very cute."

This was the first time Spencer even had a thought about seeing another woman since Anna had died. Maybe it was too soon, but he was so lonely. Spencer couldn't deny that he was attracted to Bridget.

Bridget was thrilled that Spencer had accepted her invitation. She told Scarlett on the way home from the picnic. Scarlett was elated that her new friend was coming over for dinner and a playdate. Bridget was hopeful. Her track record with men wasn't so great. She had dated the same guy all through high school, and they'd even decided to stay in town to attend community college together. Just before graduation, he'd told her that he had met someone else. He'd broken up with Bridget and married his new girlfriend shortly after graduation. His new bride had been pregnant. Bridget had been devastated. She'd dated several men after college, but no one seriously until she'd met Kurt, Scarlett's father.

She'd moved in with Kurt after about six months. Bridget had been totally infatuated with him. Kurt was wild and sexy... sexy in a Ryan Gosling sort of way. Her friends always said he was hot. He was so different than the guy she'd dated all through high school and college. Kurt was a professional baseball player. He worked as a bartender in the off-season. When Bridget had found out she was pregnant, Kurt said he was happy, and Bridget believed him. He hadn't wanted to get married, because he said their relationship was fine the way it was. When they'd had the ultrasound that found Scarlett's amputated arm, it was too much for Kurt. He'd told Bridget he wasn't prepared to be a father and especially not to a handicapped child. He would help to support their daughter financially but did not want to be involved in her life. He'd moved out a week later and had not even returned for Scarlett's birth. Bridget never accepted any of his calls, and she certainly didn't want any of his money. He'd turned out to be an incredibly selfish bastard, and she wanted nothing to do with him.

Bridget's father had been furious. She was afraid of what her father might do if he ever saw Kurt. Her parents were so supportive. They loved Scarlett and helped Bridget navigate single parenthood. They lived close by.

Bridget decided that she would make spaghetti and meatballs Saturday night because it was kid-friendly and who didn't like it? Besides, it was one of her best dishes. Her mother was Italian, and she'd watched her make meatballs and sauce since she was ten years old. She would make an apple pie, too. She wanted to go all out. She didn't dare say anything to the other nurses she worked with, but she told her mother.

"Oh, honey, be careful. Men who lose their wives are so needy and lonely. You don't want to be the rebound woman in his life."

"Mom, it's not really a date. He is coming with his two daughters. He just seems like such a nice guy, that's all. It would be nice to even have him for a friend. I hardly know him, but I would like to get to know him."

Finally, it was Saturday. The food was pretty much under control. Scarlett watched a movie on her bed, while Bridget took a nice, relaxing bath. Bridget wanted to look her best, taking time with her hair and makeup. She decided to wear her skinny jeans with a powder-blue cotton sweater and silver dangling earrings. She wasn't usually nervous about men, but she was kind of anxious about tonight.

Spencer and the girls arrived right on time. He, too, was a little nervous. He should have asked her if he could bring something. He'd stopped and bought a bouquet of sunflowers and two bottles of wine... red and white. Then he thought maybe the flowers were too much. Haley wanted to carry them and give them to whomever was Ivy's friend's mommy. Haley was more excited than Ivy about going. That was no surprise. Ivy was still so very shy. Spencer was relieved that Brad had let him know that Bridget was, indeed, single. He really didn't know much else about her, other than she was a NICU nurse.

It was a nice evening for September, but rather cool. The girls put on jackets and went outside to play on the swing set. Bridget asked Spencer to open a bottle of wine, and she put out some cheese and crackers. Sitting in front of the window at the kitchen table, they could keep an eye on the girls as they played outside.

Bridget thought Spencer was a little shy. Conversation was slow at first but then came a little more freely. She wanted to know about his life before moving to Rochester.

After a glass of wine, Spencer found it pretty easy to talk to her. She was a good listener. Bridget didn't share much about her own life. She did say that she was never married to Scarlett's father, and that he'd walked out on her when he found out about her birth defect. The conversation switched over to the kids and the hospital, which was a relief for both of them.

"I haven't had a home-cooked dinner like this in such a long time. It was delicious." Spencer even noticed that Ivy ate her dinner...all of it. Bridget had a nice way with kids. She had a craft planned for them after dinner. They were making leaf prints. It was turning out to be a good evening. After apple pie, Spencer knew it was time to go home. Haley told Bridget that her apple pie was just as good as her mommy's. Bridget smiled, but it caused an awkward silence. She packed up some leftovers for them, and they all said good-bye.

Spencer buckled the kids into their car seats. He shook Bridget's hand. "Thanks, Bridget, I really enjoyed this evening. Would it be all right if I called you sometime, and we went out without the kids?"

Bridget laughed. "Oh, do you mean like a date? For sure... I would like that."

Spencer smiled. "I'll call you." That would be a big step for Spencer.

Haley chatted about Scarlett and Bridget all the way home. "I like Scarlett's mommy, Daddy. She is so nice, and she is really pretty." Spencer was pleasantly surprised when Ivy said, "I like her, too." The girls had a lot of questions about why Scarlett was born with only part of her arm.

Spencer read the girls a story and put them to bed. He poured himself a glass of Scotch. He looked at a picture of his beautiful Anna. He missed her so much. He was so lonely. Tonight he felt hopeful. He decided that for sure he would call Bridget. It was a start.

Chapter 7

Kyle was having trouble getting over the fact that Mark had missed Lucy's preschool family picnic. Mark had come home from the bakery, taken a Vicodin, and poured himself a glass of wine. He clearly was in no shape to go. He'd said that he was incredibly busy today with an important order, and besides he'd overdone it on the treadmill at the gym. He was in excruciating pain. He'd given Kyle the cupcakes that he'd made for the picnic. He'd kissed Kyle and Lucy and told them to have a good time. He was going to bed. Lucy had cried. She'd wanted both of her daddies to be there. Kyle had appeased Lucy by telling her that they could bring Grandma instead. Pam had been elated when Kyle called, but she was also concerned about what was going on with her son and his partner. She loved her son-in-law, but she could also see that he had changed. Kyle told her it was because of his chronic back pain.

When Kyle and Lucy got home, Kyle found Mark sleeping soundly... softly snoring. He always worried when Mark took Vicodin and then drank alcohol. Mark insisted that it was only wine, and it would be fine. Kyle didn't know what to believe anymore.

Mark was already up and making Lucy breakfast when Kyle got out of the shower. Lucy was telling him all about the picnic. "Mark, my mother said she would take Lucy tonight. Let's have dinner just the two of us. We need to talk."

"Okay, sounds great," Mark said. "I'll make a reservation at Angelo's and meet you at six? Can you pick Lucy up at daycare and take her to your mom's?" Mark was glad that he had a light day. He had no weddings this weekend, and most of today would be spent meeting with potential customers. He knew that he and Kyle needed to spend some time together, just the two of them. Mark always packed Lucy's lunch. He always put something special in there. Sometimes it was a special treat he'd made for her at the bakery, sometimes it was a sticker, or it could be a photo or a silly picture that he had drawn. Mark had quite an imagination... it could be just about anything. Today it was a little elastic beaded bracelet. Lucy adored Mark. Kyle had to admit that sometimes he felt jealous when Lucy reached out to Mark before she would reach out to him. Maybe it was because it turned out that Mark was her biological father. They'd used a mixed sample for insemination, but they'd had to have DNA testing after Lucy was born for the adoption. It was Kyle who'd had to adopt Lucy. Kyle loved her so much. He tried to tell himself it didn't make any difference.

Angelo's was special for Kyle and Mark. It was where Mark had proposed. He was already there when Kyle arrived. Kyle couldn't help but think how handsome Mark looked tonight. His face looked relaxed and not so strained like it looked when he was in pain. He had ordered a bottle of their favorite Chianti. After some wine, and when their entrees arrived, Kyle began the discussion. "Mark, I'm worried about you. I'm worried about us. I hate what this pain is doing to you. I think you are getting too dependent on the Vicodin, and I hate it when you also drink when you take it. You're just so out of it all the time... too tired for Lucy and too tired for me. We used to have great sex... not so much anymore."

"Kyle, I'm just in so much fucking pain! Do you think this is who I want to be?"

"I guess I'm frustrated because you never try anything else for relief. You never wear the TENS unit or keep the physical therapy appointments."

TENS stood for transcutaneous electrical nerve stimulation. It was a device that could be worn even when Mark was working. It worked by sending stimulating pulses across the surface of the skin and along the nerve strands. It was supposed to prevent pain signals from reaching the brain. Mark said it gave minimal relief, and he found it too cumbersome to wear at work. He did not appreciate some of the comments his physical therapist had made to him, so he'd quit going. He wouldn't even consider acupuncture when Kyle had suggested it. Kyle had gone to an acupuncturist for years for his migraine headaches.

"That stuff isn't working for me," Mark said. His tone was a little belligerent.

"Maybe we should go back and talk to that surgeon that Brad Williams suggested. He said that your last MRI showed bone spurs in your spine and that removing them would probably give you some relief."

"Kyle, you know how I feel about surgery." His father had died from complications after routine surgery for hip replacement.

Mark could be very stubborn. Kyle said what he needed to say, and he didn't want to ruin the first date night they had had in a long time. Mark reached out for Kyle's hand. "I'll try to take it easy on the meds. I hired another assistant to help out at the bakery, and maybe I can be off my feet more. You and Lucy are everything to me. I'll just have to figure out a better way to deal with the pain. Maybe I will try the

49

acupuncture. Will you make an appointment for me with the girl that you see?" Mark didn't think it would work, but he would go to appease Kyle. He had to do something, because his doctor was starting to give him a hard time about refilling his narcotic prescriptions, and he hated the tension it caused in his marriage.

Mark had called his doctor's office just this morning asking for a refill. The nurse had said it was too early for a refill, and the doctor wouldn't write the prescription. Mark had talked to a guy whom he sometimes bought a little marijuana from. He'd bought a few Percocet pills from him, but they cost seventy-five bucks apiece. The guy said he'd given him a deal since he was already a customer. Kyle could never find out. He was very straight, at least when it came to drugs. He rarely even smoked a joint.

That night Mark reached out to Kyle and they made love...something they hadn't done in a while. He loved Kyle and really wanted to get their marriage back on track.

Chapter 8

Beverly had the appointment for the CVS coming up on Monday. She was so nervous about it. If it turned out that the baby was normal, she felt like she should continue the pregnancy. How could she abort Brad's child? However, deep down in a place that Beverly didn't like to think about, there was a voice telling her that it was her body and her choice. She had every right to terminate the pregnancy whether the baby was normal or not. She had been given enough challenges in her life where she had no choice but to accept the circumstances and deal with them. She knew this time she had a choice. She could make this problem go away. She loathed herself for thinking like that, but knew it was true. She tried to remember what the counselor at Planned Parenthood had said to her that helped her to make the decision before. But she knew this was different. This was Brad's baby. She made herself sick thinking about the abortion. Brad found her in the bathroom vomiting when he came home.

"Oh, I was hoping that nausea was finally under control. I haven't seen you sick in a while."

Beverly wiped her face and rinsed out her mouth. "I think that when I'm nervous, it just gets me going. I'm okay now." She didn't want to tell him that thinking about abortion was what had triggered it this time.

"Do you think you would be up to going to dinner with Peter and Susan Saturday night? It might take your mind off of Monday's appointment for a little while." Peter was a neurosurgeon and Brad's partner. He had also been her husband's partner. He and his wife, Susan, had introduced Brad to Beverly. The Dwyers had gone to Paris with them for their wedding and were their attendants. Beverly wondered if Brad had told Peter that she was pregnant.

"Brad, have you said anything to anyone? Have you told Peter?"

"Oh God, no, I wouldn't do that… not yet anyway."

"I haven't told anyone, either. Maybe a night out wouldn't be such a bad idea. Tell Peter we will join them for dinner."

Beverly took care dressing that night. She thought she looked a little pale, so she applied a little more blush and played up her eye makeup. She wore an apricot silk dress. It was a flattering color. Her breasts were already fuller. Brad said he loved the pregnant Beverly. He said it was hard for him to keep his hands off of her. He wanted to make love to her before they left. How could she say no? He was so tender and adoring. They were a little late for dinner. The Dwyers were already on their second cocktail when Brad and Beverly arrived. Beverly felt pretty good, almost normal. Pete wanted to get her a drink. She said she would wait and have a little wine with dinner. Beverly saw Susan raise her eyebrows. The ladies wanted to hit the restroom before their entrees came.

"Bev, you're not drinking tonight? What's going on with you? You look a little different. Brad can't keep his eyes off of you, and you look like the cat that swallowed the canary."

Beverly was dying to confide in her friend. She had to tell someone. "Susan, you are not going to believe this, but I am pregnant!"

Susan gasped, "*Oh, my God!*" She went to give Beverly a hug and could see that there were tears in her eyes. Susan couldn't read her. "How do you feel about this, honey?"

"Shocked and confused, but Brad is thrilled. Please don't tell anyone. I'm not ready to tell anyone else until I make it out of the first trimester. Can you wait to tell Peter? Besides Brad and the people at my doctor's office, you are the only person who knows.

"I'm honored that you shared your secret with me. By the way, you look beautiful tonight. I won't tell anyone. I promise." Susan knew that Beverly had told her all that she was ready to talk about. She also knew that Beverly was three years older than she was... that would make her forty-eight.

The ladies went back to the table. Everyone was enjoying their dinner. Beverly ate most of her meal. She ordered pasta with chicken and artichokes in a light cream sauce. She knew that pasta would agree with her. She had a few sips of wine, but that's all. She passed on dessert. It had been a nice evening. Brad said that Helen was baby-sitting Martina, and they had to get her home. They said their good-byes. It was an early evening. Beverly couldn't believe she'd told Susan about the pregnancy. She was glad that she hadn't given her any more details. She didn't want to tell her about the CVS.

The next day at mass, Beverly noticed that Brad went over to light a candle and say a prayer. It seemed like a private moment. She didn't want to ask him who the candle was for. She knew it was probably for their baby. Beverly didn't know what to pray for because she didn't know what she wanted. She just asked God to give her the strength to accept whatever it was she had to deal with.

After lunch, Brad and Beverly took Martina to the apple farm to pick apples. She loved it. There was a petting zoo there, and they were giving pony rides. Beverly was pretty tired when they got home. Martina wanted apple pie, but Beverly didn't have the energy to make it. She said that she would make another apple dessert that was just as yummy. She made apple crisp, and Brad ordered a pizza. Brad put Martina to bed while Beverly took a bath. She was exhausted and hoped that she would get a good night's sleep. Tomorrow would be a big day. Brad got into bed and kissed her. He told her that he loved her. He stayed up to read in bed. Beverly fell right to sleep.

She saw Erica and Johnny during her sleep all through the night. There was no particular dream. She just kept seeing their faces. Toward morning, her sleep was lighter and she started tossing and turning. She became restless and felt some cramping. She drank some water from a bottle at her bedside table. She got up and went into the bathroom. She was spotting. She didn't know what to think. At first she was anxious. Then she remembered reading that a little spotting could be normal in the first trimester. Then it occurred to her that maybe she was having a miscarriage. It troubled her that she hoped it was true. Brad was awake when she got back into bed. She told him.

She saw his furrowed brow and the concern in his eyes. "Let's not jump to any conclusions. We'll find out soon enough what's going on." He kissed her and then got up to shower. Beverly went downstairs to make coffee. Today the smell of the coffee brewing didn't even bother her. It smelled good. She decided to have a cup. She started boiling water for Brad's poached eggs and put English muffins in the toaster. Beverly went up to shower while Brad ate and checked his email. She didn't know what to think. There was still some light spotting. She got Martina up and dressed. Brad took her to preschool.

They didn't talk on the way to their appointment. Neither one of them knew what to say. They waited anxiously in the waiting room. Beverly looked around. There were a lot of pregnant women, but nobody who looked her age. The few women she did see who were in their forties or fifties certainly did not look pregnant and were probably there for menopausal complaints. She remembered sitting there with Erica just four years ago. God, so much had happened. She hoped that she would be called soon. She had to have a full bladder for the ultrasound. She felt like it was about to burst.

They were finally ushered into an exam room and waited for Dr. Renaldi. Beverly told him about the spotting. He said, "Well, let's take a look." He applied the gel and put the transducer on her abdomen. "I'm sorry," he said. "There is no longer a fetal heartbeat. You have had what we call a missed abortion or fetal demise. It often happens because of chromosome problems with the fetus, which is a strong possibility considering your age." Dr. Renaldi took hold of Beverly's hand. "I'm very sorry." Beverly looked over at Brad. He had tears in his eyes. She was ashamed to admit that she felt nothing. Dr. Renaldi went on to explain her options for treatment. She could have a surgical evacuation of her uterus or vaginal application of misoprostol tablets. The drug would cause the uterus to contract and expel the products of conception. Dr. Renaldi went over the side effects of the drug, as well as the treatment protocol and follow-up. He stated that it was a highly effective treatment, but she could still opt for the surgical abortion if she wanted. *There was that word: abortion.* Beverly didn't think she could bring herself to have an abortion whether the fetus was living or dead.

Dr. Renaldi stepped out of the room so that she and Brad could talk. Now Brad had tears streaming down his face. Beverly just looked at him and shook her head. "I'm sorry, Brad, I know you had hopes for this pregnancy."

He kissed her. "It's okay. It was obviously not meant to be."

Beverly only felt empty and numb. *What's wrong with me? Why am I not crying?* "I think that I would rather take the misoprostol for treatment." They left with her prescription and instructions.

Brad took the rest of the day off. He picked Martina up at preschool and took her to the zoo. It was a beautiful day. Beverly told him that she would be fine. She inserted the first of her misoprostol tablets and went to lie down on the couch. She thought if she put a movie on it would distract her. She was still having trouble sorting out her emotions. She couldn't deny that she was relieved that she was no longer pregnant, and the decision about ending the pregnancy had been made for her. Then she felt anger. It was just another shitty thing that had happened to her. Now, three of her children had been taken from her. She couldn't count the first one, because she had made the decision to make that baby go away. Beverly felt like she had let Brad down. He deserved better. She decided to call Susan. Maybe talking to Susan would give her some perspective and help to pass the time. *God, I'm a mess!*

Beverly had stopped seeing her therapist about a year ago. Dr. Martino had helped her through her grieving process after Tom died. He'd given her support through single parenthood and helped her to navigate her feelings in her new relationship with Brad. She'd continued therapy with him after Erica died. She didn't think she would ever have survived without his support. Well, today, maybe Susan could help. Beverly got them both a glass of wine. There were no warnings about not drinking alcohol while using the medication. She told Susan the whole story. She even told her the part about the abortion in college. Beverly thought it was part of what was complicating her feelings even more.

"Honey, I can understand your feelings. I for sure wouldn't want to have a baby now, and I'm forty-five. I admire how you and Brad are raising Martina. You could have just as easily let Ruby have Martina. You are a good person, Beverly, and you have been so strong through so many hardships and challenges. Brad loves you and he adores Martina. He will be okay."

"Oh, Susan, you should have seen how sad he was. He cried. Why is it that he cried and I didn't?"

"You have been through so much. I think you are just numb right now."

"Maybe this baby didn't make it because I really didn't want it. There, I've said it!"

"Bev, you said the doctor told you there was a high rate of miscarriage in women your age, and the baby most likely had some sort of chromosome problem. That's why this happened."

"I had decided that I was going to continue the pregnancy if the CVS was normal. I'm glad I didn't have to make the decision of what to do if the fetus wasn't normal."

"I guess God or Mother Nature made the decision for you. I just wish you could close this chapter in your life. You are always so hard on yourself."

After two glasses of wine, Beverly was starting to feel a little more cramping. Susan left, and she got the heating pad and some Motrin. Brad came home with Martina. He had stopped at Wegmans for a rotisserie chicken. He said he would make some rice and green beans. It had been a long day. After Brad gave Martina a bath, he read her a story and put her to bed.

"Daddy, is Mommy still having problems with her tummy?"

"She is, sweet pea, but the doctor gave her some medicine today. I think she will soon be feeling better."

Beverly was already in bed. Brad kissed her and asked her how she was feeling. "I love you, Beverly. I just want you to be okay." He held her all night long.

Beverly had vaginal bleeding, a little heavier than a period, for about three days, then it tapered off to spotting. She thought this whole ordeal was almost over, but it wasn't. Now she was crying... all of the time. Maybe it was the hormonal changes, or maybe she was finally grieving. She was inconsolable at times. Brad wasn't sure what to do. He called Dr. Renaldi, who suggested a support group for women adjusting after perinatal loss. He knew Beverly would never go for that.

"I guess I was afraid to want this baby. I couldn't risk losing another child, but I did, and now I'm so sad. Oh, Brad, I don't understand why I'm being so punished. It really challenges my faith and love for God."

"Beverly, I think some of what you are feeling is normal after a loss. Your therapist has always helped you before in your times of grief. Maybe you should go see him again." She thought maybe she would.

Chapter 9

It took a few weeks, but Spencer finally mustered up the courage to call Bridget. He planned to take her to dinner on Saturday night. He was nervous and wondered if he was really ready to do this. It took him back to junior high when he'd had to get up the nerve to call Maggie Morgan and ask her to the eighth-grade dance. He wanted to take Bridget somewhere nice, but nothing too formal. Spencer asked Brad Williams about a restaurant recommendation. He liked getting to know Brad, and even though Brad was probably ten years older, they had become friends. Brad had invited him to his country club to play golf with him and his partner, Peter Dwyer. Brad suggested his favorite Italian restaurant, Angelo's. He said it was popular and everyone loved it.

Spencer's nanny, Lizzie, agreed to come and watch the kids. They were curious about where he was going. He decided that it was probably best to tell them the truth. Their daddy was going on a date. He didn't think it was a good idea to tell them it was with Bridget. They seemed accepting when he told them.

"Who is the date with, Daddy?" asked Haley.

"Oh, she is a new friend I met."

Spencer was astonished when Ivy asked if he was going to kiss his date good night.

"Of course he is, Ivy!" giggled Haley. Spencer didn't know what to say. It was such an awkward moment.

He picked Ivy up and said, "I don't know, but I am going to kiss you, and then I'm going to kiss your sister, and I have to get going. You girls be good and have fun with Lizzie."

Lizzie smiled. She was amused. Lizzie thought Spencer was pretty cute... not really hot, but cute. He looked like the type of guy who would be a pediatrician. She hoped it would work out for him tonight. He seemed so sad all the time. She took the girls into the kitchen to start dinner. They were making homemade pizza. It was getting close to Halloween. After dinner, they watched *It's the Great Pumpkin, Charlie Brown* on TV. They were each allowed a story before bed. Ivy picked *Cinderella*, which was her favorite. She wanted to be Cinderella for Halloween. Haley asked Lizzie if she thought their daddy would get married again.

"Oh, honey, probably someday. Your daddy's still young."

Ivy had a meltdown. "I don't want to have a wicked stepmother!" she said. Ivy was crying now. Her big sister tried to comfort her.

"Don't worry, Ivy, if Daddy does get married, he would only marry somebody nice like Mommy."

"Haley's right.

Your daddy would only choose someone special... someone pretty and kind." Ivy stopped crying. Lizzie went downstairs and brought up her guitar. She played and sang for the girls. When she saw Ivy's eyelids drooping, she kissed them, said good night, and turned out the light. There were enough bedrooms in the house for the girls to each have their own room, but they shared a room and slept together in a queen-sized bed. Ivy needed the security of having her sister close by. Ivy slept holding her sister's hand. The room was painted

60

lavender. It had a white canopy bed with a pink-and-lavender-flowered quilt. There were several framed pictures of the girls with their mother in the room. Spencer's wife had been beautiful. *God, what a horrible tragedy it was.* Sometimes it brought tears to Lizzie's eyes when she thought about it. She was glad that she'd found this job. She felt needed.

Bridget was psyched about her date with Spencer. He seemed like such a decent guy, although she had been wrong about so many men before. Scarlett was staying over at her parents' house. She and Spencer had agreed that it was probably best that the girls didn't know about their date. Bridget had bought a new outfit. She hadn't bought any new clothes in a while. She wore a skirt and sweater with heels. She knew men always liked to see a woman in heels. Bridget was petite, so she could always wear heels without being taller than the guy she was with. She hoped that it didn't look like she was trying too hard. She dated now and then but really not that often. It was challenging being a single mom and working full time. Although her parents adored Scarlett, she didn't like to take advantage of them for childcare. Besides her parents, she only had one sitter whom she trusted to take care of Scarlett.

Spencer poured them each another glass of wine. Conversation was becoming a little more relaxed, and now it seemed more focused on single parenthood. Spencer told Bridget about his challenges with Ivy since his wife had died. Because she was just two when her mother had died, it was really hard to tell what was in her head. How much did she remember about her mother? How much did she understand? Spencer just knew that she wasn't the same kid anymore. She had always had a strong attachment to Anna, but she wasn't so fragile. She had been a normal two-year-old. After his wife died, she seemed to become unglued so easily. She was wary and shy. Spencer went on to say that his father was good with her, and his new nanny was building a trusting relationship with her.

Bridget listened intently to everything that Spencer was telling her. She knew that he was still in a lot of pain. Then he said, "That's enough about me, tell me more about yourself, Bridget."

"I don't know, Spencer, there's not all that much to tell. I love my job in the NICU. I love helping those struggling little babies overcome their problems and transition to their new world. Their success stories bring me a lot of joy and satisfaction. Right now, my world is my job and being a mom to Scarlett. It has been a journey. I don't even see her as a little girl with a disability anymore. She is just my Scarlett."

There was only so much she wanted to share with him. A lot of her story was about failed relationships and struggles to help her daughter overcome problems with her disability. She was tired of those stories, and besides, Bridget was someone who didn't want to dwell on the past but wanted to look to the future. She was resilient. Bridget was also a fixer. She wanted to help heal this new man who'd entered her life. He needed her. The men in Bridget's failed relationships had never needed her.

Bridget invited Spencer in after he brought her home. She told him that her dad had taught her how to make Irish coffee, and it was one of her guilty pleasures. "It's good for what ails you," she said with kind of a wicked look in her eyes.

"Okay, it wasn't hard to convince me. I would love to have Irish coffee with you," Spencer said. It was mid-October, and the nights were getting much cooler. Bridget turned on the flame in the gas fireplace that was in her living room. Spencer sat down on the couch and felt comfortable. Bridget was in the kitchen brewing the coffee. She brought out the coffees, kicked off her shoes, and joined him on the couch. Spencer knew where this was probably going, and he hadn't had sex with a woman in a long time. He didn't want to appear too needy, and he didn't want to disrespect Bridget pushing sex on the first date. He thought it best to follow her lead.

Bridget had already cautioned herself before she left for the evening. While she was putting her makeup on, she'd looked in the mirror and said, "Bridget O'Connell, as much as you may want to, do not have sex with this man on your first date."

After he finished his coffee, Spencer kissed her properly and thanked her for a really nice evening. He said that he wanted to see her again soon. Bridget felt the heat in his kiss. She knew that he would be calling her.

Spencer got home a little later than he'd anticipated. Lizzie was watching *Saturday Night Live* on TV. She was huddled under an afghan. He asked her how the girls had been.

"Oh, they were fine. Ivy cried a little during our *Cinderella* story. She had some questions about stepmothers, but she calmed down easily. The girls are excited about Halloween. I hope you had a nice evening."

"Thank you, Lizzie, I did."

Lizzie put her jacket on and kissed him on the cheek. "Good night, Spencer, I'll see you on Monday."

Spencer wondered what that was all about. She almost always called him Dr. Harris, even though he told her it was okay to call him Spencer. She never kissed him or even hugged him.

Spencer shrugged it off. She was young... only twenty-two years old. He guessed that kids that age were just more demonstrative now. He noticed that with his residents.

Chapter 10

Ruby had called Beverly and asked her if Martina could come spend the night. She and the girls were planning on making cut-out cookies for Halloween. She loved spending time with her granddaughter. Sometimes Ruby thought that Martina didn't have a strong enough connection to her father's family. She did, however, look African-American. She looked like her father, but she had her mother's vibrant green eyes and turned-up little nose. Ruby had had to teach Beverly how to do Martina's hair. Martina loved it when Ruby did it in all braids with little colored beads. Beverly hadn't mastered that yet, but she was able to wash it and style it in other ways. Ruby had had to show her what products to use.

The twins adored Martina and loved to play with her. Danielle and Denise missed their big brother so much. Martina was their connection to him. Ruby couldn't believe the girls were already in eighth grade. She knew they would be a big help when the babies came; however, they were at that age when they were getting a little boy-crazy. Ruby was strict with her girls. No way was there going to be any more teen pregnancies in her family.

Ruby asked Beverly to stay for a cup of tea when she came to drop Martina off. The last few times that Ruby had spoken to Beverly, she hadn't seemed like herself. "Beverly, is everything okay? You have been quiet and seem a little sad."

Beverly didn't want to share her loss with Ruby, but then again, maybe something Ruby would say could help in some way. She and Ruby had shared so much in the past. They were a good support for each other. "Oh, you are not going to believe this. I, too, was pregnant, but had a loss at ten weeks. Everything was fine at the first ultrasound and then there was no heartbeat." Beverly's voice cracked when she spoke. "I have to admit, I was conflicted about the pregnancy, but now I'm so sad."

Ruby reached over for her hand. "Oh, Beverly, I'm sorry. God has certainly challenged you as a mother. How is Brad handling your loss?"

"Oh, you know Brad. His biggest concern was for me. He was sad and disappointed, but he stayed strong for me. He was so hopeful that maybe he would finally have a biological child of his own."

"Every day I thank the good Lord for Martina," Ruby said. "I know how much Brad loves her, and he has been such a good daddy to her. She talks about him all the time."

"I know Ruby, Brad and I are lucky to have Martina. Enough about me, how are you doing? Pregnancy is still going well?"

"I have to admit a twin pregnancy was much easier when I was younger, in my twenties. I get so tired, and I'm just twenty-five weeks. Look how big I am already! Mario helps out as much as he can, but he is so busy with his job and school, too. He so much wants to be a nurse anesthetist. He's smart. I know he can do it. It's hectic because he has to go to Buffalo three times a week for classes. We for sure will appreciate the money when he graduates and gets his license. I think my doctor will let me work as long as my blood pressure is okay and I don't have any problems with preterm labor."

"Ruby, you never cease to amaze me. Are you sure you are okay with Martina tonight?"

"Oh, for sure I am. The girls will look after her. She's never any trouble."

Beverly thought a lot about Ruby on the way home. She had always admired her. Beverly had had an affluent and privileged childhood. Both of her marriages were to successful physicians. She never had to worry about money. Ruby's financial situation was a little better now that she was married to Mario, but she still struggled with her finances. Ruby had had to work extremely hard her entire life.

Beverly thought it might be helpful to make a few meals that Ruby could put in her freezer for nights she was too tired to cook. She also thought about giving her Martina's crib and asking if she and Brad could buy the crib for the other baby. She was glad she'd stayed to talk to Ruby... it kind of got her over her poor-me mood. Beverly had days when she couldn't even stand herself. She had been seeing her therapist, Dr. Martino, again. It was helping, but she was still quite depressed. Since her miscarriage, her thoughts were always dominated by everything she had lost in life... her son at age four, then her husband, Erica at age eighteen, and lastly the baby who never was. She was still haunted by her initial feelings about wanting to abort the pregnancy. Dr. Martino had told her that she couldn't control her feelings, but it was how she acted on her feelings that mattered. He urged her to stop feeding the *guilt monster.*

She decided that she would stop at Wegmans and pick up some lamb chops... Brad's favorite. She would make him something really nice for dinner. She would also make garlic smashed potatoes and roasted Brussels sprouts. For dessert, she would make an apple tart. She knew a shop in the city where they made their own lavender ice cream, which would go great with the tart. She wanted to put a little romance back in their marriage. Brad had been so patient with her lately. She just wanted to go back to the way things were before the pregnancy. Sometimes she forgot that Brad had suffered a loss, too. She vowed to try harder to put the miscarriage behind her.

Ruby sat at the kitchen table and watched as the girls made cookies with Martina. She had made the cookie dough and frosting the night before, which made the project a little easier. It was Martina's job to put on the sprinkles after the cookies were cut out, baked, and frosted. They were all having fun, but the kitchen was a big mess. There was flour, orange frosting, and sprinkles everywhere. Martina climbed up on Ruby's lap with a cookie. "Grandma Ruby, are there really two babies in your tummy? I want to see them."

"Oh, we will have to wait a bit. They are still growing." Just then, one of the babies gave Ruby a swift kick, which Martina could feel in her bottom. She was delighted.

"I think they're dancing!" Martina said.

"You're right," Ruby said. All of a sudden, there was a flurry of activity in her belly. "Did you know that one of the babies is a boy and one is a girl?"

"What will they look like? Will they have black skin like me? I hope the girl has black skin."

That was the first time that Ruby had ever heard Martina ask about black and white. It took her by surprise. She was three now; she was bound to have questions. They had decided that Martina would be told about her birth parents when she started asking. The time had probably come.

"The babies will have black skin because Grandma Ruby and Papa Mario have black skin. We are their mommy and daddy."

She could tell that Martina was thinking it over. Her little brow was furrowed. "But I have black skin and my mommy and daddy have white skin." Besides the twins, no one was there to help Ruby out with this. She wanted to say the right thing. Danielle and Denise looked at Ruby and wondered what she would say. "Baby girl, I think we should talk about this when you are a little bit older and can understand."

"No! I want you to tell me now! I'm not a baby anymore!"

Ruby went upstairs and got out the picture of Dwight and Erica that was in her dresser drawer. It was their prom picture. She tried to remember to put it away when Martina was there. *It's time for her to see this picture.* Martina got back up on her lap. "This was your first and true mommy and daddy. His name is Dwight, and he was my son. This pretty girl is Erica. Her mother was who you call Mommy now…Beverly. Jesus called Dwight and Erica to heaven, so you needed a new mommy and daddy. Beverly and Brad wanted a little girl and now have you. You have a black family and a white family. We all love you."

"Okay, but why did I come out black?"

Ruby took a deep breath. I don't know. I guess Jesus chose black."

"Good!" Martina said. "Can I have another cookie?" They all laughed. Martina went on to talk about her Halloween costume. Ruby was relieved that the birth discussion was over. She hoped that she'd handled it all right.

Mario was working the evening shift. When he got home, Ruby was already in bed. She couldn't get comfortable, and she couldn't stop thinking about what Beverly had told her and also about all of Martina's questions. "Are the babies keeping you up?" He put his hand on Ruby's belly. He could feel all the squirming going on. He kissed Ruby and started rubbing her back. He asked about her day. This was Ruby's weekend off. Mario was hoping that she would take the time to rest, but it sounded like she had been busy all day. Ruby told him about Beverly and all the questions that Martina had asked.

Mario worked a lot of cases with Brad in the OR. He respected Brad and knew that he was a highly skilled neurosurgeon. His patients usually did well. He was a great father to Martina. Mario had his reservations about Beverly. She was a complicated lady. Mario was very much in love with his wife and happy in his marriage, but Ruby came with a lot of baggage.

Dwight's father, who was also the girls' father, had been in prison most of his adult life. His original offense was armed robbery. Parole violations had landed him back in prison. He had a cocaine problem and a nasty temper, which he'd often taken out on Ruby. Supposedly he had found the Lord in prison. He still wrote letters to Ruby professing his love and asking for her forgiveness. He had been brought to the funeral home in shackles to see his son.

Mario had his own baggage, too, but not as much. His son, Anthony, was now fifteen. He was a good kid who worked hard in school and stayed out of trouble. He played both varsity football and basketball. Mario had never been married to Anthony's mother. Her name was Keisha. They'd never had a serious relationship...mostly had sex now and then. It wasn't that Mario didn't like her. He just didn't see a future with her. Keisha was a party girl who didn't take life seriously. She'd completely ignored the fact that it was possible she could be pregnant, and then she'd been too far along to get an abortion. Mario had found out about the baby after the fact. Keisha had paid him a visit, with Anthony in her arms, and said he was a daddy. Mario knew she slept around some and had insisted on a paternity test. Mario was indeed Anthony's father. She'd said she didn't want to be a mother and relinquished full custody to Mario. He'd never heard from her again. Mario had been living at home with his mother and going to college at the time. His mother had helped him with the baby. Once Anthony had started kindergarten, they'd moved out. He would be forever grateful for his mother's help. Sadly, his mother had had a stroke and died a year after they moved out. His mother's name was Lillie Mae. He wanted to name his baby girl after her grandmother. Mario couldn't believe they would be a family of five now. He prayed that everything would go all right.

Chapter 11

Kyle was an accountant. He was a junior partner in a big accounting firm. He had done well in his career. So, of course, he managed the finances for the family. Mark used a different accountant for his business. His bakery was called Sugar Plum. In keeping with Mark's wicked sense of humor, he sometimes referred to himself as the sugar plum fairy. He had a good reputation in the small-business community and was a very talented pastry chef. A wedding cake from Sugar Plum would be special... decadent, delicious, beautiful, and unique. Mark worked hard and took pride in his craft. Lately, his enthusiasm was dampened by his pain.

Kyle studied the bank statement for their joint account. Mark had recently made a lot of ATM withdrawals. Kyle wondered what he needed so much cash for. It didn't take long for him to figure it out. He suspected that maybe it was for drugs, because he was having problems getting his narcotics prescriptions refilled. Kyle hating thinking it but feared it might be true. *How will I have this conversation with him?*

Mark walked in the door with Lucy. He had taken her to buy her Halloween costume. They were both laughing. Mark was always "Poppy," and Kyle was "Daddy." They'd decided on this before the results of the paternity testing had come in. Mark and Kyle rarely brought up the fact that Mark was Lucy's biological father. Mark said that he loved being called Poppy.

"Daddy," Lucy squealed, "Poppy and I had the best time ever! We bought my Snow-White costume, and then we went out to lunch, and then Poppy took me for a mani." She showed Kyle her nails with the little pumpkin decals. She wrapped her arms around Kyle and gave him a big hug. Then Mark said, "One, two, three, group hug!" This was the Mark that Kyle had fallen in love with.

Mark was in a good mood. He'd had a great day with his little girl, and he wasn't in pain. He was able to score three OxyContin tablets. It was a longer-acting medication and managed his pain much better. His dealer charged him one hundred dollars for each pill, insisting it was a good price. He made wedding cakes that sold for over a thousand dollars. He felt justified in spending the three hundred dollars if he was in pain. Mark knew that he couldn't keep shelling out that kind of cash for pills without Kyle finding out. He knew that he was becoming dependent on narcotics, but he didn't know what else to do about his pain. He quickly went through his prescribed medication and had no choice but to buy pills on the street, which wasn't hard, but very costly. Yesterday he was at the shop working on an elaborate wedding cake for an important client when the sweating and agitation had started. It was hard for him to focus, and he didn't have the patience to do the piping on the cake. He'd had no choice but to get some pills so that he could finish the cake.

He was having problems with insomnia. Mark knew it was probably a withdrawal symptom. He would be up tossing and turning all night. That's when the self-loathing would start. He would think about Kyle and Lucy and how much he loved them. He would also think about his business and his employees. People depended on him. He knew he had a problem. *God, I'm a fucking junkie...I'm buying drugs on the street.*

Kyle didn't know who he could confide in. He was close to his mother, but this wasn't something he felt he could share with her. She adored Mark. His mother had always been so supportive of his relationship with Mark and was a wonderful grandmother to Lucy. Kyle was estranged from his father. His father could never accept the fact that his son was gay. His only sibling was his sister, Colleen. She was okay with her brother being gay but was not a proponent of gay marriage and did not support his and Mark's decision to be parents. Kyle had been close to his sister growing up, but not anymore. She had become a hard-nosed conservative bitch. She was an assistant in the Manhattan district attorney's office and only seemed to care about her career ambitions. She'd married a guy with similar views to her own. They didn't have any kids.

Mark's sister, Sophie, was different. Kyle loved her. He and Mark spent a lot of time with Sophie and her boyfriend. She was a lot younger than Mark...a few years older than Kyle. Lucy was crazy about her aunt Sophie. Kyle thought that if there was anyone he could confide in, it was Sophie. He thought that he would give her a call and maybe meet up with her for lunch.

They met the following week. "Oh, Kyle, I've been worried about him, too. Do you really think he is buying drugs on the street?"

"I suspect he is. He goes through his prescribed meds really fast, before it's time for a refill. He's been making a lot of cash withdrawals from our joint account."

Sophie had tears in her eyes. "Oh, my God, Kyle, what are we going to do?"

"Maybe we should talk to him together. We are the two people he trusts most in this world. Would you be willing to do that, Sophie? We could have kind of an intervention with him."

"Let me think about it, Kyle."

Kyle hated upsetting Mark's sister. He guessed he probably shouldn't have shared so much with her. They agreed to keep in touch. For now, Kyle decided to let it be.

For a while, things seemed to be a little better. Mark said he was getting some relief from the acupuncture. Kyle wondered if that was really where the relief was coming from.

Chapter 12

Spencer ran into Bridget in the hospital cafeteria. He asked her if she had plans for Halloween, which was Friday night. "I'm probably just taking Scarlett trick-or-treating for a while."

"Why don't we take the kids together?" Spencer said. "It would be fun."

"There are not many kids in my neighborhood, so I was going to go on my parents' street, but we could go in your neighborhood if you want. Scarlett would probably love to go with your girls."

Spencer jotted down his address on a paper napkin and told Bridget to come about five o'clock. He told her he was looking forward to it.

Bridget was really excited. She was hoping this relationship would go somewhere. Scarlett was thrilled to be going trick-or-treating with her new friends. They arrived promptly at five o'clock with a pan of homemade macaroni and cheese. Bridget also brought a salad. She put dinner in the oven and Spencer handed her a beer.

"Cheers! Happy Halloween," he said. Bridget smiled with a mischievous look on her face. She was dressed as a sexy witch. Spencer hadn't even thought about wearing a costume.

"It was so thoughtful of you to come with dinner. I was just going to order pizza, but this is so much better."

"I thought the kids should have some dinner first, so they wouldn't be hungry and wanting to eat so much candy."

After they finished eating, Spencer put the dishes in the dishwasher while Bridget helped the girls with their costumes. Ivy was Cinderella, Haley was the Little Mermaid, and Scarlett was a ballerina. They looked adorable and seemed to be having a great time. Bridget took their picture, Spencer got Bridget and himself another beer, and they headed off. It was the perfect night for Halloween...a clear, starry night and about fifty-five degrees. The kids got tired after about forty-five minutes, and they headed back.

"Stay for a while?" Spencer asked.

"Okay, the kids are having so much fun." They'd changed out of their costumes and were sorting through their candy.

"Daddy, can we have popcorn...please?" asked Haley. Spencer and Bridget agreed that it was probably better that they have popcorn than more candy. He put a bag in the microwave and poured some cider.

Bridget looked around a little. Spencer's wife was all over the house. She was very pretty. They all looked so happy.

"Why don't you girls watch a movie?" He started a DVD for them in the den. He put another bag of popcorn in the microwave and opened up two more beers. He and Bridget sat in the living room. Spencer put on some music. "This is fun," he said. He leaned over and kissed Bridget. "I was worried about doing the Halloween thing this year. Last year the girls went to spend the night at my sister-in-law's house so that I wouldn't have to deal with it."

"I'm having fun, too," Bridget said. The girls were asking for another movie. Spencer made his girls put on their pajamas. He said that Scarlett could wear some of Ivy's.

"Oh, thanks, that's good," Bridget said. "This way I can just carry her to bed when we get home." She and Spencer were having a serious make-out session on his couch. The girls were so quiet. Spencer went in the den to check on them. All three of them were sound asleep. He covered them up with a blanket.

He came back in the living room and took Bridget by the hand. "The kids are asleep." There was a first-floor bedroom in the house that Spencer used as a guest room and office. Spencer started undressing Bridget and had her on the bed in no time. She seemed surprised but was a very willing participant. Spencer wanted to take his time, but it had been so long. He later held Bridget in his arms. He didn't know what to say. Bridget said, "That was nice." They laid in silence for a while, Spencer holding her and stroking her hair. Bridget turned and looked at him. He had tears in his eyes.

"Spencer...it's okay." She stroked his cheek and kissed him. She rolled over on top of him, and they made love again.

It was well after midnight. Bridget said they had better be going. They both got dressed. Spencer carried Scarlett to the car and buckled her into her car seat. He kissed Bridget and said, "Thanks for tonight."

On the ride back home, Bridget was filled with mixed emotions. She was happy to have Spencer in her life, but she also felt so sad for him. She could feel the tears coming on. She could hear her mother's voice in her head cautioning her about needy and lonely men.   Spencer had seemed so restrained. She was caught off guard tonight. She really hadn't thought their relationship would include sex for a while. Maybe her mother was right. It was always hard for her to see a man cry. She would often see the fathers of her little patients cry when they were overwhelmed or things weren't going well. She remembered her own father's tears when Bridget had told him his granddaughter would be born with part of her arm missing. The tears in Spencer's eyes after they'd made love for the first time were leaving her unglued.

Spencer had his own thoughts about the evening. After he carried the girls up to their room, he sought solace in a glass of Scotch and his picture of Anna. *I feel like I just cheated on my wife. God, I'm such a mess.* He wished he could call his dad, but it was way too late for that. His dad had been fifty-two when his mom had died. Although he'd never remarried, Spencer remembered some of his father's lady friends. Maybe his dad could help him sort this out. He decided he would call him in the morning.

Chapter 13

Beverly couldn't seem to dig herself out of the big black hole of depression that she'd fallen into after she'd lost the baby that she really hadn't wanted. She found herself back in full grieving mode. She was grieving for Tom, for her son, Johnny, for Erica, and she guessed for the baby who was just taken from her. The worst times were when Martina was at preschool and Brad was at the hospital. That's when she would get out her old photo albums with pictures of her and Tom, so young and so much in love. She saw a picture of herself pregnant with Erica. She was radiant... beaming. Beverly remembered the joy she felt when she'd found out she was pregnant. She'd paged Tom, who was in the OR. One of the nurses had called her back to tell her that he was in surgery. She'd gone to the hospital and waited in the family waiting room. He'd come down to the waiting room when he was out of the OR to tell his patient's family how the surgery had gone. After they were done talking, she'd grabbed him to tell him her news.

She for sure had not felt that joy this last time. She'd felt nothing but dread. How could she feel that way about a life that she and Brad had conceived? Now she hated herself for feeling that way. She loved Brad; why couldn't she love his child?

Then there was her precious little Johnny. Beverly couldn't believe that he'd gone through all those surgeries and hospitalizations and died anyway. He'd died during a routine follow-up procedure... a cardiac catheterization. The doctor was supposed to come back to the room and tell them that everything was good, but something had gone wrong, and her little boy was dead. Beverly looked at the picture of Tom with Erica on one knee and Johnny on the other. Johnny was of course holding Bob, his teddy bear. He went everywhere with Bob. Beverly ran up to Martina's room to get the friendly old bear. Erica had insisted that they keep it for her baby. Beverly sat clutching Bob to her chest and cried. Johnny's birthday was right before Halloween. It was always a difficult time for her.

Beverly put the picture albums away and poured herself some Chardonnay. Martina was spending the afternoon with Helen. Brad was picking Martina up on the way home from the hospital. Beverly knew she was lucky to have Helen, who thrived on being a great-grandmother. She helped out a lot with Martina, and just like Erica, Martina adored her. She called her Granny. Helen would turn eighty next month. This year her birthday fell right on Thanksgiving. Beverly marveled at her energy and her always positive outlook.

Martina ran into the house wearing a little orange knitted cap, complete with a green stem. Beverly knew Helen had made it for her. She looked like a little pumpkin and was delighted. Beverly was on her third glass of wine. Brad could tell she had been crying and having another bad day. Beverly hadn't even thought about dinner.

"I think we should take our little pumpkin out to dinner tonight," Brad said. They took Martina to her favorite restaurant, the Village Café. Beverly knew that she probably shouldn't order any more wine. She was hungry because she'd never gotten around to eating lunch. They ended up having a pleasant dinner, and Beverly was feeling a little calmer and more relaxed. Martina wanted ice cream for dessert. Beverly and Brad had coffee.

Martina was chatty. She was excited about Halloween. Ruby's girls, Danielle and Denise, were planning on coming over to take her trick-or-treating. They were all going as mice... the three blind mice.

"Did you know that Grandma Ruby has two babies in her tummy? I hope the girl baby will be black like me and Danny and Nisey. My real daddy was black. Grandma Ruby showed me his picture. Don't worry, Daddy, I love you, too." Beverly looked over at Brad. He just raised his eyebrows and smiled.

"I love you, too, pumpkin." Brad hoped that Martina wouldn't start talking about her real mommy. He didn't think Beverly could handle talking about Erica tonight. He was surprised that Ruby had already had this conversation with her. He had thought that they would all tell Martina together. Brad just accepted it... like he'd learned to accept everything since he'd met Beverly and walked into her complicated life.

Later that night, he and Beverly talked about it. "I'm surprised Ruby didn't tell me that she talked to Martina," Beverly said. "That's not like her."

Brad shook his head. "Maybe Martina just started asking questions, and she had to begin a conversation she wasn't prepared to have. We should probably all get together and talk about it before she starts asking more questions. Mario tells me that Ruby is not quite herself. He says she seems a little overwhelmed and quite emotional with the pregnancy. We will all figure it out."

Now Beverly was crying. Brad was so worried about her. He had seen her through some extremely emotionally tough times, but this deep depression that had settled in since the miscarriage had him worried. He was glad the she had an appointment with her therapist the next day.

Beverly didn't know what she would do without Dr. Martino. He knew her so well. She had started seeing him after her husband died, and had been seeing him regularly up until about a year ago. She had been feeling so much more confident and happy. She had finally been able to set aside her heartbreaks and tragedies. She had been happy and secure in her new marriage and was finding joy in being a mother to Martina. She felt like she had fallen flat on her face again with the pregnancy and miscarriage.

Dr. Martino looked at her with his soft brown eyes and said, "Beverly I am concerned about you. I see such deep sadness and remorse. You have endured a very cruel insult to your womanhood, and none of it is your fault. Of course, you had mixed feelings about bearing a child at age forty-eight. I really do think that any woman would. Wouldn't you have felt the same way about finding yourself pregnant at age forty-eight with Tom's baby?"

Beverly shook her head. "I don't know... probably."

"I'm sure that when Brad married you, he never expected you to bear a child for him. If he was looking for a woman to have a child for him, I'm sure he would have sought out a younger woman. Brad was attracted to you and fell in love with you. Had you ever talked about trying to have a baby together?"

"No. He did tell me that his first wife was younger than him, and she had made it clear that she didn't want to have children. Brad found out about a year after his divorce that she had remarried and was pregnant. He said that it hurt and confused him. He always tells me how much he loves being a father to Martina. I think he does think of her as his daughter and not his granddaughter. I love Martina, but in my heart, she is my granddaughter."

"She is your granddaughter, but in reality, you are now her mother. Your adoption papers say so. Doesn't she call you Mommy"?

"She does, but I really don't deserve to be anybody's mother. The first-time motherhood knocked at my door, I had an abortion because being a mother was inconvenient for me at the time. If I had paid more attention to Erica after Tom died, she probably wouldn't have gotten pregnant. I should have watched her more carefully during her pregnancy. She deserved a better mother. Then there's Johnny. What did I do when I was pregnant with him to cause him to be born with such a serious birth defect? I can't help but feel that not wanting this last baby caused by body to miscarry." Beverly was sobbing now.

"Wow, that's a heavy burden you insist on carrying. There's nothing I can say to you that will assuage your guilt about that abortion you had in college. Abortion is a complicated matter, and I'm sure you did what was best for you at the time. Babies are born with birth defects to healthy women all the time, just as healthy people become ill with terminal illnesses. Sometimes we just don't know why. If I recall, you were very supportive of your daughter after your husband died. You accepted her interracial relationship and her pregnancy. The genetic problem, Factor V Leiden, is what caused the blood clot that led to her death. Lastly, Beverly, you probably had a miscarriage because that is what happens most often when women conceive in their late forties."

"But I can't seem to get past all of this. These feelings haunt me and immobilize me. I just can't seem to get back to being me."

"I think you may be suffering from postpartum depression, Beverly. Your hormones have taken you on a wild ride, and it is for sure adding to the change in your mental and physical well-being."

"I thought postpartum depression was what happened after you gave birth and couldn't cope with being a new mother. I remember being a little blue after having Erica and Johnny, but only for a little while and never like this."

"Beverly, postpartum depression can happen after pregnancy loss, too. It is complicated by the fact that you are also grieving."

"Grieving for a baby that was barely there?"

"Yes, you told me that at your first ultrasound they gave you a picture of your developing baby and you heard its heartbeat. Am I correct?"

"It was just a fetus," Beverly said.

"Beverly, you lost your baby. You have suffered so much loss. I think maybe this time you may need more help in recovery. I would like to prescribe an antidepressant. I would like to try one of the newer antidepressants, Lexapro. It is less likely to cause bothersome side effects. It is generally well tolerated. After a few weeks, I think you may feel better. Try to go back to doing things that have always brought you comfort in the past. I know you like to paint. You have told me it has been therapeutic in the past. You have expressed a lot of remorse about your initial feelings of not wanting to be pregnant, even though it was Brad's baby. You feel like you have betrayed and disappointed him. Maybe you should focus on your relationship with him. Loving Brad got you through that tumultuous year after your husband died. Figure out ways to find joy as a mother to Martina. Three-year-olds are delightful. Try and have fun with her. Come back next week, Beverly. I'm confident you will get through this and feel like your former self again. Please, do get that prescription filled."

Beverly knew that all of what Dr. Martino said was true. She hoped the medication would help. She went to the pharmacy to pick up her prescription and decided to stop in the shop that she used to own to see Pam. Pam had always been a wonderful friend to her. She had supported Beverly through some awfully rough times.

Pam was thrilled to see her. She showed Beverly a sweater that had just come in that she thought would look lovely on her. Beverly bought it and convinced Pam to take a break for lunch.

Beverly was tired of talking about her miscarriage. Pam didn't know about it. She and Pam talked about Martina and Lucy. They loved that their granddaughters had ended up enrolled in the same preschool class.

Beverly and Pam had spent Thanksgiving together since the year Beverly's husband had died. It all started when Erica had started seeing Dwight. Ruby had to work that Thanksgiving, and Erica had asked Beverly if Dwight and his sisters could have dinner with them. Ruby had come later when she got out of work. Pam was having tension in her own family, because her son, Kyle, had just come out, and no one wanted to include his partner, Mark, for Thanksgiving dinner. Beverly had thought it would be fun to mix it up and invite them, too.

Of course Helen had also come. Everyone had enjoyed the day so much that they'd decided to continue the tradition. The celebration had grown to include Mario and his son and, of course, Brad, Martina, and Lucy. Beverly and Pam started the planning. After Halloween, Thanksgiving was right around the corner. They wanted to make it extra special this year, as it would also be Helen's eightieth birthday. They both marveled at Helen's energy. If you didn't know her, you would think she was seventy or even sixty. For Helen, age was only a number. It was never a barrier to deter her from what she wanted to do in life.

After lunch, Beverly stopped to fill her prescription. As she was waiting for it to be filled, she had an idea. Dr. Martino had suggested that she paint. There was a photo that she'd taken in Paris on her honeymoon with Brad. It was a café where she and Brad had had lunch. Beverly thought she could recreate the scene as a watercolor painting. She knew Brad would love it. She stopped at the hobby store to get some of the painting supplies that she would need. Helen had agreed to pick Martina up at preschool today, as she always did on days that Beverly had an appointment or meeting. Beverly wanted to do something nice for Helen. Helen loved ice cream. She stopped at the dairy and picked up a quart of pumpkin ice cream for her. Beverly stayed to have a cup of tea when she got to Helen's. Martina and Helen were busy in a game of Candy Land when she got there.

After such an emotionally draining morning, it turned out to be a good day. She put a chicken in the oven to roast. She had a martini chilling in the refrigerator for Brad. She put on her new sweater and fixed her hair and makeup. Brad walked in and smiled when he saw her. He kissed her. They had a pleasant dinner, with, of course, Martina doing all the talking. Beverly gave her a bath. Martina asked her to play a song on her violin before putting her to bed. "Please, Mommy. You haven't played a song for me in such a long time." How could she not play for her?

Brad was already in bed reading when she came in from Martina's room. Beverly put on her nightgown and slipped into bed with Brad. She reached out for him, and they made love. Brad was relieved. She hadn't been very interested in sex since her miscarriage. Beverly seemed like her former self tonight.

Chapter 14

For a while it seemed like Mark was doing better. Kyle asked his acupuncturist. Mark was indeed coming once a week for treatment. Kyle didn't notice anything more out of the ordinary on his bank statements. He wanted to believe that Mark was doing better. They seemed to have their marriage back on track.

Mark had found his own solution to his problem. He did go to acupuncture, because he didn't want Kyle to find out otherwise. Maybe it was helping a little. He was able to negotiate a stronger prescription from his primary care doctor, but he'd had to sign a pain contract. Mark signed the contract because he wanted to make sure he was able to continue to get his prescribed medication. He knew he had to be careful about violating the terms of the agreement. Mark had found out a way to get additional pain relief when he needed it that didn't cost so much money. He'd discovered heroin. It was a quick fix, and for ten or twenty bucks, he could get what he needed. He knew a few dealers he could go to. He was reluctant at first. No way did he want to get into an IV drug habit. He really didn't want to have a drug habit at all. He only used it as a last resort when withdrawal symptoms were too much, and he only snorted it. It gave him immediate relief. Mark knew he was playing a dangerous game, but he felt like he had no choice.

It was his sister Sophie's birthday. He and Sophie were tight. Before Mark had met Kyle, Sophie was all he had. Their mother was an alcoholic who'd abandoned the family when Mark was in high school and Sophie was just in kindergarten. Their father had been a wonderful man. They were blessed to have him after having such a disappointing mother. His death five years ago was heartbreaking. It was hard to accept how things could go so wrong after a routine surgery. The hip replacement was supposed to improve the quality of his father's life, but it had ended it. Mark knew his fear of surgery was somewhat unreasonable, but he couldn't help it. Besides, from what he read, there was no guarantee that a laminectomy would cure his pain, and there were risks. The risks appeared on the surgical consent like the fine print in a contract... something that you should pay attention to but did not.

Sophie and her boyfriend were coming for dinner tonight. Kyle had spent most of last evening making lasagna. He was a good cook. Mark could bake, but it was Kyle who was adept at savory dishes. Kyle even made fresh pasta noodles. He was also planning on making his killer Caesar salad, which he could put together tonight. Mark was bringing home one of his signature cakes... tiramisu cake. He had decorated his sister's cake beautifully.

It was a nice evening. Lucy was so excited that Aunt Sophie and Jimmy were there. She had worked very hard at making a birthday card. Mark and Kyle really liked Jimmy, Sophie's boyfriend. He was an easygoing guy who seemed to accept his girlfriend's unconventional family without judgment. He brought a very nice bottle of Chianti for dinner. Mark knew he probably shouldn't have wine, but he had a glass anyway. Abstinence from alcohol was in his pain contract. *Who would find out?* Mark had never told Kyle about the contract. Kyle worried about Mark mixing alcohol with the narcotics. When Mark poured himself a second glass, Kyle couldn't help but look over at Sophie. He could tell that she was thinking the same thing.

"Mark, do you really think that's a good idea?" Sophie said.

"What?" Mark said.

"You know… drinking wine when you are taking pain medication for your back."

"Okay, so I won't have any more." Up until now, it had been such a pleasant evening. He didn't want to spoil it. He passed his glass over to Kyle. Lucy was getting tired. It was time to serve the cake. Mark went into the kitchen to put on the coffee and take the cake out of the refrigerator. He was feeling agitated and broke out into a sweat. He wished his sister hadn't called him out on the wine. It probably would have taken the edge off, so now he felt like he had no other choice. He went to the bathroom and snorted a little heroin… just a little. He was able to get the candles lit on the cake and bring it out.

After cake, Kyle said he would put Lucy to bed. "No! I want Poppy to put me to bed." She kissed everyone good night, and Mark got her ready for bed. She was always read at least one story before bed. The rule was no more than three. They were both asleep before Little Red Riding Hood reached Grandmother's house. After an hour, Mark was still in Lucy's room. Kyle went in to check it out. He could hear Mark's snoring before he even opened the door. Kyle tried to jostle him awake, but he was out cold. Mark stirred but didn't awaken.

Kyle went back out to the living room. "I guess they were both pretty tired," he said. He didn't want to worry Sophie, but he was concerned about how soundly Mark was sleeping.

"Is he okay?" Sophie asked.

"I think so. I'll keep an eye on him, but maybe we should have that talk with him."

Kyle knew that Mark would be embarrassed about falling asleep and not saying good night to his sister. Kyle felt badly about that, but he was also angry. *How could Mark let this happen?*

Mark was in the kitchen with Lucy making pancakes when Kyle got up the next morning. Mark had never come to bed. "Poppy slept in my bed all night, so I didn't even need my night light. He's making blueberry pancakes. Do you want some, Daddy?"

Kyle poured himself coffee and sat next to Lucy at the breakfast bar. "Of course I do, honey. Did you and Poppy save any bacon for me?"

Mark looked contrite. "Kyle, I'm sorry that I conked out last night. We had a crazy busy day at the shop. One of my assistants called in sick. I will call Sophie and apologize."

"It's okay, man, we knew you were tired."

Mark called Sophie anyway. Sophie wanted to meet him for coffee. She decided that maybe it was best if she talked to her brother by herself.

"Mark, I'm worried about you. I know your back pain has gotten worse and that you are having problems managing your pain. I'm concerned that you are getting too dependent on the Percocet or the Vicodin or whatever it is that you are taking."

Mark frowned. "Is that what Kyle told you?"

"I can see it for myself. You are not you lately. You seem a little out of it. I worry, Mark, because of Mom. I know that people can have a genetic predisposition to substance abuse problems. I don't want that to happen to you. I love you, Mark. I can't let that happen to you. Hey, I know you're in pain. I know you aren't using the drugs to get high, but that doesn't mean you won't get dependent on them. I can't help but worry about where this is going."

Mark reached out for his sister's hand. "Honey, I'm not Mom. I'm working closely with my doctor, who is prescribing my meds. He even made me sign a pain contract. I'm going for acupuncture. I'm trying. I've got a business to run, and I can't work without meds to help control the pain."

"But Mark, why would you be mixing drugs and alcohol?"

"God, Sophie, it was just a glass of wine... my bad."

"Okay, I don't want to upset you. Just be careful. We love you. Kyle and Lucy and I couldn't bear it if anything happened to you."

"I know, Sis, but nothing is going to happen to me. I've got it under control." Mark wiped the tear that was running down his sister's cheek.

The little talk that Mark had with his sister made him feel like shit. When he got home, Kyle and Lucy weren't there. He remembered where he had a joint stashed. He went out in the backyard and smoked it. Now he was ravenous. He went back inside and cut a huge piece of lasagna and put it in the microwave. By the time he was finished eating, he felt better.

Chapter 15

Spencer hadn't talked to Bridget since Halloween night... the night they'd had sex for the first time. Spencer couldn't help but wonder if maybe he was rushing into things with Bridget, but then he decided that it had kind of been their third date. He hadn't dated in such a long time. He didn't know what the norm was. Back in the day, he would have thought nothing about having sex with a woman after they had been out three times. This was different. There had been an emotional connection with the sex. Maybe that was what was bothering him. Bridget was so nice. He didn't want to lead her on.

Spencer wished he had somebody he could talk to about this. He did try to talk to his father. It was an extremely awkward conversation. His father said, "Son, I was much older than you are when Mom died. I'm sure it was a little different. Women in their fifties have all kinds of hang-ups about their bodies. They weren't all that easy to get into bed. My relationships were more about companionship and friendship. There wasn't all that much sex. If it was sex that I was after, I would have pursued younger women. I really wasn't all that interested. I didn't have the desire or energy. Your mother was the love of my life. None of the relationships after her seemed to work out. If I did have sex with a woman, it wasn't like I was making love to her. There was no emotional connection. Spencer, you're a young man. It's okay if you fall in love again. I know Anna would want that for you."

Spencer guessed if he had gone to that bereavement group for younger widowers, he might have been able to get some better insight. He had to give his father a lot of credit for even having the conversation with him. Spencer did remember coming home for break in college and seeing a prescription bottle with his dad's name on it in the medicine cabinet of his bathroom. It was a prescription for Viagra. Maybe his dad was getting a lot more than he was willing to share with him. His father was such a gentleman.

Spencer met up with Brad Williams as they were both walking out to the parking garage at the end of the workday. Brad asked him if he wanted to get a drink. It sounded so normal and appealing, but he knew he had better check with Lizzie to see if she could stay a little later. She said that she would be glad to stay and that the kids were fine.

Brad ordered a martini and Spencer had a Scotch. "Are you seeing Bridget O'Connell?" Brad asked. Spencer admitted that he had been out with her a few times. "Good for you. She's very nice and such a good nurse... beautiful, too."

"How did you know?" asked Spencer.

Brad chuckled. "Actually, Martina told me. She said that Scarlett told her. Kids don't miss much. You know my wife was a new widow when we first met. Her husband had only been dead a few months when I first started seeing her." Brad told him the whole story.

"Those first relationships after a spouse dies can be complicated. It was difficult for both of us. Beverly couldn't let go of her husband, and I felt like I was competing with him even though he was dead. He was always so present in our relationship. I tried to be patient and earn her trust. She had to realize that I loved her, and I wasn't trying to replace her husband. She had to learn to love *me*."

"I guess that's how I'm feeling, too. It's hard for me to completely let go of Anna, and when I do, I feel guilty, like I betrayed her. Bridget's wonderful, but I'm still so raw. I don't want to hurt her because of my confusion."

"Hang in there. Be patient with yourself. Bridget's no dummy. She probably understands how vulnerable you are."

Spencer stayed with Brad longer than he had planned. When he got home, Lizzie had already fed the kids, and she was helping Haley with her homework. Ivy was coloring. She had a plate of food set aside for him. Spencer apologized for being so late. "I was happy to stay," Lizzie said.

"Lizzie made meatloaf," Haley said. "She made yummy mashed potatoes, too. It was really good." Lizzie was trying so hard. She was even cooking more, which Spencer really appreciated. She told Spencer that she had looked in her mom's recipe file for kid-friendly recipes. Her mother had made notations on a recipe if the kids had liked it. Lizzie always made sure the girls had some kind of vegetable. Tonight, it was broccoli. She was good with Ivy. Spencer thought that Ivy was doing much better. After a little while, she got her coat and gave each of the girls a hug. She looked at Spencer and smiled. "Good night, Spencer, I'll see you in the morning."

Lizzie had a big test the next day. She'd stayed at her job a lot longer than she had anticipated, but she didn't care. She really didn't think of it so much as a job anymore. She loved the girls, and she had to admit, she had a little crush on Spencer. She felt needed. He paid her generously. It was a win-win for everybody.

"We really like Lizzie," Haley said. "I wish she could stay for dinner every night."

"I like it when she plays her guitar," said Ivy. "She sings pretty songs."

Spencer didn't even know about the guitar. He was glad things were working out so well. The move to Rochester had been a good idea. He liked his job, and he found working with the residents to be rewarding. He decided to give Bridget a call to see when she was free to go out again. She had said that she was off this weekend and Saturday would be fine. Spencer was planning on taking her to a movie.

Bridget was thrilled that Spencer had called her. She was a little disappointed that he hadn't called before this, but she sensed that he was still having a hard time moving forward after his wife's death. Maybe it was the sex. She reassured herself that it was he who'd initiated it. She remembered how melancholy he'd gotten afterwards. *Oh, be careful, Bridget.*

Scarlett wasn't there when Spencer went to pick Bridget up. She was spending the night at Bridget's parents' house. Bridget greeted him with a warm smile. Spencer felt a little guilty for waiting so long to call her, so he'd decided to bring flowers for her. He'd chosen a bouquet of salmon-colored roses. She was clearly delighted. "Spencer, you are so sweet." She rewarded him with a kiss. After the movie, they went to a bar that featured a great piano player and singer. They stayed to listen and have a drink.

Although the music was good, they both decided they would rather go back to Bridget's than stay and have another drink. It was still before midnight when they left. It was kind of like they read each other's minds... anxious to get back to

Bridget's house and maybe into the bedroom. It was exactly what they did. Spencer was glad that Lizzie had told him to stay out as late as he wanted. She'd said she had a paper to write.

Spencer was able to keep his feelings in check. He just focused on Bridget. She was funny and sweet and beautiful. She was good in bed. Spencer wished that he could spend the entire night with her, but he knew it was time to go.

"Bridget, I wish I could stay. I hope you understand that I would stay if I could. We will have to figure out how to make that happen soon."

Bridget kissed him. "I know. It's just another challenge of single parenthood. See you soon?"

"Yes, for sure, I'll call you." Spencer took off. He felt better about things. It had been a good night. Lizzie was sitting at the kitchen table working on her laptop when he got home. She asked him about his night, and they talked a little bit about the girls. After she shut down her computer, she put on her coat, and again there was that kiss on the cheek.

"Good night, Spencer." He still felt a little uneasy about that. He wondered if Lizzie had a boyfriend.

The Sunday forecast was rain all day. Brad called Spencer and asked if he wanted to come over and watch football. The Buffalo Bills were playing the Philadelphia Eagles. It was supposed to be a good game. Brad remembered that Spencer was from Philadelphia. "Bring the girls. They can play while we watch the game." Spencer was thrilled with the invitation.

Brad had a great house. There was a large, well-equipped playroom. The girls were having a great time. Every now and then they would emerge and ask for a snack or run up to Martina's bedroom. Brad's wife watched the game with Spencer and Brad. Spencer thought she was very attractive. Looking at her, it was hard to believe that she was Martina's grandmother. At halftime, Beverly asked Spencer if he and the girls would stay for dinner. "I made a lot, hoping that you would stay," she said.

"Thank you. That would be great." Beverly poured herself another glass of wine and got more beers for the guys. She refilled the bowl with the guacamole. Spencer couldn't stop eating it. He thought it was delicious, with just the right amount of heat. She also put out some cheese and crackers. It was a pretty exciting game. The Bills won with a field goal in overtime. Brad told Spencer how, when he'd moved to Rochester, he'd discovered how crazy Bills fans could be. He and his partner, Peter Dwyer, had gone to Buffalo a few times to catch a home game.

Spencer thought dinner was delicious. Beverly was an incredible cook. She made chicken enchiladas, a tossed salad, and homemade cornbread. She made a kid-friendly version for the girls. For dessert, she made these incredibly decadent brownies. It had been such a fun afternoon. Of course, the girls didn't want it to end.

Spencer was in such a good mood when he got home. He put the girls to bed and read them a story.

"Daddy," Ivy said. "I like houses where there are mommies. Will we ever have a mommy again?"

"Oh, honey, I don't know, but I think so. But if you do have a new mommy, I will make sure she is kind and loves you. I promise."

"Maybe Lizzie can be our mommy," Ivy said. Spencer was speechless. He wanted to say the right thing.

"I'm glad you like Lizzie and that she takes such good care of you, but she is your nanny."

Haley held her sister's hand. "Don't worry, Ivy, it will be okay."

Chapter 16

Ruby got her purse and swiped out for the workday. She was exhausted and still had to go to her doctor's appointment. She was glad that Mario was able to take her today. She waited in front of the hospital, watching for his car.

"Baby, you look tired." He leaned over to give her a kiss. "Maybe you should ask the doctor about getting you out of work."

"Mario, you know I want to work as long as I can. I was hoping to hang in there until thirty-two weeks." She was twenty-eight weeks now. "It was just busy today because two nurses called in sick. There's a nasty cold going around."

The nurse at the clinic took her blood pressure and raised her eyebrows. "Ruby, that's a little high today. Your blood pressure is 140/88. Your norm has been about 120/70." Her doctor wasn't happy about her blood pressure, either.

"Ruby, are you having any headaches or abnormalities with your vision?"

"No, I feel fine. I'm just a little tired today. I just got out of work."

He looked at her feet. They were a little swollen, but nothing out of the ordinary, considering she was carrying twins and had been on her feet all day. "Your urine dip was negative... no protein. Are the babies active?" He listened to each of their heartbeats.

"Oh, they're crazy active."

"I want you to do a twenty-four-hour urine collection so that I know what your baseline is, in case you do develop problems with your blood pressure and preeclampsia. I think it's time to go out on disability. I want you to get as close to term as possible."

"Are you sure I need to stop work now? I was hoping to work until thirty-two weeks."

"I am, Ruby. I want to see you carry these babies until at least thirty-six weeks. I don't need to remind you that you aren't as young as you were when you had your first set of twins. We need to be prudent."

Ruby knew it was the right thing to do. Life was always hectic, especially with Mario being in school. She was tired. It would give her time to prepare for the babies, and the holidays were right around the corner. She was always worried about money. Lately she had put in a fair amount of overtime because her unit was understaffed. The extra money had helped. She could forget that now.

"Ruby, I want you to lie down on your left side, and we will check your pressure again in about fifteen minutes." Dr. Lewis left the room and went to write a note to excuse Ruby from work for the duration of her pregnancy. Something was nagging him. He was concerned about Ruby's condition. He was quite fond of her. She had been his patient for twenty years now. He thought she was a remarkable woman, and he knew that she had been though a lot in her lifetime.

The nurse came back in to recheck her blood pressure. It was 132/84. Dr. Lewis came back into the room. "Well, that's a little better. Mario, I want you to check Ruby's pressure twice a day. Call me if that systolic is 146 or greater and the diastolic

90 or greater. Please take it easy, Ruby. I want to see you every week now."

Ruby was quiet on the ride home. Mario looked over at her. "Oh, baby, you've got to be good. Leaving work now is the right thing to do. Don't worry, we'll be fine. Some of the OR nurses are trying to get rid of some of their call time. I can for sure grab a few hours that way. It will help out with money for Christmas."

Ruby got the mail on the way into the house. She saw the letter with the return address: Attica Correctional Facility. *"Oh, Jesus, what does he want?"* She ripped open the letter. Jerome had been writing her more often since Dwight died. Ruby knew that Jerome was trying to show remorse for all of the pain he had caused her. He always started his letters by telling her how much he loved her. This time he wrote to tell her that he remembered his son's birthday and prayed for his soul every day. He said that he was also praying for her and his girls. Jerome went on to say that the love of Jesus was saving him. If she could find it in her heart to forgive him and love him back, he would for sure be saved and could be a new man. He closed by saying that someday they would be a family again.

In a very small and deeply buried place in Ruby's heart, there was love for Jerome, but he was a viper. He could be dangerous. He, however, was the father of three of her children. That would never change. Ruby had been taught about the power of forgiveness by her own father, who was a Baptist minister. She had forgiven Jerome, but she couldn't forget. She couldn't forget the beatings. She could never let him into her life again. Ruby ripped up the letter and tossed it into the trash.

Ruby got a call from Beverly to confirm the Thanksgiving plans. Beverly wanted to know how Ruby was feeling and if everything was going well with her pregnancy. Ruby told her how the doctor had taken her out of work. "Ruby, I have a lot of time on my hands, just come for Thanksgiving. You really don't need to bring anything. You should be resting."

"Beverly, it's really no trouble. I want to bring my usual dishes...my candied sweet potatoes and my macaroni and cheese. The girls will help me. We are all looking forward to it."

"Okay, Ruby, we will see you about two o'clock then? Martina is so excited. Please take care." Beverly knew that once Ruby had her mind set on something, there was no changing it. She knew that taking it easy would be hard for Ruby. Beverly wanted to help, but accepting help didn't come easily to Ruby. She lived life on her own terms.

Ruby had a tumultuous sleep. In her dreams she could see Jerome. His face was handsome, and he kissed her. Then he had his angry face and showed her his gun. In her dream she was pregnant. He grabbed her and slammed her against the wall. Ruby cried out in her sleep. "No! Don't hurt my babies!" It awoke Mario. He held her. She was crying, and her heart was pounding. She wouldn't talk about it.

Chapter 17

Lucy was excited that she was going to Martina's today for Thanksgiving. Grandma was coming, too. She was proud that they were bringing the cut-out cookies decorated like turkeys that Poppy had made. They were also bringing a birthday cake for Martina's granny. Her daddy was helping her pick out her dress. "I hope Poppy's back feels better before we go to Martina's, Daddy. I hate it when Poppy's back hurts."

"He'll be all right, honey." Kyle brushed her hair and tied the ribbon around her ponytail. Kyle knew he wasn't as good at doing Lucy's hair as Mark was. "There, look how pretty you are today. You are a princess." Lucy twirled around in her dress. She put her arms around Kyle.

"I love you, Daddy. "Can we play Candy Land until Poppy's ready to go?"

"Sure, honey, you go set up the game, and I'll go see how Poppy's doing."

Mark was just getting out of the shower. Kyle went over to him. "Are you doing okay? I know you had a pretty restless night."

"I'm much better now." Mark reached out for Kyle and held him tightly. "I love you, Kyle. It's going to be a good day. We have so much to be thankful for. We have each other, we have Lucy, and we just bought a great house." In the spring, they had moved into their new house. It was an arts-and-crafts-style house that was built in 1918. It had been beautifully restored by the previous owners. Once they had Lucy, they'd known that they needed to move out of the city. Their new home was in a suburb just next to the city. The house was brick and stone and had beautiful woodwork and leaded glass inside. It had a gourmet kitchen and a great yard for Lucy.

Kyle looked forward to Thanksgiving every year since this gathering of friends had started four years ago. He remembered how beautiful Beverly's daughter, Erica, had been. Her boyfriend, Dwight, had been just as handsome as she was beautiful. How sad it was that they were gone, but this Thanksgiving tradition was a wonderful tribute to them. Beverly was a great hostess.

The guys were involved in the football game. The ladies had their own gathering in the kitchen. Kyle looked over at Mark. He saw that he had a glass of wine. That always made Kyle uneasy, but he could see that Mark was barely touching it. Martina and Lucy were having a great time.

Brad asked Mark how he was doing with his back. Kyle was interested in his answer. "Well, Brad, I really think the acupuncture is helping. I'm coping."

"If you ever change your mind about exploring surgical options, I'm sure my colleague, Fred Thomas, would have a lot of good information to share with you. As a neurosurgeon, his entire practice is devoted to the treatment of back pain. He has had a lot of success, which has earned him quite a national reputation."

"Oh, Dr. Thomas is good," Mario added. "I love working on his cases."

"Thanks, I'll give it some more thought."

Kyle knew that Mark would never go for it. He was much more into pharmacology... way too nice of a word. Mark was into drugs.

Martina and Lucy were playing with their American Girl baby dolls. Beverly had bought a doll that was black for Martina. *Did she really have a choice?* Martina had named her doll Jasmine. Beverly and Brad had been amused when she'd said that it was a good name for a black baby. The girls ran into the kitchen with their dolls and said that they needed to warm up their bottles. Martina had an announcement. "Grandma Ruby has two babies in her tummy. One is a boy and one is a girl. The babies will be black like me. The girl baby will be named Lillie Mae. That was Papa Mario's mother's name. I wish the baby's name could be Nancy."

"You don't know that they will be black!" exclaimed Lucy.

"Oh, yes, I do!" Martina said. "Of course they will be black, because Grandma Ruby and Papa Mario are black."

Lucy was perplexed. "But you turned out black and your mommy and daddy are white."

"Oh, girls, it really doesn't matter, does it? God chooses boy or girl and black or white. He knows what's best for everyone," Helen said. She reached out and put her arms around both of the girls. She hugged them. "I think *your* babies are really hungry. You better get them fed and put them down for their naps. Maybe we can play a game while they are sleeping." Helen was always great at diffusing a difficult situation.

Beverly was glad that conversation was over. She looked over at Ruby and smiled. "More wine, anyone?" She filled Ruby's water glass. Ruby looked very tired.

Helen reached over and took Ruby by the hand. "Ruby, dear, why don't you go upstairs to the guest room and lie down for a little while before dinner. I'll keep the girls quiet so that you can rest."

"Please do, Ruby," Beverly said. "Come on, I'll walk you up." Beverly sat down in a chair next to the bed. "Will you let me help?" she asked. "I want to take care of the babies' room. Martina's crib is still in perfect condition, and I can get another one to match. I looked, and they still sell the same model. You can use her changing table, dresser, and rocking chair, too. It's not being used now and is just being stored in the basement. You know how I love to decorate. I really want to do this. I can pick up some samples of paint colors, and you can choose what you think you would like. Remember the mural I painted for Martina's nursery? I would love to do something similar for the new babies' room. It will be fun! I will think of something that would be good for a little boy or a little girl. We can get Danielle and Denise in on the project. They will love it. I'm sure Helen would love to make curtains. Please Ruby, let me do this."

"Thank you, Beverly. That would be nice." Ruby thought it was very nice, but she really wanted to do the nursery herself. She had to admit that she really didn't have the energy for it, and money was tight. This was a very generous offer. Deep in a dark place in Ruby's mind was a voice that said, *"Does she think that we can't provide for our own babies?* Then she felt awful about thinking that, because Beverly had always been so kind to her, and her offer was so sincere. Ruby's relationship with Beverly had always been a little complicated. Ruby closed her eyes, and she was actually able to drift off to sleep.

Beverly and Pam chatted while they made the final preparations for dinner. Beverly was so happy for Pam. She had a new man in her life. She was seeing a retired high school principal. His name was Sam. Beverly hadn't met him yet. She hoped it would work out for her. He was coming over later for a drink.

Dinner was finally ready. Ruby came down and looked better. Mark was starting to feel anxious, and his damned nose wouldn't stop running. Kyle looked over at him a little suspiciously. Mark decided he better do something before everyone got seated at the table. He knew that snorting a little heroin was out of the question. His nose was too runny, and it was too risky in someone else's bathroom. He had splurged and bought a few OxyContin tablets for just this situation. He went to the kitchen for a glass of water and took a pill without anyone noticing. He stayed to help in the kitchen. Beverly put him on carving the turkey and garnishing the platter. *Thank God the Oxy kicked in.* Helen got Martina and Lucy seated at the table. Brad gathered everyone else to the table and said grace.

Brad always knew just the right thing to say.

"Those seated at this table are bound by friendship, family ties, and misfortune. But God has made it all work out somehow, and for that we are thankful. We are all so fortunate to have found each other, and now we are blessed in so many new ways. Lastly, God bless this abundant feast and the hands that have prepared it. We are truly grateful."

"Martina and Lucy, do you want to say the grace that you learned in school?" The two girls stood up and held hands.

"Thank you for the world so sweet.

Thank you for the food we eat.

Thank you for the birds that sing.

Thank you, God, for everything.

Amen."

Then Mark raised his glass for a toast. "To Erica and Dwight...they made this tradition possible."

Kyle looked over at Mark and smiled. Drug problem or not, he loved his husband.

Tears were dried and everybody started eating. Beverly's table was beautiful and the food was delicious.

Finally, coffee and dessert were served. Everyone sang "Happy Birthday" as Helen blew out the candles on her cake. She walked around the room and hugged everyone there. After dinner, drinks were poured and Sam arrived.

Everyone loved meeting him. Sam was charming. He was a widower who had lost his wife to cancer. Lucy took to him immediately. She had even asked him if he would be her grandpa. That made Kyle so very sad. Her real grandfather, his father, would have nothing to do with his son, who was gay, and for sure would not approve of his marriage to Mark or their having a child. He knew it probably tugged at Mark's heart strings, too, as Mark was very close to his dad, who'd never lived long enough to see his grandchildren.

It was late when everyone finally left. Lucy ended up staying for a sleepover. Martina was thrilled. Brad drove Helen home.

It had been a wonderful but exhausting day. There was a lot of pillow talk that night.

Chapter 18

Spencer had decided to take call for Thanksgiving so that he wouldn't have to work for Christmas. His father drove up to spend the Thanksgiving weekend with him and the girls. Haley and Ivy were thrilled that Grandpa was coming. His dad was a great cook... pulling off a traditional turkey dinner was well within his skill set. Bridget was so sweet. She insisted on baking an apple pie and pumpkin pie and sending them over. She was spending the holiday with her parents and younger sister. Spencer loved having his dad there. He was such a stabilizing force in his life. His dad was there when Bridget dropped off the pies. Spencer was able to introduce them.

"Bridget's beautiful, son, and she seems very nice. How are things going with her?"

"Oh, Dad, I guess they're going all right. It's all just a little complicated with the kids. She has a little girl who's in Ivy's preschool class. When we're together with the kids, we really can't be intimate. On date nights, it's like we're in high school. We have to be home before curfew... the babysitter's curfew."

His father chuckled. "I get it, son."

"It's hard enough loving another woman after Anna. Did I say 'love'? What I meant to say was that it's hard being with another woman after Anna. Dad, you know how much I loved her. Bridget's wonderful, and I'm very attracted to her. I'm afraid to move forward, and I always have to consider the girls."

"Son, you're a young man. Let yourself love again. If it's meant to be, it will work out some way. Here's an idea. I'm in no rush to get back to Philly. Why don't you and Bridget get away for a weekend? I can stay here with the girls. Maybe it would help you to sort out your feelings."

"Oh, Dad, that's a great offer. I like the idea." Spencer remembered what Brad Williams had told him. He'd said that early in his relationship with Beverly, he'd taken her to New York for the weekend. It was Christmastime. He said it had really jump-started the relationship.

"How about Cape May?" his father suggested. "There is always something going on there at Christmastime."

"Dad, how can I take her there? It's where Anna and I met and where we were married."

"Oh, right, probably not there then… a terrible suggestion."

"There's a really quaint village on one of the Finger Lakes that someone told me about… Skaneateles. He said that he takes his wife there every year. He said that it's always decked out for Christmas, and that they have some kind of Dickens theme going on. It's not that far from here so we could drive, which would make arranging things a little easier. When I was here doing my residency, we did a wine tour of the Finger Lakes region. It's beautiful country. I'll ask Bridget tomorrow night if she's free to go.
Thanks, Dad."

Spencer had plans to take Bridget out the Friday after Thanksgiving. Her younger sister was home from college and agreed to babysit. His Dad would be with his girls. Spencer got tickets to a performance of the Rochester Philharmonic Orchestra. He was looking forward to the evening. Scarlett answered the door. "Hi, Dr. Harris, Mommy's almost ready. She looks really pretty tonight."

Spencer smiled and picked up Scarlett for a hug. "I'll bet she does, Scarlett." He introduced himself to Bridget's sister, Megan. Bridget did look beautiful... stunning. She wore a red silk sheath dress that showed off her curves beautifully. She had her hair up with dangling earrings. Bridget had great legs, which she showed off with some sexy heels.

"Bridget, you look lovely tonight." He kissed her on the cheek and helped her with her coat. Bridget kissed her daughter and they were off.

Spencer wanted to kiss her when he got her in the car, which he did. Her perfume, though it was subtle, almost made him dizzy. He kissed her again. *Get a grip, Spencer,* he said to himself.

The concert was great. Spencer was happy that Rochester offered some decent cultural experiences, something he'd always enjoyed living in Philadelphia. They went out for a drink after the concert. Bridget liked merlot. He ordered a good bottle of merlot and an appetizer for them to share. They chatted about their Thanksgivings.

"Bridget, my dad has offered to stay in Rochester for a while. He really misses the girls, and I think he is kind of lonely. Would you be able to get away for a weekend before Christmas? Could you have your parents watch Scarlett?"

Bridget reached for his hand and smiled. "I would love to. I'm sure my parents would take Scarlett, but I'm not off until the second weekend in December. Would that work?"

"I'm sure that would be fine. We can try to leave after work on that Friday. I'll make the arrangements. Imagine…two nights together."

They finished their wine and Spencer drove her back home. He walked her to the door and kissed her. She looked at him and said, "Spencer, please come in." She took his hand and led him into the house. "My sister has her own car. You can stay for a while. This has been such a wonderful evening. I don't want it to end."

They chatted a few minutes with Megan, and she said good night. Spencer walked her out to her car. Bridget checked in on Scarlett. It was less than five minutes before Spencer was unzipping Bridget's dress and had her on the bed. Spencer couldn't help himself. Sex with Bridget was always fantastic. Afterwards, he held her.

He hated going there in his head, but sex with Bridget was wild and crazy. Sex with Anna had been passionate but more tender and reserved. Sex with Anna was an intensely emotional experience. Sex with Bridget was all about physical gratification. He hated the comparison, but that's the way it was. He never asked her, but he didn't even know how old Bridget was. He wondered if she was much younger than him. Anna and he were the same age. *I shouldn't be thinking about Anna when I'm holding another woman.*

"Where are you, Spencer? Where did you go?" Bridget asked.

He didn't know what to say. "I'm sorry, I just had a moment." He kissed Bridget to reassure her. "It's wonderful being with you. I can't wait to get away and have you for the entire night and then see your face when I wake up in the morning."

"You can do that tonight. Your dad is with the girls and probably already asleep. You can stay."

"As much as I'd like to, I probably shouldn't. What would Scarlett think about seeing me here in the morning? My girls wouldn't like it if I wasn't there for them in the morning. They wouldn't understand."

"Oh, Spencer, that's why I like you so much. You are such a considerate man. You are so principled. Make love to me again before you leave me."

Spencer thought he was falling in love with Bridget, but he couldn't help but wonder if it was too soon.

It was after two A.M. when Spencer finally got home. Bridget was right. His dad was already in bed. Spencer had a hard time falling asleep. It suddenly occurred to him that the Friday after Thanksgiving was the very first time he had made love to Anna after meeting her that September. How ironic that tonight was a big step in moving forward with his relationship with Bridget. Spencer knew he was torturing himself with these comparisons. He finally fell asleep. The next day he had to go to the hospital for a while to check on a few patients. He was happy for the distraction. He ran into Brad Williams at the hospital. They decided to go to a nearby pub for lunch.

Spencer told Brad about his plans to get away with Bridget. Brad was happy for him. He wanted to confide in Brad about his conflicted feelings when he was with Bridget. "I am still so in love with my wife. I'm starting to have feelings for Bridget, but I can't get my wife out of my head when I'm with her."

"Your feelings for Bridget shouldn't diminish the love you still have for Anna. Anna is the mother of your children, and I'm sure you will always love her. Let yourself live again. Beverly and I went through all of this. It's all very complicated...I know."

"Hey, how old do you think Bridget is?"

Brad looked puzzled. "Why do you ask? I would think that she's in her late twenties or thirty, maybe."

"Yeah, that's what I think, too. She's probably a bit younger than me."

Brad smiled and said, "That's a good thing, right?"

"Right," Spencer said.

"Hey, she's cute and sexy and smart. She seems warm and sincere. Just see how it goes."

"Good advice, Brad, thanks."

Spencer and his dad took the girls to a movie when he got back from the hospital. Later his dad made dinner. They had a glass of wine while he was cooking. "Dad, you don't mind staying another two weeks?"

"No, I love the time with the girls. I always get a bit lonely around the holidays since Mom died. Why don't we get a tree tomorrow? It will be fun." Last year, Anna's sisters had come over and put up a tree and decorated it for him. He wanted to try harder this year. He felt like he'd really let the girls down last year.

Spencer knew his father never put up a tree anymore. He always spent Christmas at one of his brother's houses. He was glad that this time with his father was good for both of them. Spencer's mother had died right before Christmas. This year would mark twenty years. This was probably a difficult year for his dad, too. Spencer's father was his hero. His dad never showed any weakness. After his mother died, his father had just pushed forward with getting his sons through high school and college. He'd gone to their weddings and baptisms of grandchildren, always alone. His father was a rock, but insightful, kind, and gentle, as well. Spencer would never forget how his father had cared for his mother as she was dying. As much as he admired his father, Spencer wanted his story to turn out differently. He didn't want to be alone the rest of his life.

Spencer called Lizzie to tell her she could have the next two weeks off. She was actually okay with it because she had a lot of work to do for school. Spencer insisted on paying her anyway.

The girls were so excited about decorating the tree. Grandpa made everything more fun. Haley asked if they could buy an angel for the top of the tree instead of putting up a star. She said that the angel could be Mommy watching over them. Spencer took them shopping to find just the right angel. It was such a precious idea, how could he not? Spencer thought it was kind of a lot of work to put up a tree, considering he was planning on taking the girls to Philadelphia for Christmas, but he knew a Christmas tree was an important part of Christmas for kids. They would enjoy the tree until they left for Philadelphia on Christmas Eve morning. Spencer told the girls he was writing a letter to Santa telling him that they would be at Uncle Bill's house on Christmas morning. He knew that he needed to spend Christmas Eve with Anna's family. Christmas Day would be with his family at his brother's house. It was just too soon to spend Christmas without both families. Spencer was determined to make it work.

Chapter 19

Business was booming at Sugar Plum. December was always busy, with wedding cakes, cakes for Christmas parties, and people requesting Mark's beautifully decorated sugar cookies. Mark hired temporary help. He was working long hours. Long hours meant more pain. It had been a busy, hectic Saturday at the shop. Pam was taking Lucy for the night so that he and Kyle could have dinner and do Christmas shopping. They would put up the tree on Sunday. Mark was looking forward to the evening with Kyle and the fun of putting up the tree with Lucy. *But God, I'm in so much pain. I just need to feel good.* He needed something to get him through the rest of the weekend. It was pretty easy to buy drugs on the street in Rochester. He knew that he could walk down a few blocks from his shop and buy a few packets of heroin on the street corner. He did just that. As he was walking back to the shop, a police car pulled up next to him and two cops got out. They had watched him buy the drugs and were arresting him for possession. They took the heroin, asked for ID, handcuffed him, and told him to get in the car. Mark was panicked. He couldn't believe it had come down to this.

At the police station, he was fingerprinted and booked. He was allowed to make his phone call. He knew Kyle would be furious. He was relieved that Lucy was with Kyle's mother. Mark was so ashamed. *Merry fucking Christmas!* He called Kyle, who came down to the station with one of their friends who was an attorney. Mark would never forget the look on Kyle's face when he walked in.

The quantity of heroin in his possession was very small. He was charged with a class-A misdemeanor. Mark had never been arrested before. His record was clean. His attorney convinced the desk sergeant that he was a respected businessman and that he didn't use drugs for recreation. He had a narcotics prescription for pain control and only resorted to heroin when he needed additional relief. They released Mark after he paid a preset bail of five hundred dollars. He was given a date to appear in drug treatment court.

Kyle drove Mark home. He was a mess. He was crying and was having some mild symptoms of withdrawal. Kyle was understandably angry at first, but now he just felt sorry for Mark. He knew that he had a big problem. He loved this man. Somehow, he would help him get through this. Mark took his prescribed evening dose of OxyContin and hoped it would kick in soon. Kyle made pasta, and they talked through dinner. Kyle said he wanted Mark to go to rehab after Christmas. He reassured Mark that he loved him, but he couldn't stay in a marriage with a drug addict. He went on to say that he would get a divorce and sue for custody of Lucy if Mark didn't get clean. Mark couldn't believe that Kyle threatened him with a divorce and taking custody of Lucy. He knew he must be very angry.

Mark didn't know how to tell Kyle how sorry he was. He begged for his forgiveness. Kyle said he could forgive him, but he would never forget. He said for the sake of their marriage and their daughter, Mark had to go to rehab. Mark was crying again. He kissed Kyle and said, "Okay." He went to bed.

Kyle wanted to call Sophie because he needed to talk, but he couldn't bring himself to upset her, too. Kyle was so wound up. He was worried about Mark and his marriage. *What will happen in drug court? Will Mark have to go to jail? What about*

Mark's business? He hated that people might find out. He poured himself a glass of wine and got out his computer. He needed some kind of distraction. He decided to do some Christmas shopping online. He also did some research on opiate addiction and addiction specialists in Rochester. That night Kyle was too hurt and angry to sleep with Mark. He slept in the guest room.

Mark was up before Kyle the next morning. He had made cinnamon buns, which were Kyle's absolute favorite. Kyle could smell them baking. Mark was also frying up bacon and working on the eggs. Kyle walked into the kitchen and poured himself coffee. He said, "Let's try to move forward from yesterday. We'll get through Christmas and then get you some help." He went over and hugged Mark and they sat down for breakfast. After breakfast, they were going to get Lucy and take her to get a Christmas tree.

Mark vowed that he was only going to take his prescribed OxyContin. He would do his best to deal with any withdrawal symptoms. He realized now, it was about so much more than pain control. It was about cravings and getting high… feeling good. His love for Kyle and Lucy had to get him through this.

Mark and Kyle had an appointment with an addiction specialist the following week. He suggested that Mark would benefit from a methadone program because it would help to control his pain but also reduce his cravings. He also said that it might be better for him to seek treatment away from Rochester. He knew of a good facility in Syracuse. After his inpatient stay, and once he was stabilized on methadone, he could come back to Rochester, and he would continue to oversee his treatment. Mark and Kyle felt comfortable with Dr. Lamb and were hopeful that his plan was the answer. He gave Mark a letter that he could show the judge when he went to drug treatment court the following week.

Drug court was a humbling experience. Mark looked around at the others who were waiting their turn to appear before the judge. Some of the defendants looked pretty normal and others really skanky. Mark's attorney argued his case. He showed the judge Mark's prescription for OxyContin and explained his problems with chronic back pain. He also informed the judge that Mark was a respected businessman and last year was given an award for Small Businessman of the Year. He submitted Dr. Lamb's letter, which showed his intent to get addiction treatment.

The judge looked over his reading glasses at Mark. "Sir, heroin possession is a serious crime. I can see you were in possession of a very small amount.

However, you have still committed a class-A misdemeanor, which can be punishable by up to one year in jail. I understand that you are a family man and your substance abuse problems stem from a medical issue. You seem earnest in your desire to get your problem under control. You will not have to do jail time but will be responsible for a one-thousand-dollar fine and will have to follow up regularly with the court. You will have to do some community service. Good luck to you."

Mark and Kyle both breathed a sigh of relief. As they were walking out of the courthouse, Mark saw Melanie, the surrogate they'd used to give birth to Lucy, walking down the hall. She was deep in conversation with someone. Mark asked Kyle, "Did you see Melanie? What if she fucking saw us before we got in the elevator?"

"I didn't see her," Kyle said. Later they found out that she was clerking in the DA's office until she finished her last year of law school and passed the bar.

Chapter 20

Beverly wanted to move forward on her project to decorate Ruby and Mario's nursery. She wanted to get it done before Christmas. She was worried about running out of time if Ruby had the babies early. She had made a pot of tomato basil soup, and she was planning on taking it over to Ruby's with some paint-sample cards. She and Ruby had already decided that they would do the room in primary colors so that it would be good for both a boy and a girl. Beverly was glad to see that Ruby was resting when she got there...not sleeping but resting on the couch. Beverly still thought she looked tired.

Beverly asked her how her doctor's appointment had gone this week. Ruby looked at her and said, "Blood pressure is a little elevated." She went on to say that her doctor wasn't overly concerned because there was no protein in her urine and her non-stress test was good.

"What's a non-stress test?" Beverly asked.

"They monitor the babies' heartbeats to see if they accelerate with fetal movement. If they do, it is a reassuring sign that the babies are getting adequate amounts of oxygen across the placenta."

Beverly sliced the fresh bread that she'd brought and ladled them up some soup. She assured Ruby that she'd made the soup with low-sodium broth.

"Beverly, you are so good to me, and I thank you for taking charge of the nursery. I've got to admit that I don't have the energy for it." They looked at paint colors after eating and decided on a soft yellow. Beverly described her idea of painting one of the walls with big red and blue polka dots. I can paint a big teddy bear down in the corner." Ruby loved the idea. Beverly told her she would have liked to paint something more elaborate like she did for Martina's room, but didn't think she could get it done in time.

"Helen will make polka dot curtains and a matching cushion for your rocking chair. We will paint the trim white, and it will look nice with the white furniture."

"It sounds perfect to me... adorable!" Ruby said.

They chatted awhile about Martina and the rest of the family. Ruby wanted Beverly and Brad to come along with Martina to her sister Sarah's house for a little while on Christmas Eve. "And please bring Helen."

Beverly had gotten to know Sarah and her husband, Henry, when Erica and Dwight were dating. She thought that they were very nice people. She knew it was important to Ruby that Martina would spend some time with her father's family during the holidays. Ruby had said on more than one occasion that she didn't want Martina to forget her black heritage. Martina was becoming more curious about it every day.

Beverly was glad that she didn't own the shop anymore. She managed to keep very busy. There was so much to do before Christmas, and she wanted the room done before then. She was hoping the painter could finish the room this week, and next week she could paint the accent wall with the polka dots and the teddy bear. The new crib would be delivered next week. Mario was borrowing a truck from a friend, and he was coming over to get Martina's old crib and the rest of the nursery furniture. Beverly had already seen the fabric that she wanted for the curtains and cushion. She could stop and purchase it on the way home. Helen could get started sewing. Beverly made some measurements in the room before she left.

She was excited to do this for Ruby and Mario. Beverly was always happy when she had a project. It kept her from dwelling on things that made her sad. She was still having problems with depression. Antidepressive medication and weekly therapy sessions with Dr. Martino seemed to be helping. He encouraged her to stay busy and to do things that she could control and that would give her satisfaction. Too much had happened in Beverly's life that she couldn't control, the last being her pregnancy and miscarriage.

Mario got home. He had class tonight. He took one look at Ruby and said, "Oh, babe, you look tired." Mario couldn't shake the worry he had for Ruby and the babies. He checked her blood pressure before he left. It was her normal, but he thought she looked so damned tired. He also thought that she got short of breath too easily, but she had a big uterus pushing up on her pleural space. He knew a little bit about OB because in school he was going up to the birth center with his preceptor to put in epidurals. He knew that most OB patients were generally pretty healthy, but when things went bad, they could go really bad. He wanted Ruby to get as close to term as possible with the twins, but he was so worried about her. Mario wanted his wife back…his strong, healthy, energetic wife.

Chapter 21

Clinic was winding down. Spencer couldn't wait to get out of there so that he could start his weekend with Bridget. He'd booked a reservation at the inn in the town of Skaneateles, and they also had a dinner reservation there that night. The girls didn't say too much about him going away for the weekend. When Anna was alive, he and Anna would sometimes get away for the weekend, and the girls would stay with their grandparents. He said he was going away with a friend from the hospital. It was kind of the truth. Spencer couldn't help but notice how beautiful Bridget looked when he went to pick her up. She had a powder-blue cashmere scarf tucked around her neck, which made her eyes even bluer, and tonight they seemed to sparkle. He noticed that she liked to wear the color blue. Spencer was determined to make the weekend about more than just sex. He wanted to get to know Bridget better. He was embarrassed that he didn't even know how old she was. Bridget was hoping it was the beginning of a long-term relationship. She was tired of being single. She sensed that Spencer was still having trouble letting go of his wife. Bridget wanted to be more than a warm body in his bed. Men always thought she was good in bed. On the other hand, she was afraid of falling too hard for him. She didn't want to get her hopes up and be hurt once again.

The ride to Skaneateles was a little more than an hour. "Oh, Spencer, this place is charming. I love it!" He brought their bags up to the room. Their room even had a gas fireplace. It was very inviting. When Spencer booked the room, he'd arranged for champagne to be chilling when they arrived. As much as he wanted to, he didn't think he should just peel her clothes off already. He wanted it to be more tonight... more of a seduction. As for Bridget, she was trying not to appear too eager.

Spencer said, "It's such a beautiful night. We have a lot of time before dinner. The town's all lit up. Let's have some champagne and then take a short walk." He uncorked the bottle and filled their glasses. "Here's to us... Merry Christmas." He kissed her. She was probably expecting him to just throw her on the bed, but instead they sat in front of the fire and enjoyed the champagne. Neither one of them said much. They just enjoyed the moment. Spencer helped her on with her coat and put her scarf around her neck. He kissed her again. "I have plans for you later tonight, pretty lady." Bridget loved that Spencer was romancing her.

The air was cool and crisp. It was a clear night, and the stars were out. There were Christmas lights everywhere. Carolers were singing on the street corner. "Spencer, this is wonderful. I haven't done anything like this in a long time. With work and being a single mom to Scarlett, I don't have much time for me. I'm sure it's got to be the same for you."

"Oh, it is. I have to admit, I'm still having some problems with grief. I miss my wife and the wonderful life we had. Moving to Rochester has helped. Meeting you has helped."

Bridget had hoped Spencer's wife wouldn't be joining them this weekend. It seemed like in some way she was forever present. Bridget didn't have that much experience with grief. Her parents and all of her grandparents were still alive. No one close to her had ever died. Her experience with death was mostly when one of the babies in the NICU died. She knew that had to be different. She did know what it felt to be lonely. If loneliness is what brought her and Spencer together, so be it.

They went back to the inn for dinner. They had the best table in the dining room, in the corner near the fireplace. It was quieter so that they could talk. Spencer reached across the table for Bridget's hand. He said, "Bridget, you never talk about yourself. I know so little about you. I don't know much about your family... only that you have a sister in college and that your parents help you out with Scarlett. I am embarrassed that I don't even know where you went to college or how old you are."

Bridget smiled. "Are you worried that I'm too young for you?"

Now, Spencer smiled. "I don't know, maybe."

Bridget said, "Okay, Dr. Harris, I'm twenty-six. I got my associates degree from Monroe Community College and last year got my B.S. at Nazareth College. I have only one sibling... Megan, who you have met. Is the interview over?"

"You already passed the first interview, with flying colors. Why did you want to be a nurse?"

"It probably started when our family dog, Heidi, had a litter of puppies. She was a dachshund... you know, they call them wiener dogs. Only one of the five puppies survived Heidi's difficult delivery, and even he wasn't doing too well. My mom said it was because of my persistence that he finally made it. Heidi and her puppy slept in my room. I fed him with an eye dropper until he was strong enough to nurse with his mother. I made sure he was warm and held him when he whimpered, which was all the time. I was only ten, but I was on a mission. I named him Snoop. My mom said I would be a nurse someday."

"I love that story," Spencer said. *Okay, she loves babies and puppies. That sounds good so far.*

"High school and college were a struggle for me because I wasn't focused. I had problems with ADHD. I was kind of a party girl. When I got pregnant with Scarlett, I realized that I needed to settle down. I love my job, and I love being a mother."

"It shows. Thank you for sharing all of that with me." Spencer realized that she was very different than Anna, but he was attracted to Bridget's spirit. Who was he kidding? He was attracted to everything about her.

A jazz band was warming up in the bar as they were finishing dessert. Anna never ordered dessert. He loved that Bridget had no reservations about ordering the decadent chocolate layer cake and that she ate every bite.

They went to the bar and ordered after-dinner drinks. Spencer asked Bridget to dance. He held her close. He couldn't help nuzzling her ear as they were dancing. They listened to the music, ordered another drink, and danced a few more times. Spencer and Bridget went back to their room. That night Spencer had the best sex of his life. *Is it awful that I think that? We both had a lot to drink, but so what? It's turned out to be such a fantastic night.*

The next morning, they were both a little hungover. Spencer rolled on his side. "I need a nurse." Bridget kissed him. She wrapped a sheet around herself, got out of bed, and rummaged through her overnight bag. She brought out a bottle of ibuprofen and poured him a glass of water. She took two tablets herself and went into the bathroom. She brushed her teeth. There was this awesome pedestal tub. She started the water and poured in some bubble bath. She put on a robe and went back out into the bedroom. She took Spencer by the hand and led him into the bathroom. She dropped her robe, and they got into the tub. She reclined in his arms, and they enjoyed the moment. "This must be heaven," she said. As soon as she said it, she wished she hadn't. *Does the word* heaven *make Spencer think about his wife?* He seemed unfazed.

It was well after noon before they finally were dressed and emerged from the room. The maid had already knocked on the door twice. They were famished. After lunch, they walked around town and did some shopping. There was ice skating at the community center. Spencer and Bridget skated for a while. "Oh, Spencer, this is so much fun! I haven't been skating since I was a little girl."

That night was another fabulous dinner. This time it was at an Italian restaurant, which actually had its own bakery and vineyard. It was almost like they were in Tuscany. A violin player strolled from table to table. He stopped at their table and said that he would play a special song for the "sweethearts."

Later, back at the inn, there was, of course, more sex. This time it was slower, more deliberate, and more passionate. "I think I'm falling in love with you, Bridget O'Connell." Bridget was afraid to say anything. She didn't want this fairy tale to ever end. Men had said they had fallen in love with her before, but it never lasted.

"Spencer, let's just take this slow."

Bridget fell asleep in Spencer's arms, but he had a hard time winding down to sleep. When he finally did, he had a dream about Anna. He almost never dreamt about Anna. He and Anna were in the shower. He was shampooing Anna's hair, and he made love to her in the shower. Then there was that familiar feeling that you often feel when you are sleeping... like you are falling out of bed. It startles you and wakes you up. He was crying when he woke up. *God, I'm such a mess.* He looked over at Bridget and was relieved that she was sleeping soundly.

His girls were happy to see him when he got home. His dad was driving back to Philadelphia in the morning.

It was back to reality on Monday. Lizzie was there bright and early to get the girls ready for school. She told them that when Haley got home from school, they could bake Christmas cookies. "We missed you so much, Lizzie!" Ivy said.

She hugged the girls. "I've missed you guys, too. I love your Christmas tree!" She walked Haley down to the end of the driveway to wait for the school bus. She kissed Haley and said, "Have a good day! Remember cookie baking when you get home!" Haley waved from the bus until Lizzie was out of sight. When Lizzie got back inside, Spencer was putting on his coat to leave. She kissed him on the cheek. "Have a good day, Spencer." As much as Spencer liked Lizzie, that kiss still made him uncomfortable.

Lizzie drove Ivy to preschool. The girls had told her that Spencer had a date with one of the mothers in Ivy's preschool class. She wondered who it was. It wasn't hard to figure out that it was probably Scarlett's mom. Lizzie checked her out. She didn't think that Scarlett's mother was much older than she was... probably only by a couple of years. She was pretty but not beautiful like Spencer's wife. On the ride home, she thought about Spencer and the girls. She loved the part she played in their lives. Lizzie even thought it would be nice to make the arrangement permanent. Maybe Spencer could fall in love with her, and they could be a family. She was bored with the guys she had been seeing lately. Spencer was so much more. It would be nice to be a doctor's wife. *Hey, it doesn't hurt to dream.*

When Spencer got to the office, even before checking his schedule and reading his email, he called a florist. He sent Bridget a dozen white roses with sprigs of holly. The card read, "Thanks for a wonderful weekend. Love, Spencer." He wasn't going to deny his feelings. He was falling in love with Bridget, but that didn't mean he wasn't still in love with his wife.

Chapter 22

Melanie had seen Kyle and Mark at the courthouse. She was curious as to why they were there. Being a clerk in the DA's office, it was easy for her to find out who had been arrested and why. She couldn't believe it. Mark had gotten picked up for heroin possession! She didn't think Kyle and Mark were the type that would use drugs, and especially not heroin. *Who did I give up my beautiful baby girl to?* She'd never expected this. Now she was worried about her daughter's safety. Melanie wondered if the judge even knew Mark was raising a child and if Child Protective Services was involved. She didn't want to talk to anyone at work about this, because she didn't want anyone to know that she'd sold her egg and rented out her womb to pay for law school.

Melanie had always felt good about her decision to be a surrogate. Now she had serious doubts. She couldn't concentrate on the brief she was writing. She wondered if she should just make a visit to Kyle and Mark's house. She had agreed that she would not be a part of her daughter's life. Melanie didn't want to violate that agreement. She didn't think going there herself was a good decision, but she was genuinely concerned about the welfare of her biological child. Melanie decided to file a complaint with CPS. After all, if drugs were being used in the home, it met the definition of child neglect because it put the child in imminent danger of potential harm. She hated playing hardball, but she thought she had to do it.

A week before Christmas, Kyle picked Lucy up from preschool and decided to stay and work at home for the rest of the day. The doorbell rang. The woman at the door said she was a caseworker from Child Protective Services and a complaint had been filed. Lucy was in the living room working on a floor puzzle and watching TV. Kyle and the caseworker, Mrs. Carpenter, talked in the kitchen. She said that the complaint stated that there was concern that drugs were being used in the home. With a child in the home, it posed a potential for danger or neglect. Kyle explained the situation. He said that he'd known Mark, his husband, took prescription narcotics, but had never seen him use heroin. He had been totally unaware of his heroin use until the arrest, and Mark had told him he only snorted the heroin when he was in pain and his prescription wasn't covering the pain.

Mrs. Carpenter asked Kyle if it was okay if she looked around. She asked to see Lucy's room and also asked to use the bathroom. Kyle was sure she was going to look in the medicine cabinet. He himself had done so after Mark was arrested… both bathrooms. She also looked in the refrigerator and the kitchen cupboards.

Kyle asked, "Who made this complaint?"

"I cannot tell you that unless that person wants to be identified. I must say, though, it looks like Lucy has a stable home here. Your house is lovely. I will still need to talk to your husband, and also to the person who filed the complaint to obtain some additional information."

Lucy walked in and climbed up on Kyle's lap. "Daddy, what are you talking about?"

"Lucy, this is Mrs. Carpenter. We were talking about Poppy's sore back and the medicine he takes to make it feel better."

"It's true," Lucy said. "Poppy has a lot of trouble with his back. Did you know that my Poppy is a very good baker? Do you want a Christmas cookie?"

Kyle put three cookies on a plate and placed them on the table. Mrs. Carpenter picked up a beautifully decorated cut-out of a Christmas tree and took a bite.

"You're so right, Lucy. This cookie is delicious and so pretty, too."

She asked for Mark's cell phone number. "I do hope we get this all straightened out. I'll meet with your husband, and the three of us will meet again."

Kyle was so relieved when she was finally gone. He couldn't believe it had come down to this. He had that sinking feeling about losing Lucy again. It wasn't hard to figure out that it might have been Melanie who'd filed the complaint, or maybe it was the court. The judge hadn't said anything about CPS. He couldn't help thinking that maybe the complaint was justified. If Mark ever brought syringes in the house, it could be dangerous for Lucy. Mark swore he never injected the heroin. Kyle hoped that was true. Lucy was only three. What if she got curious and got into something she found? Mark was Lucy's biological father. What would happen if Mark overdosed and died? Then Kyle worried that he could lose Lucy to Melanie.

Kyle's head was spinning. *What a fucking nightmare!* He was worried on so many levels.

It was a week before Christmas; the bakery was very busy. Kyle wasn't surprised that Mark was late getting home. He told Mark about the caseworker's visit. "I told you I saw Melanie," he said. Kyle had saved Mark a plate of food from dinner. After Mark ate, he put Lucy to bed, and he and Kyle talked.

"Mark, part of me wants to take Lucy and go live at my mom's house until you can get clean. I'm so afraid of losing Lucy. I don't trust Melanie anymore. Maybe if Lucy and I live at my mother's, it will help to appease her."

Mark looked deeply wounded. "Kyle, this is Lucy's home. It's a week before Christmas. Don't do this! Maybe we should meet with Melanie and talk to her. We could invite her here. She could see our home and see that Lucy is happy. Lucy doesn't have to know who she is."

Kyle was not the trusting person that Mark was. He thought it was a horrible idea. He thought that if Melanie saw Lucy, she would know that she was an amazing little girl. She might have regrets. She might want her back. Kyle thought it was best that they meet with their family law attorney, who specialized in these matters. He'd been involved in their surrogacy arrangement and the adoption. It wasn't the same attorney that they'd used for Mark's arrest. Maybe a meeting should be arranged with both of the attorneys present. Kyle thought it was best to be proactive. Kyle wished he could consult his sister. She was shrewd. Working for the DA in Manhattan, she knew New York State law. Colleen could be such a bitch, and he definitely didn't need to hear her *I told you so*. Besides, he didn't want her to know that Mark was a drug addict.

Mark convinced Kyle that they should spend Christmas together at their own house as a family. It would be their first Christmas in their new home. He would meet with the caseworker and convince her that his drug problem was in no way affecting his daughter. "Come on, Kyle, you know it

137

isn't." They would meet with their two attorneys. Mark again assured Kyle that, after the first of the year, he was going to Syracuse for rehab. "Please, Kyle, let's just be together for Christmas." Kyle wanted that, too.

Kyle told Mark he was really tired and was going to take a shower and turn in. Mark said he needed to catch up on his email. He said he would put the garbage dumpster and recycling bin out to the curb.

It had been a horrendous day for Mark. He had spent hours on this cake for an important client's Christmas party. His assistant had dropped it. They'd both had to stay late to remake the cake, because it needed to be delivered first thing in the morning. Now this! Mark still had a few joints stashed away in the garage. He needed to chill out. He went out to the garage and lit up.

Maybe it was because it was just before Christmas. Things calmed down over the next few days. Mrs. Carpenter hadn't called yet, and Kyle and Mark's meeting with their attorneys was scheduled for the week after Christmas. Mark called Sophie and told his sister what was going on. Kyle called his mother. They were both surprised but unconditionally supportive and understanding.

Mark invited Brad and Beverly Williams over for coffee on Christmas Eve morning. They would bring Martina, and the girls would play for a while. Mark had made cinnamon rolls. Kyle and Mark were so proud of their new home. They wanted to show it off. Lucy was so excited that Martina was coming. They were going to exchange presents. It was a nice start to the holiday.

Later in the day, Kyle's mother was coming for dinner. She was bringing her new boyfriend, Sam. Sophie and Jimmy were also coming. Kyle spent most of the day cooking. He was making braciole, which was stuffed flank steak simmered in a rich tomato sauce. He was serving it with a side of pasta, a tossed garden salad with balsamic vinaigrette, and garlic bread. Mark made cannoli. Kyle was looking forward to the evening. He and Mark were taking Lucy to the family mass at four o'clock. The mass was geared to children. Some of the older children would be dressed like Mary and Joseph and the Wise Men. The younger kids would be angels and shepherds. A real baby would be in the manger. Lucy's preschool was affiliated with the church. Her little friends Martina and Scarlett were angels, too. She was so excited.

Everyone decided to join them at church before dinner. Watching the Nativity was too precious to pass up. Dinner was delicious and everyone was having such a good time. Mark's arrest was like the elephant in the room. Of course, no one mentioned it, but everyone knew it was there. Everyone seemed to let it go for the night.

Christmas Day was just Kyle, Mark, and Lucy. It was such a relaxing day. Lucy was delighted with all that Santa Claus had brought for her. Lucy was so into her new toys. Kyle and Mark played with her almost all day. They watched a Christmas movie together later in the afternoon. Kyle and Mark had the same thought. It was probably the last really good day the three of them would have together in a long time.

Chapter 23

Martina was chatting up a storm in the backseat as they were driving home from visiting Kyle, Mark, and Lucy. She was absolutely ecstatic about Santa coming, and she couldn't wait to put on her angel costume for the Nativity at church. Beverly got a call from Ruby's sister, Sarah. "Beverly, the babies are here! They were born about an hour ago. Everyone is doing well. Little Mario Jr. weighed in at four pounds, six ounces. Lillie Mae was four pounds, ten ounces. They're both seventeen inches long. Ruby's okay but extremely tired. We are so blessed!"

Beverly pressed Sarah for more details. Apparently, Ruby's water had broken as she got out of bed. Her labor had progressed fairly quickly. She'd had a vaginal delivery. Lillie Mae was the first baby out, followed by Mario a minute later. Sarah said, "Beverly, I'm so happy the nursery is ready. The babies are doing well. I'm thinking they won't be in the hospital for very long." She told Beverly that it would be all right to visit later in the day.

"Oh, Sarah, thank you so much for calling. Please give Ruby and Mario our love. Merry Christmas!" Beverly couldn't wait to tell Martina.

"Martina, Grandma Ruby had the babies! We can go visit her after church today." Martina insisted on stopping at Macy's to buy the babies each a present. She picked out a little stuffed lamb for Lillie Mae, and for Mario, it was a little stuffed football. Beverly and Brad were amused by her choices. They also bought little pink and blue knitted caps that came with matching blankets. The next stop was Wegmans. Beverly bought a bouquet of white roses tied up with pink and blue ribbons. She had just the right vase at home that she planned to bring to the hospital. Martina insisted on buying a bunch of pink and blue balloons.

This was turning out to be such a big day for their little girl. She was bubbling over with excitement. Brad chuckled. "I wonder how long before she understands that these babies are actually her aunt and uncle?" Beverly smiled, but then her mood turned a bit melancholy. She couldn't help but remember Erica and Dwight and how much in love they'd been that first Christmas together. Then she remembered the day that Martina was born and her brief stay in the NICU. Martina was born at thirty-five weeks. She knew Ruby's twins were thirty-four weeks today. Beverly had been keeping track. Walking up to that nursery would not be easy. It was flooded with bittersweet memories... more bitter than sweet.

As much as she loved Martina, if Erica hadn't been pregnant, she wouldn't have had the blood clot that killed her. As fond as she had become of Dwight, Erica probably wouldn't have gotten pregnant if she hadn't connected with him. These were thoughts that tormented Beverly all the time. Christmas and the birth of Ruby's babies were bringing it all back again in a big way. Beverly was still having problems accepting her miscarriage. If it hadn't happened, she would be well into her pregnancy by now. Her baby would have been an Easter baby.

Brad looked over at his wife. He felt so helpless when he saw her in such emotional pain. He was gifted in so many ways. He could perform very complicated neurosurgeries to heal a person's brain, but he didn't know how to mend his wife's broken heart.

***

Bridget had to work on Christmas Eve, but she would be out on time to go to the children's mass and see Scarlett in the Nativity. Spencer had told her how disappointed Ivy had been when she found out that she would have to miss it. She knew Spencer had taken the kids to Philadelphia first thing this morning. She was thinking about Spencer when her beeper went off. Lately she thought about him most of the time. Bridget was called down to the delivery room to be ready for thirty-four-week twins that were about to deliver. She went with one of the pediatric residents and another nurse. As soon as she got there, she knew who it was. She had seen her at Scarlett's preschool a few times. She was someone connected to Martina. Bridget wasn't exactly sure about her relation to Martina, but she knew that she was a nurse on one of the surgical floors. She'd married an OR nurse. *What a small world!*

The babies were vigorous and in pretty good shape. They were dried off and bulb suctioned a little more. Some blow-by oxygen was delivered. After vital signs and foot printing, the babies were brought up to the NICU in their isolettes for further observation and stabilization. Bridget thought that the babies were absolutely adorable, and she was happy that they seemed to be doing so well. Bridget had only been in the NICU for about two years. Before that time, she'd worked on the unit with kids who were ages three through twelve. One of the nurses who had worked there longer said she knew Ruby and that she would never forget when Ruby's granddaughter was born after a postmortem C-section at thirty-five weeks. Bridget was in disbelief. *Oh, my God, that must be Martina!* Then she heard the rest of the story. Ruby's son, who was the baby's father, had been shot. The baby was being raised by her other grandmother. *That must be Beverly!* Bridget never knew any of this. She wondered if Spencer

142

knew, because he had become friends with Brad Williams. Scarlett talked about Martina all the time.

***

Martina wanted to wear her angel costume up to the hospital so that Grandma Ruby and Papa Mario could see her in it. Martina sang the entire "Away in a Manger" hymn for them when she got there. Then she sang "Silent Night." "Grandma Ruby, the babies were born on Christmas Eve, just like Baby Jesus!" She wanted to go see them. One of the nurses got a wheelchair so that Ruby could go up with them to the NICU. Mario was with the babies. He brought them closer to the window so that they could be seen. The babies each had an IV and a feeding tube but for the most part looked pretty good. "They are so tiny!" exclaimed Martina.

Beverly couldn't fight back her tears. She hugged Ruby. "They are so precious and so perfect. I'm so happy for you."

"Don't cry, Mommy, this is a happy day."

Brad picked up Martina. "Sweet pea, sometimes people cry when they are happy. They are called tears of joy." Martina had lots of questions. She wanted to know about the IVs and feeding tubes and about the isolettes. She wanted the babies to be taken out. She was fascinated with the armholes on the sides of the isolettes. Ruby did a good job at explaining everything to her. Beverly marveled at the rapport that Ruby had with Martina. Sometimes it made her a little jealous.

It was getting late by the time they finally got home. Beverly made Martina a grilled cheese sandwich while Brad got her into her pj's. Martina wouldn't go to bed until Beverly played a Christmas song for her on the violin. Beverly played "Silent Night." They put cookies out for Santa and left a carrot for

Rudolph. Beverly and Brad were finally able to put their daughter in bed and kiss her good night.

They knew of a Chinese restaurant close by that would deliver. Brad opened a bottle of wine. He said it was his turn now. One of Brad's favorite things about Christmas was listening to his wife play "Oh Holy Night." The doorbell rang just as Beverly finished playing. It was a really cute Chinese guy wearing a Santa hat. He had their food. He sang "Jingle Bells" with his Chinese accent. It cracked them all up. Brad gave him a generous tip. It was a light and bright spot in their kaleidoscope of a day filled with so many mixed emotions.

Beverly and Brad ate in front of the fire and finished up the bottle of wine. That night Brad made love to his wife very tenderly. He held her until she fell asleep. He knew it had been a tough day for her. The tears at the hospital were really not all about joy.

Christmas Day would be low-key. Helen would come over for dinner later in the day. Beverly was still feeling a little sad. She asked Brad to call Mario to see how Ruby and the babies were doing. The babies were still doing fairly well, but little Mario had a minor setback. He was having some respiratory difficulty and needed some supplemental oxygen via CPAP. Beverly remembered that when Martina was born, the NICU nurses had told her that, statistically, premature girls usually did better than premature boys. They were going to take out Lillie Mae's feeding tube and see if she would breastfeed.

Then there was Ruby. Mario said that she had fluid in her lungs and was short of breath. Her heart rate was elevated. Her blood pressure had dropped, and she'd almost collapsed when she got out of bed. There was concern about her heart. She was having some diagnostic testing today.

Mario and Brad talked for a long time. Mario told Brad that he was worried about cardiomyopathy. Brad asked Mario if he wanted him to come to the hospital. Mario told him that he would really appreciate that. Brad filled Beverly in on everything Mario had told him. "Oh, God, Brad, I hope everything will be okay. Why don't you get showered and get on over to the hospital? Martina and I will have fun playing with all her new toys. We'll call Helen and have her come over a little earlier than we planned." Beverly packed up some sandwiches, fruit, and Christmas cookies for Brad to take to the hospital.

Chapter 24

The girls were being good in the car for the long ride to Philadelphia, but Ivy was still pouting about missing the Nativity play at church. She wanted to be an angel like the rest of her little friends. Spencer wished he could have stayed in Rochester for Christmas. It was really starting to feel like home. *Maybe next year*, he thought. He was planning on staying at his brother Bill's house. He and Bill had always been close. Spencer was fond of his wife, Heather. They had two girls, also, who were close in age to Haley and Ivy. The cousins had always played well together. Spencer had mailed the presents he had bought for Haley and Ivy ahead of time. The rest of the gifts he brought with him. He had done most of his shopping online. Lizzie had done the wrapping. Spencer knew that Heather would make Christmas morning special for all the kids. His other brother and his family, as well as his dad, would all join them on Christmas day. What Spencer wasn't looking forward to was the Christmas Eve gathering at Anna's parents' house. It wasn't Anna's sisters or Anna's father; it was his mother-in-law whom he found difficult. Irene wasn't always that way, but after Anna died, she'd become more and more critical of him. She was really disapproving of his move to Rochester. His in-laws hadn't even been up to visit yet. The girls loved Irene, so he guessed that was what was important. She called all the time to talk to them. Spencer thought that maybe Irene couldn't accept that he had moved on, and she didn't want to see him and the kids in their new home. Irene was probably afraid that eventually she would no longer be a part of her granddaughters' lives. He would never let that happen.

Actually, it turned out that Irene couldn't have been nicer. She was so happy to see them. She was in tears when Spencer walked in with the girls. She hugged Spencer and told him that he looked great. Soon after they arrived, the family all went to Christmas Eve mass. After church, Anna's father started making drinks. Harry made a nice stiff Manhattan for his wife. He opened a good bottle of Scotch and poured a glass for Spencer and himself. "Here's to you, son. We are so happy you are here with us."

Irene put out an incredible spread. The mood was festive, and everyone seemed to be having a wonderful time. The kids were all playing together in the den. Anna had always been the most reserved of the three daughters. Her sisters could be quite unpredictable, especially after a few drinks. Anna's sister Emily, who was probably on her third glass of Chardonnay, said, "So Spencer, Haley told me you are dating… some mommy at Ivy's school. Good for you!"

Oh, God, Spencer thought, *the evening had been going so well.*

"Actually, we are really just friends. We get together from time to time for playdates with the kids."

Her sister Katie decided to join in. "Oh, come on, Spencer, do tell! What are you playing on your dates?"

Spencer felt ambushed. He didn't know quite what to say. Harry came to his rescue. "Would you girls just leave Spencer be!" Spencer was relieved that Irene was in the kitchen. Then, Emily asked how the new nanny was working out. Spencer reported that she was working out well and had made a lot of progress with Ivy, coaxing her out of her shell.

"Apparently so, because Ivy said that she wants you to marry her so that she can be her new mommy." This time Harry just gave Spencer a sympathetic look and took a big sip of his drink. Spencer wondered where Emily was getting all her information. He knew it was probably Haley. She could be a real chatterbox.

"Spence, lighten up," Emily said. "We love you. Of course, you will have new women in your life. I think the girls are just obsessed with the *Cinderella* story. They're worried about wicked stepmothers. I'm sure there is nothing going on between you and the nanny."

Irene picked just that moment to walk into the room. Harry sensed trouble. He offered to get his wife another drink. "So, let me get caught up," Irene said. "You're happy with the new nanny?"

Spencer wasn't going to let himself get derailed. "Her name is Lizzie, and yes, the girls adore her. I was fortunate to find her. If Ivy has some fantasy about me marrying her, it's because she misses having a mommy, and *no*, there is nothing going on with me and the nanny. Harry, can I get you another Scotch?" Spencer was relieved when his brothers-in-law asked him to go downstairs and shoot a game of pool.

It was getting late. Irene helped the girls change into their pj's, and they all said their good-byes. Emily hugged him and said, "Spencer, I love you. Don't be a stranger." The girls were sound asleep by the time Spencer got back to his brother's house. He carried them up to bed. He had a drink with his brother, who was still putting together Christmas toys. "How'd it go at Harry and Irene's?"

Spencer laughed. "I guess it could have been worse."

Christmas Day with the Harris family was much more relaxed. He broke away later in the day to call Bridget. He couldn't let the day go by without wishing her a Merry Christmas and telling her how much he was thinking of her. They made plans for New Year's Eve. Yesterday, at his in-laws' house, he couldn't even bring himself to think about Bridget. Their house was so full of Anna. Today he had hope that he might be able to move on. He couldn't deny that he had fallen in love with Bridget. He had trouble falling asleep that night. He put in his earbuds and listened to music on his iPod. On his playlist was one of his favorite songs by the Bee Gees, "How Do You Mend a Broken Heart". He did want to live again.

Chapter 25

The first Monday after the New Year, Mark headed to Syracuse for rehab. Kyle took the day off. Despite Mark's protests, he insisted on taking him. Dr. Lamb highly recommended the facility, but Kyle wanted to check it out, besides, he wanted Mark to feel supported in this. He knew how much Mark would miss Lucy. Kyle and Mark, despite their problems, were still very much in love. They would miss each other. Together, Kyle and Mark explained to Lucy that Poppy had to go away for a while to a special place where they could help make his back feel better. She seemed to buy it and didn't ask too many questions. They just told her that Poppy would be back before she knew it. Pam was going to stay with them while Mark was gone. It would be a big help to Kyle, and Lucy would love it. January was a slow month at the bakery. Mark's assistant would be able to handle things there.

Kyle and Mark talked on the drive to Syracuse. Mark had met with the CPS worker, Mrs. Carpenter, after Christmas. He'd met her at Sugar Plum after the shop closed for the day. He thought the meeting went well. The third meeting was with Kyle and Mark at home a few days later. She also wanted a chance to talk to Lucy some more. Mrs. Carpenter had told them that it was Melanie who'd filed the complaint. She'd given permission for her name to be disclosed as the person filing the complaint. Mrs. Carpenter now knew that Melanie was Lucy's biological mother. She said that Melanie was quite disillusioned with Kyle and Mark, and that Melanie said that she planned to continue to pursue this matter. Kyle and Mark's attorney was contacted by Melanie's attorney. She was making threats about petitioning for visitation rights so that she could check on Lucy herself, for her own peace of mind.

"I guess Melanie isn't who we thought she was." Mark said. "I never would have expected this of her. She made so much noise about her willingness to help us achieve parenthood." Back when they'd first met Melanie, she had told them that her best friend growing up was adopted as an infant. She'd said that her friend's parents were wonderful people who could never have children of their own. They had always told their daughter they were blessed to have been given such a precious gift. Melanie had always envied the relationship her friend had with her parents. Melanie's relationship with her own parents was never so great. Melanie had spent a lot time at her friend's house growing up. Her friend's parents treated her like a second daughter.

"Now I'm thinking what she did for us was probably more about money," Kyle said. "Mark, you heard what Luke said." Luke Bennett was their family law attorney. "Luke said that I am in the most precarious position here because I have no biological claim to Lucy." His voice cracked when he said it. "Mark, you've got to get this under control."

All this was too much for Mark. He hated what this was doing to Kyle. He broke out into a sweat and was starting to feel extremely anxious. Lately, the withdrawal symptoms had been worsening. He hoped that they were almost there.

The rehab facility kind of looked like an upscale nursing home. They checked in at the desk. Mark and Kyle hugged and said their good-byes. Kyle told Mark that he loved him, and they took Mark to his room. Kyle tried to fight back his tears until he got to his car. He cried most of the drive home. He knew that Mark couldn't have visitors or even phone calls. Kyle stopped and bought a sandwich to eat at his desk. He thought that going into work would distract him a little. He just wanted some normalcy back. He did have a lot of work to catch up on. After all, it was the first Monday of the New Year.

Kyle got a call from Sophie. She wanted to meet him for a drink after work. She was anxious to hear how everything had gone. Kyle filled her in on everything. He had called his mother to tell her that he would be late, as he was meeting Sophie. Pam hadn't gone into the shop today, because she wanted to be available to help Kyle with Lucy. She knew it would be a difficult day for her son. Kyle decided to stay and have another drink after Sophie left. He was still nursing a big hurt.

He ordered another martini. The guy sitting next to him at the bar kept glancing his way. Their eyes met and he smiled at Kyle. Kyle sensed that he was probably gay. He had blond hair and light eyes. He was quite handsome... not handsome in the same way that Mark was. Mark had a very Latin look. His eyes were dark, and he had just the right amount of salt sprinkled in his dark hair. He was a big guy...but not fat. He worked to keep in shape. Lucy got her red hair and freckles from Mark's mother. Kyle had seen pictures of her, and Lucy bore a striking resemblance. The guy sitting next to Kyle was more his own age. He was polished and had a seductive smile. Kyle could feel his attraction to him.

The guy introduced himself. His name was Austin. He shook Kyle's hand and smiled again. He wanted to buy Kyle a drink. After two martinis and the horrific day, Kyle's guard was down. He accepted the drink offer. This guy was smooth.

Kyle and Austin chatted. Austin worked for one of Rochester's big marketing and advertising firms. He was originally from Atlanta. He exuded Southern charm and spoke with a Southern drawl. He really knew how to market himself. Kyle was ready to buy. Kyle and Mark did not wear wedding bands. Austin never asked him if he was partnered up.

Kyle knew it was time to go home. He was pretty buzzed after that third martini. He sensed where the evening could go if he didn't get out of there. He thanked Austin for the drink. They exchanged business cards, and Kyle left. He took a cab home. No way would he risk getting picked up for DWI. Pam was up watching TV when he got home.

"Mom, I'm sorry that I'm so late. It was such a hard day. I probably had more to drink than I should have, but I took a cab home. How was Lucy?" Pam reassured him that Lucy was okay. Kyle kissed his mother. "Thanks for being here, Mom." He went to bed. Pam was worried about this whole situation. She was daunted by the CPS investigation threatening her son's family. She feared that there was more going on than Kyle had initially told her.

The next evening, after Lucy was in bed, Kyle decided to confide in his mother about the CPS involvement and Melanie's threats. He explained everything.

"Oh, honey, that's got to be so scary and stressful for you. But didn't she sign away all parental rights to Lucy?"

"She did, Mom, but the CPS issue changes everything. If she and her attorney argue that we are unfit parents, the judge may award her some rights as the biological mother. Mom, only our attorney knows this, but Mark ended up being Lucy's biological father. You know we used a mixed sperm sample.

We had to establish paternity for the adoption process. I have the most to lose here."

Kyle and Mark had never shared all the details about their surrogacy arrangement and adoption with their families. They wanted everything to remain private... mostly for Lucy's sake. Pam didn't know what to say. Was it possible that she could lose her only grandchild? Pam always wondered about the red hair and freckles, but then she knew that genetics could be unpredictable. She'd just assumed that Lucy resembled the surrogate. She always told herself that it didn't matter that Lucy didn't look like Kyle. She didn't look like Mark, either. She never understood why Kyle was "Daddy" and Mark was "Poppy." It just seemed to work.

"Mom, you can't tell anyone, do you understand?"

"Of course I won't. But do you think your sister might be able to help?"

"Mom, Colleen has always been accepting of me being gay, but you know she thought Mark was too old for me. She didn't think marriage was a good idea, and she had lots of reservations about us using a surrogate, remember?"

"Kyle, she adores Lucy. I'm sure she would help you."

"I would rather wait and use the family law attorney that we have. I trust Luke. His expertise is family law. Colleen is more interested in criminal law."

"But she has some powerful connections, and she's so smart. Maybe you should just talk it over with her."

"No, Mom. Not yet, at least."

Pam hugged her son. "I am praying for you and Mark. I have no doubt about the wonderful parents that you are. Lucy's such a special child. She's smart and loving and has such a wonderful temperament. That's because of you and Mark. I'm so proud of how you've raised Lucy."

"Thanks, Mom, and thank you again for being here."

By the end of the week, Lucy was having trouble being separated from Mark and was insistent about calling him.

"But Daddy, I miss Poppy. I don't understand why I can't talk to him on the phone." Big crocodile tears rolled down her cheeks.

"You just can't, Lucy. Poppy's working very hard to get better so that he can come home soon. I miss Poppy, too."

As Kyle was leaving work on Friday, he got a call on his cell phone. It was Austin. He let it go to voice mail. The message stated that he wanted to take Kyle to dinner. He asked that Kyle give him a call. As tempted as Kyle was, he knew he didn't need another complication in his life right now.

Chapter 26

"Faith is taking the first step even when you don't see the whole staircase."

- Reverend Martin Luther King, Jr.

Ruby had been in the hospital almost two weeks now. The babies were both doing well, but Ruby wasn't improving. Imaging had shown that her heart chambers were enlarged. Her echocardiogram put her ejection fraction at thirty-eight. She had now been formally diagnosed as having peripartum cardiomyopathy, and she was in congestive heart failure. The cardiology team was quite concerned about her. They put her on digoxin, which was a drug to strengthen the heart's pumping ability and also a diuretic to remove excess fluid. She was weak and tired and becoming quite depressed. They were taking her to the nursery to breastfeed the babies, which was starting to be too tiring for her. Ruby was adamant about feeding the babies. She said that now it was her only connection to them since they couldn't room in with her. Her doctors told her that they were going to have to start to restrict her fluid intake. That fluid restriction combined with the continued need for diuretics would affect her milk supply, and they might have to start to formula feed the babies or obtain milk from a breast milk bank. This last bit of news really upset her.

The good news in all of this was that both of the babies were on room air and feeding well on their own... no feeding tubes. Their growth was steady. Only little Mario still had occasional episodes of apnea and bradycardia. Soon they might be ready to go home. Mario was worried about taking the babies home for a number of reasons. How would he take care of the babies, study, keep up with his classes, and find time to get back to the hospital to spend time with his wife? He was currently out of work, burning up his vacation time. He knew that he could take a family leave of absence. He was worried about how long he could stay out of work and still stay on his feet financially. At least if he was at the hospital, he could work, pick up his normal paycheck, and find time to break away to visit Ruby. Then there were the kids at home. Although they were old enough to take care of themselves, they needed support and supervision, too. Anthony was old enough to drive. Now that Ruby was in the hospital, Mario gave him permission to use Ruby's car, and that helped get him and the girls to school activities.

Ruby's sister, Sarah, and her husband, Henry, helped out a lot. They lived close by. The kids were used to spending time there. Sarah was having them there for dinner every night. The kids had come up to the hospital a few times to see Ruby and the babies. Mario hadn't really told them how serious their mother's condition was.

Brad stopped by every day to check on Ruby and give Mario support. He couldn't even imagine how overwhelming this must be for him. Then he thought about Beverly. *What if she had given birth to their baby and something like this happened to her?* Brad kept her updated on Ruby's and the babies' conditions. Beverly went to the hospital from time to time to visit her, though she found it difficult to go there. She never said too much about it, but Brad knew she was worried. Beverly was good at avoiding conversations that were painful for her. Sometimes she confided in Brad, but more often it would be her therapist. Brad knew that all this was probably difficult because Beverly had lost both her son and husband to heart problems.

Today, after visiting Ruby, Beverly sensed that this wasn't good, and Ruby was not getting any better. Beverly asked Brad to explain the physiology causing Ruby's heart condition. He explained it the best that he could. He explained that Ruby's heart had become weakened and the ventricles were enlarged. Her heart had difficulty pumping blood throughout her body. It caused fluid to leak out of her blood vessels and to build up in other parts her body. The accumulation of fluid in her lungs made it hard for her to breathe. She wanted to know about *ejection fraction*. He told her that it was a measure of how much the left ventricle pumped out with each contraction of the heart... fifty to seventy percent was normal. Today's echocardiogram showed that Ruby's was now down to thirty-two percent. It had dropped a few points, which meant that she wasn't getting any better, despite medication and treatment.

"Oh, God, what will happen to her? Will she die?" He held Beverly. He could see that she was frightened.

"She might get better, but it will take time. Most women with this condition do get better. She could get worse and require surgery, maybe even a heart transplant. Yes, she could die. She's young and was otherwise healthy. That's in her favor. I'm hopeful."

"Oh, Brad, what made this happen?"

"I don't know. The condition is relatively rare, but she does have some risk factors. African-Americans seem to be at a little higher risk, and she has given birth to two sets of twins. Twin pregnancies are more demanding of your heart."

He poured Beverly another glass of wine. "We'll pray for her, stay positive, and do everything we can to support Ruby and Mario through this. I have a feeling it will be okay."

Beverly loved him for saying that. She thought about Dwight and his favorite quote from Martin Luther King, Jr. "Faith is taking the first step even when you don't see the whole staircase." She guessed that they would have to have faith and take a step forward every day. But then again, life had taught her that what was at the end of that staircase was not always good. She wondered who would take care of the babies once they were ready to go home. It sounded like that might be soon. Beverly thought she might give Ruby's sister a call to offer some kind of help and also to find out if there was a plan for when the babies came home.

That night she had a restless sleep. It was the kind of sleep where you really weren't sure that you actually slept, and you dreamt heavily right before waking up. In her dream, there was a house built up on stilts on a foggy beach. She could see Erica at the top of the stairs leading up to the house. She said, "Come on, Mom, everybody's here." When she got to the top of the staircase and walked into the house, she kept seeing faces in her dream... Erica, Johnny, Tom, Dwight, and then Ruby and others she didn't recognize. But she wondered why Ruby was there and why she was going there. Beverly couldn't catch her breath when she finally woke up. She thought that maybe it was more than a bad dream. Maybe it was a panic attack. She couldn't help but go in and check on Martina, who was sleeping peacefully with her baby doll, Jasmine, in her arm.

Beverly was glad that she had her appointment with Dr. Martino today. Her panic attack had really unglued her. Dr. Martino listened to all that Beverly told him about Ruby and then her dream. "Beverly, I believe that now you think of Ruby as family, and you are afraid of loss and facing the death of another person you care deeply about, or thinking about your own mortality. All the people in your dream are interrelated because of death and some kind of heart pathology. Didn't you tell me that your mother-in-law performed CPR on your daughter after her cardiac arrest? Didn't the bullet that killed Dwight hit his aorta...the major blood vessel of the heart? Both your son and husband died after a cardiac event. Of course you're frightened for Ruby. Her condition is very serious."

Beverly nodded and said, "That makes sense." She was crying now, as she often did in her sessions with Dr. Martino. She felt safe to let her guard down. He made her feel safe in a different way than Brad did. Brad gave her unconditional love and security. Dr. Martino gave her reassurance and validation of her feelings. Together they were the perfect package. Of course, she was married to Brad, but when she was perfectly honest with herself, she knew she loved both men. Beverly knew that it was a classic case of transference, because she'd looked it up on the Internet. She'd found an article in a psychology magazine that said it was common and a normal process of psychotherapy, as long as neither. patient nor therapist acted on their feelings. The article also suggested that the patient could discuss these feelings with her therapist. Beverly knew that there was no way she could do that. *It would help if he wasn't so damned good-looking*, she thought. Once she'd described him to Pam as a combination of George Clooney and Al Pacino in his younger days while filming *The Godfather*. He was definitely a ten.

"Beverly, I'm concerned that you are now having panic attacks. If they continue, we may want to change your medication. Do you want to come back next week, or continue with our biweekly sessions?"

She smiled and shook his hand. "I think two weeks is okay. Thank you. I'll see you then." Sometimes when she left his office she felt like she'd cheated on her husband.

Chapter 27

Spencer and the girls left Philadelphia to go back to Rochester two days after Christmas. He had to work a few days before New Year's. Bridget invited him and the girls over on New Year's Eve. They were planning on a family-night celebration. Bridget was making dinner, and they were planning on going to fireworks downtown. Bridget told Spencer that Scarlett asked if it could be a sleepover. Bridget said, "I'm all for that! Do you think it would be okay... or would we be really bad parents?" Spencer thought it over for a nanosecond.

"I guess it would be okay, but don't think you'll be getting any." He laughed. "I mean, I guess it will be okay if we're discreet."

"Well, I'll just have to think about the 'getting any' part, but my couch in the living room is a sofa bed. We could move you out there before the kids wake up in the morning."

Spencer said, "Well, let's do it. I mean, let's spend New Year's together." He couldn't wait. Haley and Ivy were excited about the plans. They told Lizzie. She wasn't surprised, but she was a little disappointed. She'd missed not seeing the girls over Christmas, and she was hoping that Spencer would have asked her to spend New Year's Eve with them. She'd had the fireworks idea herself and thought they could have a family celebration. Or, if Spencer wanted to go out, she could babysit, and her boyfriend could come over. To be perfectly honest, she was hoping for the first option, because she was really thinking of breaking up with her boyfriend. She was bored with him. It was clear to her now that Spencer was interested in Scarlett's mother. He had, however, given her such a nice Christmas gift. It was a beautiful pink cashmere scarf and a generous Christmas bonus. In his Christmas card, he'd thanked her for making his life work again and for all the wonderful and special things that she did for the girls. He went on to say that she had helped to heal them. Lizzie had cried when she read it. She decided that she wouldn't give up on her dream of someday being the woman in Spencer's life and the mother to his girls. She conceded that for now his choice was Scarlett's mother.

Spencer helped the girls pack their overnight bags for New Year's. He and Bridget didn't exchange gifts, but he wanted to do something special for her. He stopped at the florist and looked at the flowers in their cooler. There was a beautiful bunch of blue hydrangeas. He thought they were perfect, because one of the most beautiful things about Bridget was her blue eyes. They were a bright blue, like the color of the sky on a sunny day. But then he remembered that hydrangeas were Cape May's signature summer flower. Cape May was all about Anna. In the end, he decided he was overthinking it and had the florist wrap them up. He also got her a gift certificate to a spa. He knew that going to a spa probably wasn't in her budget.

Bridget had made a nice dinner, but, of course, kid-friendly. She'd made lasagna. Spencer thought it was incredible. Anna was a great cook, but Italian food hadn't been in her repertoire. Spencer was on his second piece. She had a good bottle of Chianti and sparkling grape juice for the kids. They were having a great time. The kids went in to watch TV while Spencer helped Bridget clear the table and load the dishwasher.

Bridget kissed him. "I love the flowers, and thank you so much for the spa certificate. You are so good to me. I especially love the flowers. Blue is my favorite color."

"I thought they were a good choice for my blue-eyed beauty. I'm so happy we can bring in the New Year together." He held her and kissed her much more passionately than their first kiss. What he really wanted was for her to hop up on him so that he could carry her off to the bedroom.

"We better save that for later," she said, and poured him a glass of wine. He sat down and watched her make dessert. He was intrigued. She was making chocolate soufflé. She filled up the five ramekins and put them in the oven. "Scarlett loves when I make this. She wanted me to make it tonight, because she knows I only make it for special nights." They sat at the kitchen table and talked while the soufflés were in the oven. Bridget talked to him about Ruby and the babies. She knew that Spencer had become friendly with Brad Williams and knew about Martina's story. She also knew that Spencer was listed as the pediatrician for the twins. Brad had brought him up to date on Ruby's delivery and her current condition since it all had happened while he had been in Philadelphia. He had been following the progress of the twins since he'd gotten back.

"I'm happy that the babies are doing so well. I had some experience with postpartum cardiomyopathy when I did my OB rotation as a resident. Usually the women get better; at least the patient I was involved with did. I hope that is the case for Ruby. But I also know that if patients don't improve, it has a significant mortality rate. It is as much as twenty-five to fifty percent.

Bridget put her hand over her mouth and her eyes glassed over. "Oh, Spencer, that's so scary. I've gotten to know her since sometimes I bring the babies down to her room. They used to bring her up in a wheelchair, but now they don't want her to be off the monitor. I told her that Scarlett goes to school with Martina. She's such a strong woman. Her husband seems very devoted to her."

"I've met Mario at the hospital. I joined him and Brad for lunch in the cafeteria. This was before his wife had delivered. He does seem like a nice guy. Martina has quite a life story."

The timer went off for the soufflés. Bridget topped them with whipped cream and put them on a tray to bring out to the living room. The girls were delighted, as was Spencer. He had never had a chocolate soufflé. They got in the car and headed off to fireworks, which weren't far from Bridget's house. They took Bridget's car because she had a big SUV that could fit three car seats. Bridget was careful to have only one glass of wine so that she could be the driver. Spencer had drunk more. It was a clear and cold night. The temperature was only twenty-eight degrees. They sat in the car until the fireworks began and then huddled together under blankets. The girls were under one blanket and Spencer and Bridget under another. Spencer copped a feel under their blanket.

Bridget acted appalled. "Dr. Harris! You just wait!" Then she politely rubbed him in just the right place. The girls didn't hear or pay any attention to their parents. They were enchanted with the fireworks, which were spectacular and very, very loud.

After they got back to Bridget's, she turned on the fireplace so that they could all warm up. The girls wanted to watch *Rockin' New Year's Eve* and stay up until midnight. Scarlett had spent all afternoon with her hole punch making confetti. Bridget was in awe of her daughter's ability to operate the hole punch with one hand. They didn't last long, and the three little girls fell asleep on the floor in front of the TV. Bridget knew that Scarlett would be disappointed after working so hard on the confetti, so she thought they should just wake them up to celebrate at midnight and then put them to bed. At eleven forty-five she opened another bottle of sparkling grape juice for the girls, and Spencer opened the champagne he had brought. They gently woke up the girls. After toasting and kissing and a lot of confetti throwing, the girls were ready to go to bed. Bridget snuggled them all up in Scarlett's bed, which was big enough for the three of them. She read them a story and kissed them all good night. The story she chose was *Cinderella*. It seemed appropriate for the occasion because of the reference to midnight and besides, all little girls loved the story of *Cinderella*.

Then it was Bridget and Spencer time. They finished off the champagne and Bridget made them Irish coffee. They were pretty mellowed out, but the coffee was enough to fuel them up for the marathon ahead. Spencer loved sex with Bridget. She was a wonderful lover. It was so much more satisfying now that Spencer had finally admitted to himself that he had fallen in love again. He was now able to keep Anna out of his head in the bedroom. Bridget was still somewhat apprehensive about expressing her feelings to Spencer. She let him do the talking. That night after making love, he rolled over on top of her and took her face in his hands. He looked deeply into her beautiful blue eyes and simply said, "I love you, Bridget." Bridget put her finger over his lips, and then she kissed him.

"We had better move you out to the living room before we fall asleep and the girls find you here in bed with me in the morning." She put on her robe and took some sheets and a blanket out of the closet to make up his bed.

Spencer lay down on the sofa bed and said, "Nurse, can I have a back rub?" Of course, Bridget was happy to oblige. And of course, she gave a wonderful back rub. "Thank you. You sure know how to make a man happy. Having you in my life makes me look forward to the New Year. I love you." He kissed her and said, "Good night, Bridget."

"Good night, Spencer." As Bridget walked back to her room, she couldn't help but hope that January first was the first day of the rest of her life.

The next morning, Spencer awoke to all three girls jumping on him to wake him up and shouts of "Good morning! Good morning!" He could smell bacon. Bridget brought him a cup of coffee. He thought he could really get used to this. He walked into the kitchen. Bridget was making waffles. He wanted to kiss her, but he still didn't think it was a good idea in front of the girls. He looked out her kitchen window. It was snowing lightly. The kids chattered nonstop through breakfast. Bridget looked over at Spencer and smiled. She got up and poured him more coffee.

Haley said, "Daddy, look it's snowing! Can we go sledding today? You promised on the first day there was enough snow that we could go." Spencer's father had gotten the girls sleds for Christmas. "Scarlett said that she has a sled, so she can go with us."

"Would do you think, Bridget? Can you and Scarlett go sledding today?"

"We'd love to!" Bridget said she would get showered, and she and Scarlett would head over to Spencer's about eleven o'clock. Spencer knew of a park that they could go to that was close to his house. He wanted to get cleaned up, too. He and the girls took off for home.

Ivy said, "Daddy, I'm so happy that Scarlett is my friend. We had so much fun and her mommy is so nice." Spencer wondered how much she remembered her own mother. How could she remember when she was only two when Anna died? He thought about that a lot. Haley, of course, had more memories of her mother. She had only to look in the mirror. She looked just like Anna. Ivy looked more like Spencer.

Spencer and the girls were all suited up for the weather when Bridget pulled in. They found a hill that was just about right for kids their age. Spencer and Bridget stood at the top of the hill and gave the kids pushes down the hill. Spencer couldn't take his eyes off Bridget. She was wearing that powder-blue cashmere scarf that she'd worn in Skaneateles. She also wore a white fur hat. Her cheeks had a rosy glow, and her eyes sparkled. *God, she's pretty.* Spencer just couldn't get enough of her.

After a while the kids were getting cold and tired out. It was well past lunchtime. Spencer wanted to take them all out for lunch. Bridget dropped Spencer and the girls back home after lunch. He promised to call her that night.

The girls were exhausted. Spencer got them into the tub and had them put on their pajamas. They both had school tomorrow after the long Christmas break. Since they'd had such a late lunch, dinner was just canned chicken noodle soup. Spencer got the girls into bed and read them a story. Ivy said, "Daddy...was my mommy as pretty as Scarlett's mommy?" Spencer was shocked that she had asked that.

"Oh, honey, just look at her picture. Your mommy was the most beautiful woman I've ever met, but Scarlett's mommy is pretty, too."

"Daddy, I saw you kiss her, you know."

Haley reached for her sister's hand. "Of course he did, Ivy. Daddy likes her. It's okay." Spencer kissed Ivy and then bent over to kiss Haley. She whispered, "I think it's nice that you have a girlfriend, Daddy." Spencer kissed Haley again. Ivy was already asleep. He turned out the light and went back downstairs. He poured himself a Scotch. He needed to be alone with his thoughts. Now he was wondering if things were unfolding too quickly with Bridget. Now the kids were starting to notice that they had feelings for each other.

As Bridget turned onto her street, she could see that a red Jeep was parked in front of her house. While she was helping Scarlett out of her car seat, she could see someone was getting out of the Jeep. She gasped. *Oh, my God, it's Kurt!* She couldn't believe it. He walked up to her.

"Hello, Blue Eyes, it's nice to see you." She was shocked. She hadn't seen him in four years and was certainly not happy that he'd just shown up at her door.

"What are you doing here, Kurt?" She gave him an icy stare. Scarlett stood there, not knowing what to make of the situation. If Scarlett hadn't been there, she would have slapped him across the face, but she knew that she couldn't make a scene.

"I was in town for the holidays and just wanted to drop by to say hello. Can I come in?" He followed them up the walkway to the house.

"Okay," Bridget said reluctantly, but she so didn't want this.

Once inside, Kurt took off his coat and sat on the couch. Bridget told Scarlett that he was a friend she needed to talk to for a while. She asked her to pick out a movie and said that she could rest on Mommy's bed and watch it. Bridget knew that she was pretty tired and that she would probably fall asleep. Bridget got her a juice box and started the movie for her. She closed the door to her bedroom.

When Bridget returned, she could see that Kurt had helped himself to a beer from her refrigerator. "So that's our baby girl?" he said.

"She's hardly a baby anymore, and she's not *ours*, she's mine. Just leave us alone, Kurt."

"Well, I've come to tell you how sorry I am. Everything was happening too fast. I was overwhelmed and didn't think I could do it. I wasn't ready to be tied down with a kid. Hey, but I never stopped loving you, babe. I was thinking maybe you could give me another chance. What did you say her name is again?"

"I didn't say, but her name is Scarlett. She deserves better than you."

"She's a pretty little girl, just like her mama." Kurt tipped up Bridget's chin, looked into her eyes, and kissed her.

Bridget was appalled. She slapped his face. "Get out of here and don't come back!"

"Okay, okay," he said. He took his coat and beer and left.

Bridget, always the cool one, had to admit she was pretty rattled about seeing Kurt after all this time. She went in to check on Scarlett, who was sound asleep. Bridget knew she was tired and didn't want to wake her up. She covered her up, thinking maybe she would sleep until morning. The kids had eaten a big lunch and played outside for such a long time. No wonder Scarlett was so conked out. She was relieved that Scarlett had never come out to see Kurt. Bridget changed into her pajamas and put a bag of popcorn in the microwave. She poured herself a glass of wine. It had been such a great day until now.

As promised, Spencer called. "Thanks for last night, and thanks for today. The girls and I had such a good time."

"Oh, Spencer, Scarlett and I did, too. I think that sometimes Scarlett misses not having a daddy, and I know she loves being with your girls. She said that it was kind of like having sisters. I think sometimes Scarlett and I get a little lonely."

Spencer had never heard her talk like this. "You sound a little down tonight."

"You're not going to believe this... Scarlett's father showed up here when we got home! He's never even seen her, and it's been four years since I've heard from him." Spencer knew she was crying.

"I'm sorry. He's got me a little unglued."

"Hey, it's okay. I'm just sorry that he hurt you so badly and now has upset you so much."

"I'm just worried he'll come back."

"Has he ever been abusive to you?"

"No... never. Everything was fine with us until I got pregnant. He couldn't handle it."

"I don't want him to come back because of Scarlett. He doesn't deserve to be her father or have any kind of relationship with her. I don't want to see her hurt. We have been doing fine without him. You're the man in my life now."

"Bridget, I love you."

"I know. I love you, too, Spencer." There... Bridget couldn't believe she'd said it... but she did love him. She felt nothing but contempt for Kurt. After saying good night, Bridget crawled into bed with Scarlett and cried herself to sleep. Spencer poured another glass of Scotch. He hated seeing Bridget hurt. Her ex sounded like a cowardly prick.

Chapter 28

Kyle missed Mark. Lucy really missed him. It had only been two weeks. Dr. Lamb had said he would probably be there two to three weeks. Kyle couldn't help but worry. *What if he has to stay longer than three weeks? What if the methadone doesn't control his pain and he goes back out on the streets to buy heroin? What if he dies someday from an overdose? What if Melanie is granted visitation rights?* He called Luke, his family law attorney, to meet up with him for a drink. Maybe talking to Luke would help ease some of his anxiety.

Luke shook Kyle's hand, sat down, and ordered a drink. "I have bad news. Melanie is going ahead with the petition for visitation rights. She wasn't satisfied with the report from the CPS worker. I haven't seen the report, but I can't believe she has much of a case. She said it wasn't enough to give her piece of mind."

"What will happen now?" Kyle asked. He loosened his tie, finished the last of his drink, and ordered another. He was angry and now frightened. He didn't know if he was angrier with Melanie or with Mark. He was angry with himself, too, for tolerating Mark's substance abuse problem for so long. He had been in denial, right along with his husband.

"There will be a hearing. Mostly it will depend upon the judge. When we find out who the judge will be, I'll have a better idea about how it may go. I know Melanie's attorney. She's a hard-assed bitch. I know she'll play hardball."

"It's a she?" asked Kyle. He remembered that the attorney Melanie used for the adoption was a male, an older guy.

"Yes. Her name is Suzanne Sims." Now Kyle was even more worried.

"Nothing will happen until Mark gets back. I was able to delay the scheduling of the hearing until then. Do you know when that will be?"

"Not yet. I'm going to put a call in to his doctor tomorrow. I think it should be soon."

Luke finished the last of his drink. "I've got to get home. I promised my wife I'd be home for dinner. Take care, man. We'll fight this. Call me when you get news about Mark." Kyle liked Luke. His brother was gay and an old friend of Mark's. That's how he and Mark had gotten referred to Luke when they were thinking about surrogacy and adoption. Kyle knew he should be getting home himself. He knew his mother was planning on going to her book club meeting that night. In his present state of mind, another drink was a bad idea. He was paying his tab when Austin walked in.

This was a bar Kyle had frequented because it was near the building he worked in. It was definitely not a gay bar. Last time was the first time he had ever seen Austin there. He was hard to miss because he was so good-looking. Kyle had read somewhere that whenever you were tempted to act impulsively, you should remember the acronym: HALT. It stood for hungry, angry, lonely, and tired. If you were any of them, you should rethink before you acted and did something you might later regret. Kyle knew he was all of those things.

Austin made eye contact with him and came over while Kyle waited for the bartender to return with his credit card. Kyle, I was disappointed that you never returned my call."

"I'm sorry, Austin, but right now I have a lot going on in my life."

"Stay and have another drink. I'm a good listener."

"I'm sorry, I really can't tonight."

"Well, I'm sorry, too, man. The offer still stands. If you want to have dinner with me, you have my number." He put his hand on Kyle's shoulder. "You take care."

"Okay, thanks," Kyle said. He was lonely. It would have been so easy to hook up with Austin tonight, but he couldn't. He missed the intimacy with Mark. Their sex life had really suffered in the past couple of months. Kyle wondered if they would ever get back on track.

He got home and had dinner with his mother and Lucy. His mother filled him in on what was going on with Ruby. He had been so preoccupied with his own problems that he hadn't even reached out to congratulate Mario and Ruby on the birth of their twins. Kyle and Mark had become friends with Mario and Ruby. They had dinner together from time to time. Kyle knew that Ruby was about his age. Her condition sounded serious. He thought that maybe he would send a fruit basket over to the hospital and send Mario an email in the morning. He felt bad that he hadn't contacted them before this. "I don't know, Mom, I guess this year isn't starting out so good for them, either."

"The babies are doing well, though, so that's a blessing," Pam said.

"Martina told me all about the babies," Lucy piped up. "She said they are tiny. One is a boy and one is a girl. Their names are Little Mario and Lillie Mae. She even had a picture of them that she brought to school. And do you know what else? This girl in my class named Scarlett has a mommy that's a nurse. She's been taking care of the babies at the hospital."

Kyle and Pam looked at each other and smiled. Lucy had the scoop on everything that was going on. She was very smart. Not too much got by her, and she remembered everything. Kyle worried about her finding out too much about what was going on with Mark. She'd never said too much about the CPS worker, so Kyle and Mark hadn't, either. Lucy had just said that she was a nice lady.

That night Kyle had a dream about Austin. He and Austin were driving in an orange Porsche. Austin looked incredibly handsome...like a model for Polo, Ralph Lauren. They were going to Syracuse for a basketball game. As they were walking into the Dome, Melanie was up ahead. She turned around and smiled. She said, "Hey, you two...are you thinking about having another baby?" The dream was disturbing. Kyle shouldn't be dreaming about Austin. Was the dream in Syracuse because Mark was there for rehab, or was it because of Melanie, who they'd first met at a Starbucks near campus?

Kyle called Dr. Lamb in the morning. He said that Mark was doing well, but he thought he would be there at least another week, maybe two. He also said that he didn't want to bring him home too soon and risk the chance that he would relapse. Kyle was disappointed. He was hoping that Mark would be home by the end of this week.

By the weekend, Kyle was really feeling sorry for himself. Pam was going to some event with her boyfriend, Sam, on Saturday night. He was glad to see his mother happy and dating such a nice man. His father had treated her so poorly at the end of their marriage. He was such a cliché. He'd left his mom for a younger woman. Sophie wanted to take Lucy overnight. She had tickets to see the play *Annie*, which was touring in Rochester. Lucy was excited. That left Kyle alone for the night. In a weak moment, he sent Austin a text about meeting for dinner. Austin called him as soon as he got the text. Austin suggested a restaurant that Kyle was not familiar with that was a short distance from Rochester. It was in Canandaigua. Kyle was glad because he didn't want to be seen with Austin someplace in Rochester. He told Austin that he would meet him there.

As Kyle drove to Canandaigua, he vowed to himself that getting together with Austin would just be dinner. He knew he was vulnerable and nursing a big hurt. He needed to be careful. He wasn't planning on cheating on his husband. *But hadn't Mark cheated on him with his drugs?* Kyle knew that his logic was pretty convoluted.

Austin was there already with his good looks and seductive smile. He had reserved a table and was seated. Kyle shook his hand. "I'm really glad you decided to have dinner with me, Kyle. This is such a nice restaurant, and the food is good. I have a client in Canandaigua who turned me on to this place." He summoned the waiter over to get Kyle's drink order.

Kyle decided to be up front and to tell Austin right away that he was married. Austin seemed unfazed. "You said that you were a good listener. I could use a friend tonight."

"Hey, you're married, not buried. We can be friends. I don't know too many people in Rochester yet. I only moved here this past summer." He went on to say that he got his MBA with the Simon School at the University of Rochester. After a bad breakup, he'd decided to get out of Atlanta and heard of an opportunity back in Rochester.

Austin was a good listener. Kyle told him his story. After Kyle told him about Lucy, Austin showed him a picture of his own daughter, who was ten. Austin had gone to college at the University of Mississippi. He'd married a nice Southern girl from Ole Miss. He'd gotten married young, right out of college. Of course, it hadn't worked out. He was gay. His first serious relationship with a man had ended badly, too. He talked about how much he missed his daughter and his complicated shared custody arrangement. He said that his ex-wife had become extremely bitter and was trying to exclude him from his daughter's life. Kyle realized he had misjudged Austin. He wasn't the smooth, flashy guy he had thought he was. He was sincere and probably needed a friend as badly as he did. Kyle still found him quite attractive, but both men knew that tonight things weren't going any further that night. They agreed to keep in touch and parted with a handshake.

Chapter 29

Ruby didn't think she could stay in her hospital bed one more minute. She felt like life was passing her by. She had never been this helpless. She had never been ill in her entire life. The only time that she had ever been hospitalized was for childbirth. It was in her nature to be a caregiver...not a recipient. She hated being the patient. She was not someone who accepted help easily. There was nothing that she could do about this. The pediatric team had told her that the twins were almost ready to go home. It would probably be next week. They brought the babies down to see her, and she was able to hold them and bottle-feed them. Breastfeeding wasn't happening anymore because of the effect of her medication on her breast milk. Their visits did tire her out. She was so worried about how Mario would manage with them at home. She knew the girls would help, but what about during the day, when the kids were at school? Mario still had work and school. She wanted him to continue to go to school. She didn't want him to give up on his plan of becoming a nurse anesthetist. When Ruby wasn't sleeping, she was worrying or praying. Some days she wondered if she would die.

Seeing Mario always brightened her day. He showed her so much love. He stopped in after work with his big smile and his "Hello, Baby." He bent over to kiss her. "I just stopped in to see the twins. They are doing so well. The team just finished rounding and asked to talk with me. They wanted to know if I would be prepared to take them home next Monday. Can you believe it?"

Ruby smiled, but there were tears in her eyes. "How will you manage?"

"Beverly and your sister have a plan. They are both eager to help out. Helen wants to help out, too. The kids can help in the evening. It will be okay."

"Oh, Mario, that is so kind, but I want to go home and take care of my own babies."

"I think you will, eventually. You're just not stable enough to go home yet. You know that the doctors said it would take awhile."

"But tomorrow it will be three weeks already. I don't think I'm getting any better."

"Baby, you will get better. Remember Dwight and his Martin Luther King quote. We can't see the top of that staircase yet, but we've got to have faith and take one step at a time. Getting Little Mario and Lillie Mae home is just another step. We haven't reached that step where we get you home yet."

"This is putting so much strain on you, Mario. What about you? How are you doing?"

"Ruby, I'm okay. I would do anything for you and the kids. I love you, but it hurts for me to see you so down. We've got to stay positive."

Just then Bridget came in with the babies. "I thought you two would like to spend some time with the babies together." She put one baby in Ruby's arms and one in Mario's.

By now, Ruby and Bridget had become acquainted. Ruby appreciated the extra attention and care that Bridget gave to her babies. They even talked about Martina and Scarlett... marveling at what a small world it was that they had become connected in so many ways. Mario had been unaware of the connection until today. Ruby introduced them. He had seen Bridget around the hospital. He thought she was pretty cute, though Mario never dated white women. Then he remembered hearing that she was dating Brad's friend… the peds doc. He was a lucky guy. There was always a lot of buzz around the hospital about who was dating whom. The medical center was a pretty big place, but news always got around fast. The TV medical dramas weren't far from reality in their depiction of interpersonal relationships in the hospital.

"When you do get the babies home, if there's any way I can, I would be happy to help." She wrote down her cell phone number and gave it to Mario. "I can't even imagine how stressful your life must be right now."

"You're right," said Mario. "Thank God we have a good network of family and friends willing to help us out."

Bridget took off. "She seems really nice," said Mario.

"She's spent a lot of time down here helping me with the babies. We've talked a lot. I'm sure her offer to help is sincere. Her daughter, who goes to preschool with Martina, was born with half of her arm missing. I've seen her. The little girl is amazing. Bridget has had her own hardships in life."

Mario told Ruby that Bridget was dating Spencer Harris. Brad had told him.

"Well, I hope it works out for her."

Mario went down to the cafeteria to buy some dinner so that he could bring it up and eat with Ruby when her dinner tray was brought in. He had class tonight and had to be in Buffalo by seven o'clock. Ruby's sister, Sarah, came in just as Mario left for class.

The sisters were close and always had been. If it hadn't been for Sarah and her husband, Henry, Ruby would have never survived single parenthood. Sarah ran an in-home day care. Henry was a city fireman. Sarah had always helped Ruby out with childcare, and Henry was like a father to her children. Dwight had always looked up to his uncle. Henry had been his hero. His firehouse had set up a memorial scholarship in Dwight's name after his death.

Sarah reassured her sister that she would be able to help with the babies when they got home. "Right now, I'm not watching too many kids. A family that left two children with me dropped out. She lost her job. So that will really free me up. Most of the time my assistant will be able to handle things, and I can go over to your house."

"I hate putting so much on you," Ruby said.

"It will be okay," Sarah said. "The nursery is beautiful. Beverly did such a good job with it. She really wants to help out. Just let her. It will help you, and I think it helps her in some way. She seems a little sad."

"I know she does. She's not quite herself lately." Ruby told Sarah about the miscarriage that Beverly had in the fall. She suspected that Beverly was still a little depressed.

"She certainly has endured a lot of loss in her life." Sarah sighed. "She's such a good mother to Martina. It has to be so hard for her. Martina is a constant reminder of how her life turned upside down after her husband died. Thank God, that Brad came into her life. How old is she... late forties?"

"She's forty-eight," Ruby said.

"That pregnancy was probably never meant to be," Sarah said. "Well, you look tired. I'm going to leave and let you get some rest." She kissed her sister on the forehead and took off. Sarah couldn't help but think that Ruby and Beverly's story could be made into a Lifetime movie. She hoped that all the prayers for Ruby would be heard. She couldn't bear it if anything happened to her sister. Being only thirteen months apart in age, she and Ruby had been like twins themselves.

She got a call from Mario the next evening. He was upset. The news wasn't good. Ruby's ejection fraction was now down to twenty-one. She wasn't getting any better.

Chapter 30

Word had gotten out that Bridget and Spencer were involved. Bridget never said anything about Spencer at work. She hated gossip. A few of the younger nurses she worked with wanted to hear all about it. She still was not secure enough in her relationship with Spencer to talk about him. She was still reeling after her unexpected encounter with Kurt. Bridget wasn't even sure how he'd found her house. It wasn't where they had lived together. She was certain her parents would have never told him. Her father would rather kill him. He'd probably run into one of her friends at the bar he used to work at. Kurt could be very charming and manipulative when he wanted something. Bridget wondered when Scarlett would start asking more questions about her daddy.

Spencer stopped into the NICU to see if Bridget could have lunch with him. She told him that she could meet him in the cafeteria in about fifteen minutes. He told her that he would be waiting for her. Bridget noticed a few raised eyebrows at his appearance in the NICU. He was usually in the clinic or sometimes on one of the pediatric units if he had a patient who was in-house. After Bridget signed off to another nurse, she met him in the cafeteria.

"Hey, sexy nurse-lady," he said. "I don't know too many women who look as cute as you do in scrubs."

Bridget smiled. "Sure, you come into the NICU, and now you've got everybody talking."

"So what, you're the lady in my life. I don't care who knows it." Spencer wanted to see her that weekend.

"My parents have been asking about you and want to know when they can meet you. I know that's a big step. What can I say? Since Kurt, they have become very protective of me...my dad, especially."

"I can handle meeting your parents. I would like to meet them."

"Oh, Spencer, are you sure?"

"Why don't we take them out for dinner? Would Angelo's be okay? I can make a reservation for Saturday night."

"That's fine. I'll ask my mom tonight and give you a call."

Spencer knew that their relationship was getting serious. Since Bridget's parents helped her out so much with childcare, he knew that he would need to meet them soon. He hoped that Lizzie would be free on Saturday night to stay with the girls.

Spencer and Bridget ran into Mario as they were leaving the cafeteria.

Spencer and Mario shook hands. "Congratulations on the birth of your twins. I understand that your wife is having some issues with her heart. That's got to be tough."

"The babies are about ready to go home. I'm a little anxious about that," Mario said. "It's been a long time since I've been around a newborn, and them being preemies, it makes me even more nervous."

Spencer gave him his card. "Feel free to call me anytime day or night...for advice, questions, or concerns. I would be glad to help out."

"Thanks, that's really kind of you. Our kids, Ruby's girls and my son, are patients of the clinic, so it's nice to have the medical director looking out for us."

"I'll make sure that I'm involved in the babies' final physicals before they are discharged. I'll get in touch with their NICU attending."

"Hey, thanks again, Dr. Harris."

"Please... it's Spencer."

"You were so nice to him," said Bridget.

"I didn't know their other kids were patients of the clinic."

"Ruby must be devastated that she can't go home with her babies. I'm so worried about her. She told me that her ejection fraction dropped again."

"That's worrisome," Spencer said.

After seeing Bridget in the middle of the day, it was hard for Spencer to concentrate. It was hard to deny his feelings for her, but there were always the naggings doubts. *"Am I moving forward too fast? Am I just lonely and like the sex? Is she too young for me?"* He realized that he was in pretty deep if he was moving forward with meeting her parents.

He was reading over the documentation that one of his residents had written after seeing a patient. It was the first time today that he noticed the date. Today was Anna's birthday. She would've been thirty-seven today. Then he was flooded with sadness and regret. How did he not remember until one thirty in the afternoon that it was his wife's birthday? He felt awful. He sent Brad a text to see if he wanted to meet up for a drink after work. He called Lizzie to see if it was okay if he got home an hour later than usual. She was fine with it.

When he met up with Brad, he told him what was on his mind. "I think you're being a little hard on yourself," Brad said. "I'm sure if you woke up with your wife this morning, you would have remembered that it was her birthday."

"Anna would have been thirty-seven today. Bridget isn't even twenty-seven yet. Do you think she is too young for me?"

Brad smiled. "Oh, come on... no. Younger is good. She seems to have maturity beyond her years. You have children the same age. I think that it's okay. She's not some party girl you met online or in a bar. Your relationship evolved. My advice to you is that you let it continue to evolve."

Brad went on to tell Spencer about his ex. "My ex-wife is a nurse. She, too, is ten years younger than me. But she is nothing like Bridget. Her MO was to marry a doctor. She told me from the get-go that she didn't want to have any kids, which always bothered me, but I thought she would change her mind. She was very self-involved. She got bored with me and moved on. As the Carly Simon song goes, she got 'a brand new shiny boy.' He was a younger guy and a rising star in orthopedic surgery. It was a nasty divorce, and she made out well financially. I don't think she ever loved me."

Spencer took a long sip of his Scotch. "Women can be dangerous."

"I don't get that vibe from Bridget," Brad said. "She seems genuine."

"She wants me to meet her folks."

"Big step," said Brad. "Let's make plans for you and Bridget to have dinner with me and my wife soon. I'd like to get to know her better."

When Spencer got home, Lizzie had the girls involved in coloring. Haley said, "Look, Daddy, we're making birthday cards for Mommy. She can look down from heaven and see them."

It hit Spencer like a punch in the gut. He looked at Lizzie. "How did you know?"

"Haley told me." She was only six, but she was a really smart little girl with an incredible memory. Nothing got past her. Lizzie said that their grandmother also called to talk to them after school.

"Grandma said we should say a special prayer for Mommy today because it's her birthday," Haley said.

"Is Mommy going to come home tonight for her birthday?" Ivy said.

"No, Ivy. Mommy's home is in heaven now," Spencer said.

 Haley took her sister's hand. "It will be okay, Ivy. We will still have cake and blow out the candles."

"There's cake?" Spencer asked.

"We made a cake with Lizzie after school." The cake was on the dining room table. Ivy took his hand and brought him in to see the cake. It was even decorated with *Happy Birthday Mommy*. "Can Lizzie stay for dinner and have cake with us? Please, Daddy," Ivy said.

"Can you stay, Lizzie?"

"Of course I can. Dinner's in the oven. Let's set the table, girls."

Lizzie had a meatloaf and baked potatoes in the oven. She got the green beans out of the refrigerator and put them in a pan. Dinner smelled great. Spencer knew it would be easier to get through this dinner if he had a drink. He opened a bottle of merlot and offered Lizzie a glass. He knew she was over twenty-one.

She had butter and sour cream for the baked potatoes, and she was frying up bacon for the green beans. "My mom always made green beans with bacon. That's how she got us kids to eat our green beans. She was a great cook. I hope you like the meatloaf. It's her recipe. The girls have really liked it when I made it before."

"It smells delicious. Lizzie, this is all so very thoughtful." The look that he saw in Lizzie's eyes was a look that he had seen before. It was the kind of look women gave men when they were interested in more. It was a sensual look directly into his eyes. Spencer always thought of Lizzie as a sweet girl. The look in her eyes was a big-girl look. In college when a girl looked at him like that, he knew he could probably get lucky that night. Spencer knew she had kind of a crush on him. He cautioned himself to be careful. *But really, the woman I'm involved with isn't much older than Lizzie.* He was haunted by thoughts like this all the time. He was thankful for having found such a good nanny for the girls but didn't want the complication of her developing feelings for him. A Mary Poppins-type nanny would have been so much easier.

After dinner and cake, the girls asked Lizzie to play her guitar for them. She was pretty good. Ivy loved the "Puff the Magic Dragon" song. Afterwards she did the dishes and cleaned up the kitchen while Spencer put the girls to bed. It was getting late, so he told them that he would read only one story. He kissed the girls good night and turned on their night light. As he was leaving, Ivy said, "Daddy, I love Lizzie. I wish she could be our new mommy." He had no idea what to say, so he just said, "We're lucky to have Lizzie. Now you two better go to sleep. Sweet dreams. I love you."

When he got downstairs again, Lizzie was playing her guitar and singing an old Joni Mitchell song that he recognized, "The Circle Game". "That was nice," he said. "Thank you for all you did tonight."

"I love the girls, Spencer. I would do anything for them. I would do anything for you." His cell phone rang; it was the page office. He was on call tonight. He was grateful for the distraction and hoping that Lizzie would leave.

"I'm sorry, Lizzie. I've got to make a call to a patient's mother. Thank you again. I'll see you tomorrow."

She got her coat and kissed Spencer on the cheek. "Take care, Spencer. I know this was a tough day for you. Good night." Tonight Spencer was relieved that the kiss was on his cheek. He was worried that Lizzie might try to really kiss him... on the lips.

The call was about a little boy who had a temp of 104.2. His mother said his fever persisted despite Tylenol, Motrin, and a tepid bath. She couldn't get him to drink any fluids, and she was worried that he was dehydrated. Spencer advised her to take her son to ED. He remembered that this mom was usually pretty calm and capable. She sounded overwrought. He would check in the morning to see if the kid had been admitted.

After the call, he wanted to go for the Scotch but thought he had better not. He'd had the drink with Brad and a glass of wine with dinner. He was on call. He got his wedding video off the shelf of the bookcase and put it in. There was his beautiful Anna. He couldn't believe that it was only eight years ago. There they were dancing to "When a Man Loves a Woman". He stopped the video. *This is torture.* He went into the kitchen and poured himself a glass of milk and cut another slice of cake. After he was finished, he got out the *Journal of Pediatrics* that came in the mail today and took it up to his bedroom. He thought a really boring research article might put him to sleep. He dreamt heavily. In his dream he was on a merry-go-round with Haley and Ivy. Lizzie was watching them from behind the gate. She was smiling. He was late for work and needed to get to the hospital. The merry-go-round wouldn't stop so that he could get off. It was one of those dreams where you felt frustrated and anxious. You couldn't do what you needed to do. The dream was probably sparked by the "Circle Game" song that Lizzie had been singing. Those painted ponies went up and down, and round and round most of the night.

Finally, his cell phone rang and woke him up. It was the page office again. This time it was about a kid who'd fallen out of bed and had a cut on his forehead that wouldn't stop bleeding. Spencer again advised the parent to take the kid to ED because cuts to the forehead often bled heavily and needed stitches. The fall was from a top bunk. Spencer was also concerned about a concussion. He hated bunk beds. He would never forget a case he'd followed as a resident. Six-year-old twin girls were playing on the top bunk, and one of them had fallen out and landed on a hardwood floor. She was knocked unconscious and suffered a bad subdural hematoma. She'd never woken up from her coma. Her parents had had to make the painful decision about taking her off life support. He couldn't image something like that happening to one of his little girls. Spencer's mind was now very active. He didn't end up getting much sleep that night.

Chapter 31

A month after Mark left for rehab, he was finally coming home. Kyle told Lucy, and she was so excited. She wanted to have a little party for him. Kyle told her that they would have a party after Poppy had been home for a few days. They would invite Grandma and Sam and Sophie and Jimmy. Kyle helped Lucy make a banner that said *Welcome Home, Poppy!* Kyle wasn't so sure that a party was a good idea, but Lucy had her heart set on it. Kyle had to admit that he was a little nervous about picking Mark up in Syracuse. He knew that Mark's drug addiction wasn't entirely his fault, but he thought that Mark should have gotten help before it had reached the point that he was hooked on heroin. He'd also found Mark's marijuana stash in the garage. That wouldn't have really bothered him if it weren't for the other drugs. They'd both a smoked little weed from time to time but had made a pact that that would stop after they got Lucy. Kyle was still hurt and disappointed. He was also angry that because of Mark's drug arrest, they had the CPS issue looming over them. In addition to all of these feelings, Kyle now felt guilt. He had been meeting up with Austin at the bar that was close to where they both worked. One night when Kyle knew that Lucy was having a sleepover at Martina's house, he'd left the bar with Austin and gone back to his apartment. The temptation was more than he could resist. He'd slept with Austin. He had to admit the sex was great. Now his life was really a mess.

Despite everything, Kyle was so happy to see Mark. He thought he looked good. He appeared to be calm and well rested. He took Mark's bag, and they walked to the car. Once in the car they just held each other. They talked all the way home. Mark thought that methadone was the answer for him right now. It had reduced his cravings and was controlling his pain. He knew that he would have to be closely supervised by Dr. Lamb in his substance abuse clinic. He would have to have regular urine drug screening and attend group therapy sessions. He also knew that he could risk expulsion from the program if he used alcohol, marijuana, or any other drugs. Kyle knew that he would have to be careful about drinking around Mark, at least in the beginning. He was okay with that.

"Kyle, I'm going to try so hard, I swear. You're not going to believe this, but I'm even thinking about having another evaluation to look at a surgical option for my back. I just want us to go back to being a family again. I have missed you and Lucy so much. I miss work. I need to get back to the shop. It's almost Valentine's Day. Tell me what's going on with the hearing. Has Luke given you a court date yet?"

"It's Monday. I'm worried, Mark. Luke said that Melanie has a very shrewd attorney. It's a woman… not the guy she used when we were working out the surrogacy arrangement. He said that hopefully we will get a compassionate judge."

"Oh, Kyle, I'm sorry that I got us into this mess."

"I know you are, Mark. I love you, and I'm glad you're back. You've got to stay strong and keep clean." Mark sighed. He looked so sad. Kyle filled him in on lots of other news, including Ruby and the serious problems she was having with her heart.

"Oh, my God, that's awful," he said. "I'm glad the babies are okay." Mark really liked Ruby and Mario. He and Mario kind of had the same crazy sense of humor. Mario's son, Anthony, worked at the bakery on Saturdays. He washed pans and helped with cleanup. Now that he was old enough to drive, he was able to make some of the easier deliveries. Mark thought Anthony was a good kid. "Do you think there is anything we can do?"

"Pray for them, I guess. Mario would probably love to hear from you. He needs the support of his friends."

Kyle told him about about his welcome home party. "I know it might be hard for you, but Lucy's missed you so much. She is so excited about it... it's just my mom and Sam and Sophie and Jimmy." Mark wanted to know who else knew that he'd gone to rehab.

"It was hard to keep it a secret. I had to tell Brad Williams because Lucy told Martina that you had to go away to get your back better. He asked me about it, so I told him. He was genuinely concerned and said it happens a lot when patients are on prescription opiates for extended periods. Mario asked, too, because Anthony told him you weren't around. Mario understood. I didn't say anything about the heroin or the arrest. Mark, everyone just wishes the best for you."

"I know. I'm still ashamed."

Pam dropped Lucy home from preschool shortly after Mark and Kyle got back. Pam hugged Mark and welcomed him home. She left to get back to her shop. When Lucy saw Mark, she jumped into his arms and squealed with joy. "Poppy! I missed you so much!" Kyle saw the tears in Mark's eyes. He left them alone and went to the kitchen to make lunch. Lucy insisted on tomato soup and grilled cheese sandwiches. She said that it was her and Poppy's favorite lunch. Kyle went back to his office after lunch. Mark wanted to spend the rest of the day with Lucy. She made his homecoming so much better.

He decided to take her to the bakery. She always loved going there, and Mark needed to know what was going on with his business. Everyone was happy to see him. There were no questions asked. Mark was a good boss and his employees loved him. His assistant filled him in. January was always a slow month, and this year was no exception. There was only one wedding and the rest were orders for birthday, anniversary, and Bar and Bat Mitzvah cakes. Orders were starting to come in for Valentine's Day. There were four weddings booked for February. Lucy sat up on a stool and watched as Mark mixed up the batter for a red velvet cake. He remembered from that very first Thanksgiving when he'd first met Ruby that she loved red velvet cake. She was, after all, a girl from the South. It would be two stacked baby blocks... one pink and one blue. He would go visit her in the hospital and bring the cake. He was sure it would get eaten, if not by Ruby's family, then by the nurses and doctors. He drew a sketch to show Lucy. He saved some batter to make three cupcakes.

The cupcakes didn't take long to bake. After they were cool, he frosted them and decorated one with a K, one with an M, and one with an L ... for Kyle, Mark, and Lucy. They could have them for dessert tonight. He promised Lucy that she could come back tomorrow to watch him decorate the baby blocks. Martina had told her all about the twins. Lucy, of course, even knew their names. She informed Mark that they both had black skin... but not too black. Lucy had a commentary for everything. Mark adored her. He then took her to do one of her favorite things. They went to the salon so that Lucy could get a mani-pedi. Mark got a shave and haircut. He was happy. It had been such a pleasant afternoon, and it was so good to be home. He wondered about Kyle. He sensed something wasn't quite right.

The next day, as promised, Mark brought Lucy back to the shop so that she could watch him decorate the baby blocks cake. She loved watching her father decorate cakes. Again, she told him the babies' names so that he could pipe them on the blocks. "So, it's Mario and Lillie Mae?" Mark asked.

"No Poppy, it's Little Mario! Mario is his daddy!"

Mark chuckled. "Then Little Mario it is."

When he finished, she clapped her hands and hugged him. "Oh, Poppy, this is one of your best cakes ever!" Mark dropped Lucy off at her day care and headed over to the hospital.

Ruby still looked beautiful, even though she was hooked up to a heart monitor and had an oxygen cannula in her nose. It was hard to believe she was so ill, but she did seem a little tired and weak. She was normally a woman with so much energy and spunk. She was touched that Mark had come to visit. Ruby was happy to have visitors. She was bored and lonely a lot of the time, and the visitors helped to distract her from all her worry.

"This cake comes at a good time. The babies are going home on Monday, and I can share it with all the wonderful people who have helped to take care of us. Thank you, Mark. You even remembered how much I love red velvet cake! Now tell me about you."

Mark remembered that Kyle had told Mario that he had been in rehab, so Ruby probably knew, too. Ruby was such an easy person to talk to. She was genuine. Mark told her everything.

He even told her about the heroin and his arrest. She seemed unfazed.

"Mark, for years I lived in neighborhoods where drugs were such a part of life. I know your problem stems from your back pain and the dependence you developed on your prescribed opiates. As for the heroin, you probably simply became desperate. Addiction is a powerful thing. I'm just happy that you found help when you did. I'm so sorry about the CPS problem. If there is any way Mario and I can help, please let us know." Ruby held his hand. "You're a good man and a wonderful father. I'll pray for you."

"I'll pray for you, Ruby."

"Thank you. I need prayers and maybe a miracle." Mark didn't know that much about her condition, but he sensed it might be ominous.

Kyle spent a good part of Saturday cooking for Mark's homecoming party. It was actually just a family dinner. Lucy wanted to invite Martina and the Williams family, but Kyle thought that it might be too much for Mark. He told Lucy that it was just a family party, and she seemed okay with that. Kyle was making gnocchi when he got a call from Austin. Lucy was in her room playing with her doll house, and Mark was at the bakery. The call went to voice mail. Austin asked him to call. "Please, Kyle, just call me."

Austin had called maybe three times since that night they'd spent together. Kyle never returned his calls. He knew that he should have never hooked up with Austin. He knew that an extramarital affair was wrong and would devastate Mark. Kyle also knew that he needed to repair his marriage and concentrate on getting through the upcoming hearing. His relationship with Austin could destroy his family, but he couldn't deny the feelings he had for him. Austin had become his friend and confidant. The sex complicated their relationship, and now it had to end.

Kyle washed his hands, mustered up his courage, and called Austin. He hated doing this over the phone. "Austin, can you meet me at Starbucks at about three o'clock? We need to talk."

"Sure, man, I'll see you then."

Kyle finished the gnocchi. His Bolognese sauce was simmering. He turned off the stove. The sauce could simmer awhile longer when he got back home. Dinner was under control. Anyway, he needed to pick up bread. He called his mother to see if it was okay to drop Lucy off at her shop for about an hour so that he could run an errand. Lucy loved going to the shop, and Pam was usually okay with it. Lucy was always good there. First, he took Lucy out to lunch. He brought her to the shop and kissed his mother. "Thanks, Mom. This is something I've got to do. I won't be more than an hour."

Austin was already there. Kyle hadn't seen him since that night they'd slept together. Now his body betrayed him. His physical attraction to Austin was hard to suppress. *Thank God, we're at Starbucks.* They hugged. Hugging was accepted now… both between gay men and straight men. The smell of Austin's aftershave aroused Kyle all over again. He remembered it well. He was glad he'd chosen to wear a long overcoat.

Kyle went to the counter and bought each of them a latte and came back to the table. He managed to bring his feelings under control. "Austin, I can't see you anymore. Mark's back. It's not fair to you, and I want to save my marriage. I can't risk further damaging my relationship with Mark when we're trying to fight this issue with Lucy's surrogate mother. I'm so worried that visitation rights won't be enough. I'm worried she will want to share custody."

The hurt in Austin's beautiful green eyes was unmistakable. "I understand, but I thought we shared something pretty amazing. Can't we just be discreet? I'm willing to be the other man in your life. I don't want to give you up. Besides, we're friends."

"We won't be able to keep it to a friendship."

"Do you love him that much? Is he everything you need? Do you really want to spend the rest of your life with an older dude who has a drug problem? Come on, Kyle, don't you want more than that?"

"Look, Austin, I do love Mark. He's going through a bad time. He's the father of my child. I don't want to risk losing Lucy. I'm sure you can understand that. Besides, Austin, believe me, you won't have any trouble finding someone else. I'm so sorry. This was all wrong from the start, and I'm to blame."

Austin stood up. He shook Kyle's hand. "Good luck, Kyle." He was gone. Kyle was relieved that it was over. He wasn't going to tell Mark, either. There was no point in hurting him. Kyle had thought that he and Mark had an honest and trusting relationship. Now he guessed it wasn't so. Buying street drugs had been Mark's secret. Kyle wondered what other secrets Mark had. Kyle knew that in his mind he was trying to justify his decision not to tell Mark about his affair with Austin, but he also thought it best not to assuage his guilt with a confession. He didn't think Mark could handle it, and he didn't want to do anything to jeopardize his recovery.

Kyle hoped the dinner would please Mark. The Bolognese sauce was originally Mark's mother's recipe. Apparently, before she'd gotten too deep into her alcoholism, she was a pretty great cook. Sophie said it was Mark's favorite dish as a child. He used to help his mother make the gnocchi.

The dinner party went well. There was no alcohol being served. Everyone understood. When Mark tasted his meal, tears came to his eyes. "Sophie, this taste just like Mom's sauce."

"I found her recipe and gave it to Kyle. Oh, Mark, today's Mom's birthday. She would have been seventy-five." Their mother had died of cirrhosis that led to liver cancer at age fifty-two. Mark and Sophie shared a sad smile.

"Mom was a good cook. Everything is delicious, Kyle. Thank you. Lucy, when I was a little boy, my mother made this dinner on special days. Tonight is special, because I'm home again, and my back feels so much better."

Lucy climbed up on his lap. "I'm glad, Poppy, because I love both my daddies. My Grandma Margaret had red hair just like me. Isn't that right, Poppy?"

"She did, Lucy. She had freckles, too."

Sophie had brought an ice cream cake for dessert. The evening ended early, which was probably a good thing. Mark and Kyle put Lucy to bed together and then cleaned up the kitchen.

Kyle and Mark went to bed. They both seemed more relaxed now. They were intimate. They hadn't had sex in a long time. "Oh, my God, I've missed you," Mark said. Kyle was hopeful that their marriage would survive.

Kyle and Mark dropped Lucy off at preschool and headed to the courthouse on Monday for the hearing. Melanie walked into the courtroom and glanced quickly in their direction. She didn't seem the same. When Kyle and Mark had first met her, she was a soft and pretty college co-ed. Mark remembered that she'd worn ripped jeans and a pink turtleneck sweater. Her long blond hair had been in a ponytail. Her look now was more sophisticated. She wore her hair in a no-nonsense bob. Her suit was dark and conservative. She wore a strand of pearls to soften her look. Melanie's demeanor was a little haughty. Kyle leaned in and whispered to Mark, "She's trying to intimidate us."

"Well, she's the one who sold her body to pay for law school," Mark said. He hated thinking like that because Melanie had seemed so sincere at the time, saying how much she respected adoption and how she felt good about helping a couple who could not otherwise have a natural child. Now he thought it might have been mostly about money. The judge was a man. Mark did not know if that was favorable or not. When they had found out who would be sitting on the bench, Luke had said that he had presented cases before this judge in the past. He'd said that he found him unbiased and fair. He'd said Melanie's attorney, Suzanne Sims, was a barracuda. Both Mark and Kyle worried that family court had a reputation of being sympathetic to the biological mother in these kinds of cases.

Melanie's attorney was the first to present before the judge. She stated that her client was petitioning for biweekly

Chapter 32

"Suffering isn't ennobling, recovery is."

-Dr. Christiaan Barnard

Brad was concerned that going over every day to care for Ruby and Mario's babies would be too much for his wife. He wasn't sure it was such a great idea. Everything had been going so well up until Ruby announced she was pregnant with the twins, and Beverly found out about her own pregnancy and suffered the miscarriage. Before that they had been happy. He and Beverly and Martina were a family. He loved being a father and cherished his wife. Now his wife was fragile again, much the way she'd been when he first met her after her husband died, and then again after Erica died. This time, she wasn't bouncing back. She was still quite depressed. The miscarriage had hit her hard, and now she seemed to be treading the turbulent waters of all the grief that she had experienced in her lifetime. She was tired. His wife could be a vibrant and exciting woman. Now she just wasn't herself. Brad was worried about Ruby, too. It was possible that she might die. She wasn't getting any better. It was a disturbing thought, but it could happen. It would be devastating for everyone, but for Beverly in a unique way. Her bond with Ruby had been cemented the day Dwight and Erica had conceived Martina. Together they'd suffered the loss of their children, who were barely entering adulthood. It was all too much.

Brad kissed his wife before he headed off for the hospital. She was on her way over to Ruby and Mario's. The twins were coming home this morning. "Promise me you will be home for dinner?" Brad asked.

"I will," she said. Beverly had to admit, she had no idea what to expect. She knew how to care for a newborn baby, but twins? Mario was going to use the last two weeks of his vacation time to be home and help the babies get settled in. Sarah and Helen would help, too. When Mario did go back to work, he would be home by four- thirty or five. Since he was an OR nurse, he worked the day shift. If cases ran late into the evening, another nurse would relieve him. Beverly hoped it would all work out. Sarah would probably help Mario the nights that he had school. It all sounded so hectic. Then there was Ruby. Beverly wondered if she was ever going to be well enough to come home. She couldn't even image how it must be for Ruby to have to stay in the hospital away from her babies. She felt painfully sad for her. Beverly cried all the way over to Mario and Ruby's house.

Sarah was already there when Beverly arrived. Together they looked at the nursery to see if they had everything they needed. "Decorating this nursery and getting all the furniture was such a kind thing for you to do," Sarah said. "It's adorable and now well-stocked, too." There were boxes of diapers and wipes and formula. Ruby and Mario's co-workers at the hospital had been very generous, as were the members of their church. There were plans in place for regular meal deliveries. Sarah and Beverly sat at the kitchen table and had coffee while they waited for the big homecoming. "We can do this," Sarah said.

Beverly put her hand over Sarah's. "I think we can." There were tears in Sarah's eyes. Beverly found Sarah to be different than her sister. Ruby was such a strong, confident woman, while Sarah was softer and more vulnerable. "Oh,

Beverly, I'm so worried about my sister. What if she doesn't get better? What if she dies? She had finally found some stability and security in her life. Mario is a wonderful man and completely devoted to her. For the first time in her adult life, she seemed truly happy. Now this! Why does God continue to challenge her?"

They were both crying. "Oh, I'm sorry, Beverly, you have had your own challenges. Why does life have to be so hard?"

"Come on... this was meant to be a happy day!" Beverly said. "We have those sweet new babies to care for."

Just then, Mario walked in with Lillie Mae in his arms. He handed her off to Sarah and went back to the car for Little Mario. He handed his son off to Beverly when he came back in. Beverly looked down at his sweet little face and smiled. She wondered if he would always be called Little Mario. It suited him, although he actually looked more like Ruby. She saw a little more of Mario in Lillie Mae. When Beverly brought him up to her shoulder and breathed in his newborn scent, she was flooded with memories. It seemed like just yesterday that she and Brad brought Martina home from the hospital. She'd been nervous and overwhelmed that day, too. She hadn't known if she would be able to be a mother to Erica's child... not a grandmother, but a mother. Somehow it had all worked out. Beverly just hoped that, now, all of this would work out. The baby in her arms was Martina's uncle. *God, how my life has changed!*

There was a portable crib set up in the living room for the babies. Mario thought it was a good idea to keep them in the same crib for a while. They had shared a womb. Beverly and Sarah checked their diapers and put them down. They'd been fed just before they were discharged. Mario grabbed a cup of coffee and put a bagel in the toaster. He sat down and talked to Beverly and Sarah. His look was serious. Beverly was nervous about what he would say.

"I felt awful tearing those babies away from Ruby at the hospital. She was Ruby, though. She was stoic. I talked to her cardiologist this morning." Mario now sounded a little dark. "He said if her ejection fraction drops after today's testing, he wants to get her on the transplant list. Can you believe it? He thinks that she would be a good candidate because she is young and was otherwise healthy. She has had no medical problems up until now. It can take awhile to get a heart, so he wants to get her on the list now."

Beverly and Sarah just looked at each other. They didn't know what to say.

"I know my wife. If she's lucky enough to get a heart, she will rally. She will be okay. She's a remarkable woman."

"How long does it take to get a heart?" Sarah asked.

"Doc said he doesn't know. First, she is going to have open-heart surgery to implant an LVAD. LVAD stands for left ventricular assist device. They implant a mechanical pump that helps her heart pump more blood with less work. It helps to move blood from the left ventricle to the aorta. It will be a bridge to help her get to the transplant. If it helps to correct her heart failure, she might be able to come home until a heart is available. They are planning on doing the LVAD regardless of today's tests. Her ejection fraction is already down to twenty-two. Doc says he suspects that it is even lower now, because she is not improving.

"What did Ruby say?" asked Sarah.

"Ruby said, 'Schedule the surgery!'" She just wants to come home and do whatever she needs to do to get her life back. I'm so proud of her."

The babies were good. It was really just a matter of changing them, feeding them, and putting them back to sleep. Little Mario could be a little fussy, but Sarah was very good at calming him down. Mario was going back to the hospital to be with Ruby. It was a big day for her...saying good-bye to her babies, talking to the cardiologist about the heart transplant, and spending a big chunk of the day down in nuclear medicine having the MUGA scan. The MUGA scan would give them the most accurate measurement of her current ejection fraction. Mario hoped they would have the results by late afternoon. He took off, knowing that the babies were in good hands.

Helen picked up Martina at preschool today and brought her over to see the babies. Martina was bubbling with excitement. Beverly told her that the babies would be waking up soon to eat, and maybe she could hold them. She told Martina that she would have to eat her own lunch first. Beverly made Martina her favorite sandwich, peanut butter and banana, and poured her a glass of milk. Martina chattered away and told them all the happenings at school that day. She said that today they'd each decorated a mailbox for their valentines. "My friend Scarlett's was the best! It was so pretty. I just don't know how she does it, and she only has one arm!"

Helen smiled and said, "God gives extra help to those who need it the most. But your friend Scarlett is a smart and determined little girl."

"What does determined mean?"

"It means that you try extra, extra hard to get or do what you want. You stick with it."

"That's Scarlett, all right. Is Grandma Ruby determined?" Martina asked. Her little mind was working hard trying to figure it all out. "I heard you talking to Daddy. I know Grandma Ruby is sick. I hope she is determined so that she can get better and come home. A mommy should be home with her babies." Martina ran upstairs to Ruby and Mario's room. She brought down the picture of Dwight and Erica at their prom. "This was my real mommy. She never could come home from the hospital to take care of me. She had to go to heaven. I just want Grandma Ruby to get better and come home... not heaven. Lillie Mae and Little Mario need her."

Beverly's heart sank. She got up and got a glass of water to soothe the lump in her throat. She and Helen and Sarah were all speechless. Just then, one of the babies let out a wail. It was feeding time! The rest of the afternoon flew by. The mood lightened. They were all enamored with the precious magic of newborn life.

Brad saw Mario in line at the coffee kiosk as he was leaving the hospital for the day. He asked Mario about the latest on Ruby's condition. The results of the MUGA scan were in. Ruby's ejection fraction was now only fourteen. She hadn't had any heart arrhythmias yet, which was both surprising and fortunate. They did want to schedule her for surgery to implant the LVAD as soon as possible. Hopefully that would keep her stable and put her in a better position on the transplant list. Plans for a transplant were now a reality.

Brad listened carefully to everything Mario told him. He shook his head, "Jesus, Mario... a heart transplant. I can't begin to know what you must be feeling. We're family now. Just let me know what you need."

Mario shook Brad's hand. "Thanks, man. I need to get back to my wife."

Brad had worried that it might come down to this. Stressful times were ahead. He thought that Ruby was a remarkable woman and only hoped that she could rally through all of this. He wondered if Beverly had heard any of this latest news. Beverly was at work in the kitchen when he got home. He had stopped at Wegmans and picked up a bouquet of roses. Yellow roses were her favorite. These were yellow roses tipped with red. He laid the roses down on the counter, wrapped his arms around her, and kissed the back of her neck. Brad was happy that his wife was busy in the kitchen and not lying in a hospital bed with a failing heart. He loved her completely and couldn't ever imagine losing her.

"I decided to make Ruby's mac and cheese recipe. We could use some comfort food tonight. Brad, I know about the heart transplant. It's all so overwhelming."

He refilled her wineglass and poured a glass for himself. "We've just got to be here for each other, and be there for Mario and his family. As I've said before, I have a feeling that Ruby will be okay." Now he held his wife and kissed her on the lips. "I love you, Beverly."

Beverly put the roses in a vase and told Brad all about her day. Martina was up in her room playing with her baby doll, Jasmine. The tears came only when she told Brad about what Martina had said about her "real mommy".

It had been a long day. They put Martina to bed early. Brad was in bed with his computer researching information about heart transplants. Beverly took a bath. When she came out of the bathroom, she climbed into bed and closed Brad's computer. "Brad, make love to me." Their sex that night was urgent and powerful. Afterwards, he held her in his arms until she fell asleep.

Chapter 33

Spencer was a little nervous about meeting Bridget's parents. He had no idea what to expect, and meeting the parents in such a formal way implied that the relationship was going somewhere. He guessed that it probably was. He did know that he had fallen in love with Bridget. If they didn't both have children, living together would probably be the next logical step, but that didn't seem quite right. He thought it was probably too soon after Anna died to get married again, but was it? Anna wasn't ever coming back. Lizzie couldn't watch the girls that night, but he was able to get a high school girl in the neighborhood to babysit. Spencer had gotten to know her parents. She was a nice kid. He didn't think it would be a late night. Ivy was disappointed. She just wanted Lizzie.

"Daddy, you know how much I love Lizzie, I want *her* to come over tonight. She promised me that she would help me make my valentines for school."

"Honey, I'm sorry, Lizzie had other plans tonight. We can work on your valentines tomorrow, or maybe Amanda can help you." Ivy had a meltdown. Spencer hadn't seen her act like this in a long time. He was able to get her calmed down before Amanda, the babysitter, came. Amanda brought a video for the girls to watch. It was Disney's *Lady and the Tramp*. She also brought M&M's and a bag of popcorn to microwave. He thought it would be okay.

Spencer picked up Bridget and they met her parents at the restaurant. Her parents were young...probably not even fifty yet. They had a cocktail at the bar while they were waiting for their table. Bridget's mother, Angela, was beautiful, but she didn't look like her daughter. She had dark brown eyes and a more olive skin tone. Both Bridget and Scarlett had Mr. O'Connell's bright blue eyes. Sean was cordial but somewhat intimidating in a friendly sort of way. Spencer remembered how Bridget had said that her father was protective of her, and he sensed that Sean was sizing him up. His handshake was probably a little firmer than it needed to be. Spencer noticed that he drank Irish whiskey on the rocks. Bridget had told him that he was a cop… a homicide detective.

"So, Doctor, tell me what has brought you into my daughter's life." Bridget gave Spencer a sympathetic look.

"Please, Mr. O'Connell, call me Spencer. I met your daughter at the kids' preschool. My youngest daughter, Ivy, and Scarlett are in the same class." Spencer thought that Sean probably already knew all of this, and it was probably only a test. "I later learned that Bridget and I both work in the pediatrics department at the medical center. I moved here from Philadelphia to take the position of medical director of the ambulatory pediatric clinic."

Sean laughed and took a big sip of his whiskey. "Sounds like a match made in heaven!" He recognized the twinkle in his blue eyes. He had seen it in Bridget's eyes.

"Oh, Sean, mind your manners," Angela said. When they sat down to dinner, Spencer pulled Angela's chair out for her. Spencer could be such a gentleman. Bridget knew that it was sure to score points with her mother.

Sean wanted to know more about Spencer's life before moving to Rochester. Clearly, the discussion at the table was all about Spencer. He simplified his life story the best that he could. He talked about growing up in Philadelphia, his education, his parents, and his brothers. "My wife, Anna, was killed by a drunk driver about a year and a half ago. One of my friends from my residency program informed me about the search for a medical director to head the pediatric clinic. I always liked Rochester and thought that moving here would help me to get a fresh start. My little girls like it here and seem to be adjusting well. Meeting your daughter has helped me to begin a happier chapter in my life. I feel fortunate to have found her." Spencer reached over and put his hand over hers.

Sean seemed to be taking it all in. Spencer could see that Angela's eyes looked a little glassy. "Spencer, tell me about your little girls," Angela said. Both he and Bridget were glad that the conversation now focused on the kids. It was clear that Sean and Angela doted on their granddaughter. They were taking Scarlett to Disney World over spring break.

Dinner had been pleasant but, for Spencer and Bridget, a little intense. They were glad when they finished up their coffee and dessert. Spencer had already arranged with the waiter that he was picking up the check. It would avoid an awkward moment. He excused himself and went up to the bar to sign off on his credit card. Sean and Angela thanked Spencer for dinner and they said their good-byes. Angela had said that she hoped that Spencer would bring the girls over for dinner sometime soon. Sean said he was looking forward to spring so that he could take Spencer to his club for a round of golf. Spencer drove Bridget home. Her babysitter that night was a nursing student looking to pick up some extra money. She had a car. Spencer paid her, and she drove herself home. At last he was alone with Bridget.

"Oh, Spencer, I know my father was a little much, but I think he really liked you!" She kissed him. Spencer had Bridget undressed in record time. He loved her and just couldn't get enough of her.

"I wish I could stay longer, but my babysitter tonight is a high school girl who is a neighbor of mine. I don't want to keep her out too late. It seems like we haven't been able to see each other too much lately. I miss you."

"I know. I miss you, too. Do you have plans for tomorrow? We could take the girls to a movie and all have dinner together after."

"Okay, we would all love that. I'll check out the movie times and call you in the morning. Good night for now. I love you. I meant it when I told your parents that you have made my life so much happier." He held her face in his hands and kissed her tenderly. "I'll see you tomorrow."

Bridget didn't want to get her hopes up, but she was really hoping her relationship with Spencer would have a happily ever after. She wasn't sure if he would ever consider getting married again. She was happy that she would see him tomorrow. He didn't know it, but it was her birthday. Right now, she couldn't think of a better way to spend it.

The next morning her mother called to wish her a happy birthday. She and Bridget chatted awhile. Angela told her how much she'd enjoyed meeting Spencer. "Your father liked him, too. We were wondering how old he is."

"Oh, Mom, does it really matter? He's thirty-seven."

"Oh, really? No, it doesn't matter. I just want you to be happy, honey, and we don't want to see you hurt again."

"I know, Mom, thanks for calling. I love you. I'll see you tomorrow." Her mother was having a family birthday dinner for her the following night after work. Her sister, Megan, would be in town for the day. Scarlett had just woken up and walked into the kitchen. Bridget was mixing up batter for pancakes. Scarlett was singing the happy birthday song. She wrapped her arm around her mother and proudly presented her with a card that she had made. Bridget told her about the plans for today. Scarlett was thrilled. She loved spending time with Spencer's girls. Someone was knocking at her door. Bridget flipped the pancakes onto a plate and went to see who was there.

Oh, God... it's Kurt! He was standing there with a bunch of flowers in his hand.

"Happy birthday, beautiful, can I come in?" It was clear that he wasn't taking no for an answer. Bridget didn't want a scene, so she let him in. He followed her into the kitchen. Scarlett was sitting at the table eating her pancakes. Bridget couldn't believe that Kurt actually remembered her birthday. He never had when they were together.

"Hello, Scarlett. How are you?"

Bridget couldn't imagine where this was all going, but it was making her extremely nervous. She wanted Kurt to leave. There was an open shelf above the counter with coffee mugs. He took a mug and poured himself a cup of coffee.

"Are you Mommy's friend?"

"You could say that, honey. I'm your daddy."

Scarlett just looked at him and screwed up her little face. "Well, where have you been?" she asked.

Bridget couldn't believe that this was happening. Kurt's answer couldn't have been any dumber. "Well, honey, I'm a baseball player, and I had to go play baseball."

"Well, okay, it was nice to meet you. I've got to go. Mommy and I have plans today. I've got to get dressed." She went to her room. Bridget thought Scarlett's reaction was precious. She'd given Kurt a pretty good brush-off. She wondered what Scarlett was really thinking.

"Kurt, what is the matter with you? You just can't come here and drop a bomb like that. Would you please leave now? I have someone else in my life. It's never going to work for us. If you really do love me, you will leave me and Scarlett alone. Please, Kurt. You can't come back here again."

"Can I see Scarlett again?"

"No, Kurt. That would be too confusing for her. How is she supposed to understand that her father wanted nothing to do with her because she was born with a birth defect? I don't want to tell her that. It's too late now."

"Okay, babe, I'll go now." He left like a dog that had just been swatted with a newspaper for urinating on the carpet. Bridget dumped his flowers in the trash.

Later in the car, on the way over to Spencer's house, Scarlett said, "Mommy, it's okay. I don't want him to be my daddy anyways. I don't really like him, and I can tell you don't like him, either. And *Grandpa* really doesn't like him. I heard him talking to Grandma. He said some real naughty words when he was talking about him. They thought I was sleeping, but I heard them.

"Okay, sweetie, let's just try to forget about it for today. We are going to have fun with Ivy and Haley, right?"

"We will, Mommy. It's always fun when we get together."

Scarlett's mind was still busy trying to process Kurt's visit. "I don't have to love him because he is my daddy, right?"

"No, sweetie, you don't. He hasn't behaved much like a daddy." They pulled into Spencer's driveway. Bridget was hoping she would drop it.

"Dr. Harris," Scarlett squealed, "did you know that it is Mommy's birthday today?"

"No, I didn't, Scarlett, but we will definitely have to make it a special day." He kissed Bridget. "Why didn't you tell me?"

She shrugged. "I don't know."

The kids played awhile until it was time to go to the movie. Bridget and Spencer talked. She told him about Kurt's unexpected appearance. Spencer knew she was on the verge of tears. He didn't know what to say, because he didn't know what could be done. He wondered if there was some kind of legal recourse that could be pursued. After all, he'd deserted his child.

"Maybe you should tell your father. He could have a talk with him. I hate it that he's bothering you, and I'm sure your father would be furious and could maybe scare him off."

"A scene between my father and Kurt would be ugly. I'm just going to try and leave it alone for now. If he comes back again, I'll have to figure something out. I guess I never realized how dumb Kurt is."

Spencer hated that the incident had ruined his day with Bridget. He let the subject drop. After the movies, they went back to Spencer's and had pizza. They took the kids to the dairy for ice cream after dinner. They sang "Happy Birthday" before eating their ice cream. It ended up being a good day. The kids had fun, and he was able to be with the woman he loved. Spencer found it ironic that both Anna and Bridget had birthdays in February and only six days apart. It was a school night, so the evening wrapped up pretty early. He kissed Bridget and gave Scarlett a hug. "Thank you for telling me it was your mommy's birthday."

After he got home, he read the girls a story and put them to bed. He couldn't stop thinking about Bridget, and then he couldn't stop thinking about Anna. He decided to give his father a call. Talking things out with his dad always helped.

The next day Spencer stopped at a jewelry store in the village on the way home from work. He had seen commercials for the store on TV. He knew it was a quality place. He immediately saw what he wanted. They were brilliant blue sapphire teardrop earrings. They reminded him of Bridget's eyes. He didn't care how much they cost. He had the jeweler wrap them up. He planned to stop by the NICU in the morning and give them to her.

She wasn't free to break away when he stopped by. She said she would put the gift in her locker and open it at home. She called him later in the evening. "Oh, Spencer, the earrings are beautiful. Thank you. You are so good to me. I love you." Bridget told him not to make plans for Valentine's Day. She wanted him and the girls to come over for dinner. It fell on a Friday night... *maybe a sleepover?*

That night Bridget tossed and turned all night. When she finally fell asleep, she dreamt heavily. She had an orgasm in her sleep, which woke her up. That had never happened to her before. It was too bad she was dreaming about Kurt. She couldn't help but wonder if she still had feelings for him. Then she decided it was just because she'd always thought he was so good in bed. Still, she was ashamed that her body had betrayed her heart. Just when she thought her life was finally going in a good direction, Kurt had to stumble back into it.

Chapter 34

Lucy had preschool three mornings a week. It was usually Mark who dropped her off and picked her up, because he had the most flexible schedule. She was then dropped off at her day care after preschool. Sometimes Kyle or Pam would do the pickup on days when Mark couldn't. Today Mark had a meeting scheduled with a client about a wedding cake. This was the second meeting with this client. She was a real "bridezilla." Mark knew he had the potential to get tied up with her, so the plan was for Kyle to pick up Lucy today. A half hour before the pickup time, the kids were usually out on the playground. Kyle loved to watch the kids playing, so he left the office early, stopped for coffee, and watched the kids from behind the fence. It was an atypically mild day for February. It was more like spring. The kids were having such a good time. A lot of parents had the same idea to come early, probably because it was such a nice day. Kyle spotted Melanie. He couldn't believe she was there. He wondered how she even knew it was Lucy's preschool. He was furious.

Kyle took a deep breath. "Melanie, what are you doing here?"

"Kyle, I'm just watching the kids play, like you and the other parents."

"But you are not Lucy's parent. This is inappropriate!"

"Relax, Kyle, I've never spoken to Lucy. Sometimes I just like to see her. I want to know that she's okay."

"Look, Melanie, I don't know why you've chosen to carry out this vendetta. It will only confuse Lucy and possibly hurt her. Mark and I love her, and we are totally devoted to her."

"You and Mark aren't the people I thought you were. Mark's a drug addict and you aren't the stable, loving couple that I once met. I know about the torrid little affair that you had when Mark was in rehab."

It now occurred to Kyle that Melanie had maybe hired a private investigator to check them out. *What a nasty bitch!* "Melanie, please stop. I hate saying this, but in reality, you sold your body to pay for law school. You got what you wanted, now please leave us alone. Nothing good can come from this. Is this about Lucy, or is this about you? Are you feeling some kind of guilt now?"

"I guess I'll see you in court," she said. She took off in her BMW. *Judging by her car, I guess she's not hard up for money anymore. I wonder if she's married.* Kyle's nerves were frazzled. He decided to take the rest of the day off and spend it with Lucy. He called Lucy's day care and told them that Lucy would not be coming today.

He ran into Beverly, who was there to pick up Martina. He decided to ask her if Martina could come to their house and play with Lucy the rest of the afternoon. He knew that both of the girls would love it. She said that it would be great and gave Kyle Martina's car seat. They chatted for a while. Beverly told him that she was spending most days over at Ruby and Mario's. They talked about Ruby and her needing the heart transplant. *God, things had not gone well for anyone since they'd last seen each other at Christmas.* Beverly gave Kyle a hug and told him that Brad would be by to pick Martina up after work. Lucy and Martina were delighted about their playdate.

Kyle took the girls back to the house and made lunch. He called his secretary and told her he wasn't coming back to the office because he had a migraine. He called Luke, his attorney, while the girls were outside playing on the swing set. Kyle told him about what had happened with Melanie. He told him that Melanie had accused him of having an affair.

"Well, did you?"

"Luke, it was one time! I've ended it. I can't let Mark know. I don't want to jeopardize his recovery. Believe me, I regret it. Do you think it will come out in court?"

"Hopefully, it won't. I've looked over the new report submitted by the CPS worker, as well as the statements from Mark's doctors. The child psychologist concluded that Lucy is a happy, well-adjusted three-year-old. I think the judge will end up dismissing the case. If the judge does decide to listen to more testimony, I don't think that he would look too kindly on Melanie having you followed or showing up at Lucy's school. But maybe you should have a talk with Mark. You don't want him to find out about your infidelity in court. He's a reasonable man. I think that neither one of you wants to risk losing this case because of trouble in your marriage. Work it out. Hang in there, man. I will see you guys on Monday."

Now Kyle's migraine excuse was becoming true. He felt a headache coming on. He decided to take some Motrin and go outside with the girls for some fresh air. He grabbed his sunglasses. Kyle pushed the girls on the swings and played hide-and-seek. They all took a walk and went for ice cream. When they got back to the house, he played Barbies with the girls. After Martina left with Brad, Lucy gave Kyle a big hug. "Martina and I had so much fun today. You're the best daddy ever!" She giggled and put her hand over her mouth. "But so is Poppy."

Kyle was feeling a little better about things but decided that he and Mark needed to talk. He would find a way to tell him about Austin. Maybe it was time to explain to Lucy why she had two daddies.

That night, Kyle had a glass of wine while Mark was putting Lucy to bed. Mark seemed to be able to handle it if Kyle had the occasional drink in front of him. Mark seemed to be doing well, and that was part of the reason he didn't want to tell him about Austin. But it would be worse if Mark found out about it in court. He started the conversation by telling him about his encounter with Melanie.

Mark was furious that she would just show up at her school and agreed with Kyle that she probably had hired a private investigator. "I can't believe that she would be this mean," he said.

"Mark, there is something else that she is threatening us with. She accused me of having an affair while you were away in rehab." Kyle had a hard time controlling his emotions. "Mark, it's true, but it's over. I swear to you it was just one time. We were friends at first, but then on one lonely night, it became more. We ended up in his bedroom. Afterwards, I felt so ashamed. I broke it off with him after that night. Mark, it was hard for me when you were away. I was angry and lonely and depressed. As I said, it started out as a friendship. He was easy to talk to. He was having custody issues of his own. He's divorced and was once married to a woman. He has a daughter, too. It just helped talking to someone who understood what a gay man is up against when it comes to parenting. It ended up all wrong. I hope you can forgive me."

Mark said that he'd sensed that something wasn't quite right between them when he got out of rehab. He said that he was sorry about what he put Kyle through with his careless drug use. He knew that it was his fault.

"We've both made mistakes… big mistakes. We've both got to forgive each other and move forward. We love each other, and we love Lucy. Let's focus on being a family again. I love you, Kyle. It had to be hard to tell me about it, but I'm relieved that you did. You've always been honest. We have to go back to trusting each other."

Kyle was also relieved. He felt like he'd made the right decision telling Mark. Maybe this was just another step forward with getting their marriage back on track.

Mark couldn't help but wonder if Kyle's affair had been with a younger man. Since he had started having problems with his back, he had become insecure about the difference in their ages. Kyle was such a principled man. Mark had to admit that he was surprised about his infidelity, but Mark knew he hadn't been much of a husband lately. The opiates really affected his libido. It was difficult for him to maintain an erection. Kyle had been patient, but it was definitely a problem for them now. Mark decided he would talk to Dr. Lamb about it.

Kyle and Mark had asked Lucy's pediatrician for advice about when to talk to her about why she had two daddies. He said that when she was ready, she would probably ask. He gave them a list of children's books that featured atypical families doing normal things. The families featured in the books had same-sex parents. The books were more about the story and the adventure. The focus was not the parents. The message for a three-year-old was that there were all different kinds of families. When she was old enough to understand, they could explain that since it was a woman who gave birth to a baby, they'd needed some help to have a family. They'd found a woman who wanted to help.

That night Mark held Kyle in bed. He said, "I read that book to Lucy about the two daddies taking their little girl to the beach. She loves that book. She said that she was lucky like the little girl in the story to have two daddies. Our Lucy wants us to take her to the beach someday. Let's take her this summer. She told me about all the fun you had today." He kissed Kyle. "I think we'll be okay."

The next morning, Luke called. The judge had a death in his family. The hearing was postponed for three more weeks.

Chapter 35

Today was a big day. Ruby was having surgery to implant the LVAD. Beverly and Helen were with the babies. Sarah and her husband, Henry, wanted to be at the hospital with Mario. Beverly knew that this was the best way to support Ruby today. Ruby's family was coming in from Atlanta. They still hadn't been up to see the babies yet. Ruby's father, Reverend Tobias Washington, was a Baptist minister. Beverly remembered him from Dwight's funeral. He was an intense man. He was also a busy man. He was the pastor of a large congregation and also a community leader. Beverly remembered feeling a little intimidated in his presence. She remembered Mrs. Washington as being kind and sweet, much like her daughter Sarah. A meal was being delivered that night by friends from Ruby's church. After surgery, Mario would stay on with Ruby at the hospital, and the rest of the family would come back to the house to eat and see the babies. Beverly wanted to stay and help serve dinner. Brad was going to come after work. Martina would already be there. Helen was going to pick her up from preschool and come back with her.

Brad had explained the surgery to Beverly. She knew the surgery itself carried a lot of risk. It was open-heart surgery. He'd told her that the LVAD had internal and external components. The actual pump would sit next to her left ventricle, and a cable would come out through the skin of her abdomen. The cable would be connected to a power source, probably a battery, which would control the pump. Brad told her that hopefully, if the surgery was successful, the LVAD could keep Ruby stable until a heart was available…several months or even years. Waiting years was hard to fathom. It was possible, if she had a good recovery, she might be able to go home in two to four weeks.

Beverly remembered the hours waiting for her son, Johnny, to come out of his open-heart surgeries. It was grueling. Brad told her the surgery was expected to take four to six hours. She couldn't even imagine how anxious Mario must be. He worked every day in the OR, so he knew how things could go wrong. Beverly wanted to push away any negative thoughts. She was determined to focus on taking good care of the babies and having the house calm, ready, and welcoming for the family when they came back after surgery.

She'd had an appointment with her therapist just yesterday. Dr. Martino, as always, helped her to put everything into perspective. His office was a safe place for her to ventilate her feelings. He didn't always have the answers, but he helped her to find a way to cope. He made her feel strong. He reminded her that she was only one player in all of this, and she needed to concentrate on her part. The day of the surgery, her part was to take care of the babies. It was an important part, and Ruby would know that her babies were in good and loving hands. Much of the rest of it was out of her control, so she needed to focus on what she could control. Ruby was a strong woman, and she was in the care of a competent medical team at an outstanding medical facility. Dr. Martino knew that she believed in God. He reminded her that much of this was in God's hands. Then Dr. Martino said something that really stuck in her head.

Her daughter, Erica, had wanted to become a cardiologist or a heart surgeon. Maybe God and Erica would be looking out for Ruby. Beverly thought it was a comforting thought, but when it came to heart disease, God had let her down before... first with Johnny and then with Tom. Beverly shouted angrily at Dr. Martino when he took the God path. "Why would I trust God?"

He shook his head. "You can only do your best and hope for the best. Be positive and be strong, like you have been so many times in the past."

"I'm so sorry for that outburst," she said. "I'm just so worried."

When she talked about the surgery with Brad, he also said that much of it was in God's hands. She yelled at Brad, too. Brad said nothing more. She noticed that ever since Ruby's condition had begun to deteriorate, he lit a candle after mass every week. Brad was a humble and spiritual man. As a surgeon, he was not at all arrogant. He knew that he did not have the power to control everything. To his patients, he portrayed a gentle confidence.

Beverly tried to keep busy with the babies, but the morning hours seemed to drag. She chatted with Helen. Helen had told her that she'd gone to seven-thirty mass before coming over. Beverly wished that she had a strong faith like Helen and Brad. Finally, it was time for Helen to pick up Martina at school. She got a call from Brad. "Mario just paged me. Ruby is in recovery. The surgery went really well. It took a little longer than anticipated because they had some trouble getting Ruby off of bypass. She's stable, though, and doing well."

"Oh, thank God, Brad. You're still coming over after work?"

"I will. I love you. See you tonight."

Beverly was relieved, but she knew it was far from over. There was still that long wait for a heart. It was all so much to wrap her head around. She couldn't even imagine how Ruby did it. Today was just a step up on that staircase...that staircase where you couldn't see the top. Beverly decided to call Pam. She for sure would want an update, and Pam would share the news with Kyle and Mark. Ruby had so many people pulling for her.

Beverly and Helen got the babies fed and settled down. Brad came. He held her and Beverly cried in his arms. "Let's sit down and have a glass of wine before the family gets back here," he said. "Beverly, she did well. I want you to believe that." He tipped up her chin and looked into her eyes. "I'm concerned about you. You are so consumed by all of this. It is so much anxiety and stress. I can see what it is doing to you."

"Really, Brad, I'm okay... especially now that you're here." Beverly always felt safe when she was with Brad. He had given her so much love and security from the first day they had met. Sometimes she felt like she didn't give back enough. She failed at the one chance she'd had to really give Brad something extraordinary... their baby. It was exactly why she was not one of strong faith. She didn't trust God. Beverly took a deep breath when she heard a car pull up. Ruby's family was here. They looked in on the babies. Beverly had put them up in the nursery and turned on the baby monitor. She explained they had just been fed and suggested that they have something to eat before the babies woke up. She and Helen started putting out the food that the church ladies had brought over. Some things were warming in the oven and some dishes needed to be put in the microwave. Beverly offered Sarah a glass of wine, but she politely declined. Sarah took her aside and told her that she never drank in front of her father. Beverly noticed that Henry had a beer... good for him. He seemed to steer clear of his father-in-law when he could.

Beverly found Reverend Washington to be just as intimidating as he had been the last time she'd met him, which was at Dwight's funeral. Martina seemed to adore him. She climbed right up on his lap. Brad was good at engaging him in conversation. Reverend Washington was sweet to Helen. Helen and Mrs. Washington seemed to be having a nice conversation. The house was noisy with all the kids. There was Ruby's girls, Anthony, Sarah and Henry's kids, and of course, Martina. Reverend Washington silenced everyone for prayer. At that moment, Beverly couldn't help thinking about how she'd gotten here and how much her life had changed in less than four years. Sometimes, especially when she was with Dwight's family, her life seemed surreal. The only person here tonight that she'd known four years ago was Helen. Watching the babies together, and Helen's constant help and support raising Martina, made Beverly's relationship with her mother-in-law closer than ever. Beverly loved her now like she never had when Tom was alive. She was an amazing woman. Helen's actions had kept Erica's heart pumping, which had kept blood moving across the placenta, keeping Martina alive. Beverly had to admit that she didn't even know how to perform CPR.

As everyone was enjoying their coffee and dessert, the first cries could be heard on the baby monitor. Sarah went up with the older twins, Danielle and Denise, to change the babies and bring them down. Beverly got their bottles ready. Reverend Washington fed Little Mario, while Mrs. Washington fed Lillie Mae. They admired and fussed over their new grandbabies.

Then the reverend said that he had some news. His congregation in Atlanta had been showering them with kindness. Not only had they offered up their prayers but they had done some serious fund-raising. There had been bake sales, a rummage sale, car wash, and chicken barbeque.

Several thousand dollars had been raised. He said that he planned to pass the money on to Mario so that he could hire a nurse to take care of the babies and look after Ruby when she came home from the hospital.

Beverly could feel the heat in her face. *Hadn't she taken good care of the babies? She wanted to help care for Ruby. Wasn't it best for family to take this on? Maybe she wasn't considered family.* She couldn't help but feel hurt.

"Beverly, you have taken wonderful care of my grandbabies, and I thank you. But you need to concentrate on raising our Martina. This is too much to ask. We will arrange to see after Ruby and her babies."

"I love taking care of the babies," said Beverly, and her voice cracked a little when she said it. "I can help Ruby in her recovery, too. I took care of my son when he came home to recover from his open-heart surgeries. The money could be used in other ways to support Ruby and Mario." Brad's heart ached for his wife. She had been slighted and didn't deserve it.

"I think that this is what's best for my family," he said. "I plan to discuss this further with Mario before I leave."

Sarah gave Beverly a sympathetic look but said nothing about her father's plan. She got up to take in the dessert dishes. Beverly got up to help her. Sarah took Beverly's hand. "My father is from a different generation. He was born and raised in the South. His great-grandfather was born a slave. He is a very proud man. The mentality in the South is different. I think he doesn't like the idea of white people involved in his family's business...even if it's you and your family. I'm ashamed that he thinks this way, but I know my father."

"I guess I thought Martina made us all family," Beverly said.

"It's more complicated than that," Sarah said. "Please know that Ruby, Mario, Henry, and I feel differently. We are so grateful for all the support you have given us. I'm not sure Mario will be able to convince him otherwise. I am so sorry that my father has hurt your feelings."

"Sarah, it's okay. This is not about me. This is about Ruby." She dabbed at her eyes with a tissue and blew her nose. "I'll take a step back. After your father leaves, let me know how I can help. I'm sure it will take some time to hire a nurse." Sarah hugged her.

Brad came into the kitchen. "I think it's time for us to get Martina home. It's way past her bedtime."

Martina fell asleep in her car seat. Brad and Beverly and Helen drove home without saying much. They dropped Helen off at her house. "Helen, I'll talk to you tomorrow. I think it's best if we don't go over there tomorrow."

"I think you're right, Beverly. Good night."

Brad hated that his wife had been treated this way. He knew that she was hurt and upset, but maybe it was better that she was taking a step back. The stress was taking a toll on her.

As they got ready for bed, he said, "Beverly, I'm proud of how you have stepped in to support Ruby. Please don't let what her father said make you feel differently about what you've done. There is truth to the saying 'the road to hell is paved with good intentions'. Your intentions were good. The reverend's thinking is not very enlightened. He is a proud black man from the South. His feelings about race are still probably evolving."

"Oh, Brad. I just want Ruby to be okay. This is all so complicated."

"I really think things will settle down after the reverend goes back to Atlanta and Ruby is able to come home. I do think she will come home soon. Mario will figure things out, and I guess we have to respect his decisions."

Chapter 36

Spencer and the girls did end up going to Bridget's for Valentine's Day. He hoped it would be as much fun as New Year's had been. She and Spencer ate shrimp and had a cocktail while the kids had their dinner. Bridget let the girls frost and decorate heart-shaped cookies that she had made earlier in the day. They were having a great time. The kids put on their pajamas and got ready to watch the movie *Annie*. She was planning on a candlelight dinner with Spencer after the kids were asleep. Of course, Spencer enjoyed the dates he had with Bridget, but he also really enjoyed these occasions when they were together with the kids. They almost seemed like a family.

Oftentimes Spencer entertained the idea of asking Bridget to marry him to make the arrangement permanent, but then he would quickly dismiss the idea, because he knew it was probably too soon. He was certain about his feelings for Bridget, but he wasn't sure if Bridget was ready. He didn't know how the girls would accept having a new mother. His life was stable now, so why rock the boat? He was starting to love his job, he had a great nanny who was really connecting with his girls, and he had a wonderful woman in his life. She was kind and beautiful and smart. The sex was very satisfying. He was happy again. These thoughts rolled around in his head all of the time.

Bridget had made a wonderful dinner. She borrowed some of her mother's china and set a beautiful table for two with candlelight. She made a dish called Steak Oscar. It was a beef tenderloin steak, topped with crabmeat, asparagus, and hollandaise sauce. She also made mashed potatoes and a fresh garden salad. Spencer carried the girls into Scarlett's room, one at a time, and put them into bed. He covered them up. They were sound asleep. The three little girls looked precious all snuggled up together. Bridget put the finishing touches on dinner and lit the candles.

Dinner smelled incredible. Spencer opened the bottle of merlot he'd brought for dinner and sat down at the table. Bridget served everything, and Spencer pulled out her chair for her. He held up his glass. "Here's to us," he said. "You have gone to a lot of trouble here. Everything looks absolutely delicious. I've never had this dish before, but I can't wait to try it."

Bridget took a sip of her wine and smiled. "I love cooking for you. Sometimes I get tired of making kid-friendly food, so this is fun for me. It's Valentine's Day. We deserve something special." She slipped her foot out of her shoe and ran it up Spencer's leg under the table. "Wait until dessert."

After they finished eating, Bridget picked up their dishes and brought them into the kitchen. She took her chocolate crème brulees out of the refrigerator. They had to sit at room temperature for a while before she could torch the tops. She walked back into the dining room and said, "We have about twenty minutes to kill before dessert is ready."

"Well, let's make good use of the time," he said. Spencer picked her up and carried her into the bedroom. He hiked up her skirt. She was ready. They rolled over and she was now on top.

"Oh, my God, that was one crazy ride!" she said. She could barely catch her breath. She lay in his arms. The timer went off. Bridget had set the timer because she had worked so hard on dessert that she didn't want to get so carried away with sex that she forgot to serve it. She got up and went back to the kitchen and finished her dessert preparation. She put the ramekins on a tray and grabbed another bottle of wine, along with their glasses. "More dessert...let's have it in bed." Bridget stripped down to her sexy red lace bra and panties. She'd bought the lingerie especially for tonight. Spencer stripped down to his boxer shorts.

"You're such a naughty girl." Spencer kissed her, and she fed him the first spoonful of crème brulee. "You're a wonderful cook and awesome lover. You are the perfect valentine."

"So I guess I'm a good girl then."

"You're the best. I love you."

They heard crying from the bedroom. Spencer jumped out of bed, put on his pants, and pulled his sweater over his head. He went to the kids' room. Bridget put on her robe and followed him. Ivy was having a nightmare. He brought her out in the living room because he didn't want her to wake up Haley and Scarlett. Spencer held her. "Daddy, a mean lady was chasing me." Spencer knew the nightmare was probably from watching *Annie*. Ivy was a sensitive little girl. She became frightened easily. Miss Hannigan, the menacing lady who ran the orphanage, was probably too much for his little Ivy.

Spencer wished that there were more females involved in his daughters' lives. Aside from their teachers at school, it was only Lizzie and occasionally Bridget. They rarely saw their aunts or grandmother now. Spencer knew that Ivy adored Lizzie. The other day when Spencer was helping Ivy to make a valentine to give to Lizzie, she'd told him that she loved

Lizzie and wished that she was her mommy. "I wish that you would marry her, Daddy." It wasn't the first time she had said it. It was becoming a common theme. He thought Ivy liked Bridget, but when they were together and there was some sort of problem, Ivy always sought out her daddy. At home, it would be Lizzie, even if Spencer was there. Ivy was so emotionally attached to Lizzie. He worried about what would happen when Lizzie stopped working for them. He was sure that when she finished up her master's degree, she would want to look for a job as a teacher. She was interested in elementary education. Lizzie leaving them would be another loss for his girls, but he knew he couldn't rush into marriage because his children needed a mother.

Bridget sat in the chair and watched as Spencer tried to calm his daughter. She felt a little helpless, but she thought it best not to interfere. It took awhile, but Ivy finally stopped crying and drifted back to sleep. Spencer put her back to bed.

Back in the bedroom, it was hard for Spencer to get back into the mood. He and Bridget talked...mostly about single parenthood and its challenges. What they didn't talk about was where their relationship was going. Another glass of wine put them both to sleep.

Bridget awoke the next morning and looked over at Spencer. He was deep in thought, staring up at the ceiling. "Good morning," she said. She grabbed her robe and went into the bathroom. After using the bathroom and brushing her teeth, she slipped back into bed. She leaned over and kissed Spencer. Their morning sex made up for the night before, although they had to be very quiet. They heard the girls waking up, so that was the end of that.

Then they were a pseudo-family again. The girls were chatty during breakfast and wanted to spend the day together. Spencer was not on call and Bridget was off for the weekend, so there was no reason they could not. Rochester was lucky to have the Strong Museum of Play. Spencer had heard about it but had yet to take the girls there. Bridget suggested that they go today. Scarlett loved it, so that was the plan. Sex had gotten in the way of last night's kitchen cleanup, and there were still breakfast dishes. Spencer played board games with the girls while Bridget tackled the kitchen. He took a quick shower while Bridget helped the girls get dressed. Then Bridget took a shower and they were off for the day.

They spent almost the entire day at the museum. The girls were having a grand time. Spencer couldn't help but be impressed by the museum and all it had to offer. Ivy was especially enchanted by the butterfly garden. Spencer bought each of the girls a butterfly sweatshirt in the gift shop. It had been a good day, but by late afternoon the kids were getting tired. They said their good-byes back at Bridget's house, and Spencer took his girls home.

After grilled cheese sandwiches, a bath, and a story, he put the girls to bed. Spencer wondered what he would do with the girls on Sunday. Weekends were challenging for him because he didn't always know how to keep the kids engaged. Spencer missed Anna the most on weekends. Playing house with Bridget was fun, but when he and the girls got back home, he became lonely again.

The next day, they awoke to a snowstorm. The roads were pretty bad. Spencer knew they would be house-bound. It would be a challenging day. He made pancakes for the girls, and after breakfast he called their grandparents. He tried to make a point of reaching out to his father and Anna's parents every Sunday morning. He thought it was important for the girls to stay connected with their grandparents. Anna's mother was making some noise about driving up to visit. She and Harry hadn't been to Rochester yet. After phone calls, Spencer started a Legos building project with the girls. They were making a castle for a princess... no, two princesses who were sisters. *OMG, this was going to be a long day.*

He got a call but didn't get to his phone in time, so the call went to voice mail. The call was from Mario. He asked that Spencer call him back. He had a concern about one of the twins. He sounded a little worried. Little Mario had spiked a fever during the night to 103.4. Spencer remembered that he had given Mario his cell phone number. He knew that Mario had a lot on his plate. Bridget had told him that his wife had just had open-heart surgery to implant an LVAD. He gave him a call back.

"Doc, thanks for calling me right back. I'm a little worried. I gave him Tylenol, but the fever came right back. Both the babies have had a slight runny nose. His lungs sound clear to me. Do you think I need to bring him into the ED?"

"At the height of flu season, I hate the thought of you bringing him into the ED unless it's absolutely necessary. I can come by and take a look at him. I have an SUV that handles pretty well in this weather. Give me your address and I will be over as soon as I can. Continue with the Tylenol when it's time again."

Mario gave him his address. "Thanks, Doc, I really appreciate it."

"I'm happy to help," Spencer said. He just wondered what he should do with the girls. He didn't want to bring them along. Brad Williams lived about ten minutes away. Maybe the girls could go over there for a little while. He called Brad, and he was good with it. He said that Martina would love to play with his girls.

Haley and Ivy were excited about going over to play at Martina's house. Spencer took a quick shower and told the girls to get dressed. Haley was very good about helping Ivy pick out her clothes and helping her to get dressed. Ivy hated having her hair brushed. She had very fine hair and it was really a rat's nest this morning. It was only Lizzie that she didn't give a hard time to when it came to hair brushing. Spencer decided not to deal with it this morning. He helped the girls with their jackets and boots and got them buckled into their car seats. He was happy to see that his driveway had been plowed. Rochester winters were notoriously bad. Winters in Philadelphia were much milder. After dropping off the girls, he put Mario's address in his GPS. He lived in another suburb west of Rochester. The GPS said it would take thirty-two minutes. In this weather, it would probably take almost twice as long.

Mario's house was lively that morning, with two crying babies and three animated teenagers playing video games. He introduced Spencer to his sister-in-law, Sarah, who was helping him deal with the babies. Mario told him that he'd just taken his son's temperature and it was normal. He had given him Tylenol about a half hour ago. Spencer could see that he was taking his bottle pretty well. "You are right, Mario, his lungs sound pretty clear. Let's take a look at his ears. Oh, this one looks red. I think he has an ear infection... not surprising considering his runny nose." He listened to Lillie Mae's lungs and looked in her ears, too. "She looks okay." Spencer asked Mario what pharmacy he used and called in a prescription. Spencer offered to go pick it up, but Mario said the pharmacy was walking distance from his house and his son Anthony could go.

"Would you like some coffee, Doc?"

"That would be great. I take it with just a little cream, thanks. Tell me how your wife is doing." Spencer imagined that Mario had to be quite overwhelmed with everything that was going on in his life. Mario was grateful for the opportunity to ventilate. He said that his life was a juggling act. There was his job, going to school, raising teenagers, looking after newborn twins, and supporting his wife through her illness. Mario told Spencer that he was most worried about his wife.

"I'm so afraid of losing her," he said. "What if she dies before she gets a heart, or what if the transplant fails? I've only just found her. Our life was good. We were so happy. Having a baby together seemed like the next logical step. Now this! Cardiomyopathy is such a rare complication of childbirth. Why did this happen to her? She has endured enough in her life. I'm angry, Doc!"

"Oh, I can imagine you are. I am still so terribly angry that my wife was taken from me. She was only thirty-six years old. But Mario, there is hope for you and Ruby. People can live for years with an LVAD. When your wife does get her new heart, she can be healthy again. Don't let this crisis victimize you. My father gave me some good advice after Anna died, when I was struggling to get my life back on track and raise my two young daughters. He said, 'Son, you can be the hero in your life's story. You don't have to surrender to defeat. Mobilize all your inner resources. Stay strong.' He also helped me to realize that accepting help from others wasn't a sign of weakness."

Anthony was back with the antibiotic. Spencer stayed to make sure that Little Mario was able to take it, which he did. It was still snowing pretty hard. Spencer knew that he should probably be getting back home.

"Doc, thanks for coming today, and thanks for the talk." He shook Spencer's hand.

"I'm happy to help anytime and in any way I can. Make sure the little guy stays hydrated and continue with the Tylenol. If you sense that he is showing any signs of respiratory distress, call me right away. Maybe you should bring him into the clinic on Tuesday for me to take another look at him. You take care, Mario."

Spencer liked Mario. He seemed genuine and extremely capable. He appeared to have his act together despite the odds. Spencer was amused that Mario called him Doc. It probably was a habit from working so closely with doctors in the OR. Spencer called Brad from the car. He said that the girls were playing great together and said that Spencer should just come over later in the afternoon. Brad said that Beverly wanted to invite them all for dinner. He said that on a day like this, he was glad that Martina had something to do. Spencer was happy to take him up on his offer. He knew dinner would be great, and he could use the afternoon to catch up on his work. He also called Bridget. He told her about going over to Mario's to check on his son. He also wanted to know if she needed anything while he was out. But he really just wanted to hear her voice. He was in love. It seemed like Bridget was always on his mind.

The snow tapered off later in the afternoon. Spencer headed over to Brad's. The girls were all playing up in Martina's room. Brad had told Spencer about how Beverly had been helping to care for Mario and Ruby's twins. Beverly was anxious to hear how Little Mario was doing. She said that soon she would be relieved of her duties. A nurse was being hired to care for Ruby and the babies. It was obvious that she was not in favor of the plan. Spencer thought that Brad's wife was beautiful. She was a warm and friendly woman, but Spencer always sensed an air of sadness and vulnerability about her.

Beverly went back into the kitchen. Brad and Spencer had a drink while she was cooking. Whatever was cooking smelled absolutely delicious. Brad explained about the complicated family dynamics going on in Mario and Ruby's family. He described the imposing family patriarch of the Washington family... the Reverend Tobias Washington. Spencer sensed that Brad had his own challenges when it came to marriage and family.

Brad asked how things were going with Bridget. Spencer told him how hard he had fallen for Bridget. He was in love with her but couldn't figure out how to move forward with the relationship. At times, he entertained the idea of marrying Bridget but then was plagued with doubts. Was it too soon? Was it right for the kids? Then he admitted that he worried that sex was the driving force in the relationship.

"If the relationship is working now, why change it? Just see how it goes," Brad said.

"I want more. I want a more stable life. I miss having a wife. I want my girls to have a mother again."

"Have you and Bridget talked about marriage?"

"No. She seems a little reserved about expressing her feelings for me. We laugh and talk and enjoy each other's company, but she doesn't really say how she's feeling about us."

"Give her time. Maybe she's afraid. Maybe she is in love with you but is afraid of getting hurt. She knows that she is the first woman you have let into your life since your wife died. It's probably hard being that woman. She knows that your wife still takes up a lot of space in your head. It was much the same for Beverly and me. It seemed like I was always competing with the dead guy. Her husband was always there. Maybe Bridget doesn't trust your feelings for her. She might feel like the rebound woman. Oftentimes those rebound relationships don't work out." It was good talking things out with Brad, but the conversation was getting heavy. Spencer was glad when Beverly came in and announced that dinner was ready.

Chapter 37

It was the first Monday in March. Finally, Kyle and Mark were back in court for the hearing concerning Melanie's petition for visitation rights. Melanie and her attorney were as haughty as before. The judge said that he'd reviewed the original surrogacy agreements, the reports from the CPS worker and the child psychologist, as well as the statements from Mark's doctors. He said that there was nothing to suggest that Mr. Fazio and Mr. O'Leary were unfit to parent Lucy. Furthermore, he stated that surrogacy contracts were made for just this reason. As an officer of the court, it was his duty to uphold the agreement. After conferring with the child psychologist, he concluded that granting visitation rights would not be in the best interest of the child. It would only confuse her. Kyle took hold of Mark's hand. They both breathed a sigh of relief. Then Melanie's attorney asked to approach the bench. "Oh, Christ, what now?" uttered Kyle under his breath. The judge instructed both attorneys to approach the bench.

"What is it now, Miss Sims?"

"Your Honor, we have new evidence that suggests that Mr. Fazio and Mr. O'Leary do not have the stable marriage and home that they claim to have." She presented pictures of Kyle getting into a taxi with Austin and even a picture of them kissing in the back of the cab. "It is clear that Mr. O'Leary is involved in an extramarital relationship. How can this marriage be stable? Isn't it already difficult for a little girl to be raised by two gay men? She also lives in a home with marital discord and has a father with a serious substance abuse problem. He is a heroin addict. Clearly, these aren't the same men that my client entered into an agreement with four years ago."

"Mr. Bennett?"

"Your Honor, my clients are human. People make mistakes. Mr. Fazio is being rehabilitated. Infidelity happens in many marriages at one time or another. Couples move on. The court only gets involved in cases where the parties involved are filing for separation or divorce. That is not the case. The only reason that Miss Sims has those pictures is that she had my client followed by a private investigator. She and Ms. Waters are intent on inflicting vengeance against my clients. Perhaps Ms. Waters is having second thoughts and even regrets about her decision to become a surrogate. She knew her biological child would be raised by two gay men, so why is this even an issue now?"

"Miss Sims, I think I have to agree with Mr. Bennett. This case is closed. You need to stop harassing these men."

Suzanne Sims and Luke Bennett took their seats.

The judge banged his gavel. "Petition for visitation has been denied. Court is adjourned."

Melanie was clearly upset as she walked out of court. She was crying.

Kyle, Mark, and Luke went out for lunch to celebrate. Luke said he had a friend in the DA's office. She was a friend of his from high school. She wasn't a lawyer. She was an administrative assistant. He'd asked her if she knew Melanie. She'd told him that she didn't know her well, but she did know that she had been diagnosed with ovarian cancer last year. She elected to have both ovaries removed to decrease the chance of recurrence. Melanie was married. Her husband had some serious money. "This friend of mine from high school always knew the dish about everybody and was always willing to share it. She hasn't changed much," Luke said.

"Oh my God, that's horrible about Melanie!" Mark said. "I'm so sorry, but I guess that explains her desperate behavior. She just didn't seem like the Melanie we knew before. I'm sure she's worried about having a family of her own."

"You're right," Kyle said. "Her behavior was not only desperate but I think it was despicable. I'm sorry she had to go through all of that, but was it fair to us that she put us through hell?"

"There's nothing fair about any of this," Mark concluded. "Do you think maybe she froze her eggs before her surgery? I hope she will be okay."

"From what I understand, the cancer was detected in stage one. She was lucky. She didn't need chemotherapy." Luke shook his head. "This is a big, hot, fucked-up mess."

That night both Kyle and Mark stretched out on the bed with Lucy and each read her a story. They knew they were fortunate to have her. When Kyle looked over at Mark, he saw that there were tears in his eyes. Mark was always emotional. They talked later.

"Kyle, do you think we should let Melanie have visitation rights? She'll probably never have a family of her own." Mark was crying again.

"No, Mark, I don't. Melanie's cancer has nothing to do with this. I'm sorry that happened to her, too. It sounds like she's probably going to be okay. I don't want to share Lucy with her. I can't even believe you're considering it."

It had been such an emotionally draining day, but when the judge had closed the door on granting Melanie visitation rights, it was like the sun coming out after a storm. Despite the news about Melanie, it had been a good day. Kyle wanted to make love with Mark. It clearly wasn't happening tonight. Mark was already asleep, and he probably couldn't get it up anyway. That's when Kyle started thinking about Austin again. He remembered the night that he'd spent with Austin and how good it had been. Lately he thought about Austin a lot. He wanted the old Mark back. They used to have great sex... sex where they were both satisfied.

The next morning Mark told Kyle he was sorry that he'd fallen asleep so early. He went on to say that he knew they'd needed each other last night, but he was too tired to make it happen. "It was such an exhausting day. I want to make it up to you. I'm going to see if Sophie can come over and stay with Lucy. Let's have dinner together tonight. I'll make a reservation at Angelo's. We could use a night out."

"That sounds great," Kyle said. He kissed Mark on the way out the door. "See you tonight. I'm looking forward to it. I love you." He hoped that maybe tonight would be better.

Mark was meeting up with an old friend of his after he dropped Lucy off. It was a guy just a few years older than him. He and Mark had been friends for years. Mark knew he was a diabetic. His partner was also a bit younger than him. His friend had confided in Mark awhile ago about his own problems in the bedroom, mostly since he'd developed diabetes. His doctor had agreed to give him a prescription for Viagra. He said it had changed everything for him. Mark explained his current situation. George reached into his pocket and took out a little pill case and dropped a pill into Mark's hand. "Give it a try," he said. Then, as an afterthought, he asked Mark if he had any problems with his heart. Mark assured him that he did not. "Well, go for it," he said. Mark and George had been together many years ago when they were much younger. Now they just shared a laugh. "God, it's a bitch getting old, isn't it?" said George. Mark thanked his friend and headed over to the bakery. He called for his dinner reservation and got started on a cake.

He hadn't seen his sister in a while. It was always good to see her. When Lucy was out of earshot, he filled Sophie in on everything that had happened in court. He also told her what he'd found out about Melanie. "Oh, God, Mark, that's awful! You can't feel guilty about that or let it influence your decisions about Lucy. You had nothing to do with that. When Lucy is older and asks about her mother or asks to meet her mother, you can decide about it then. She's only three years old."

"Kyle says the same thing. Cancer sure is a powerful trump card."

"Only if you let it be. Mark, you need to do what's best for you and Kyle and Lucy." Mark knew she was right. He had his own cross to bear. He needed to stay clean, learn how to deal with the chronic pain that he still had, and keep his marriage alive. Mark and Kyle kissed Lucy and Sophie and took off for dinner.

Mark and Kyle continued to talk over dinner. Mostly they talked about Lucy and their relief that the hearing was over. "Let's put it behind us, Mark. Maybe we should take Lucy on a vacation this spring. We can take her to the beach. We've never taken her on a trip before."

"Let's do that," Mark said, but he knew that that couldn't happen when he was tied to the methadone clinic for his meds. He didn't know why he'd even said they should go. "I am finally thinking about having that surgery to remove the bone spurs in my spine. I want to make an appointment with that neurosurgeon that Brad recommended. I can't let what happened to my father cloud my thinking. People have successful surgery all the time without complications. What happened to Dad was a random occurrence. I don't want to be on opiates the rest of my life. My pain is better on methadone but not gone. I want to go back to being me again." He took Kyle's hand. "I want to go back to being a better husband to you."

They had a pleasant dinner. Mark thought Kyle seemed pretty relaxed. He was on his second martini. He could be kind of uptight sometimes. He was always a little looser after a few martinis. They didn't order any wine. Mark knew it was too early in his journey to risk expulsion from his methadone program. It was just another reason to have surgery and get off the opiates. He and Kyle had always enjoyed a good bottle of wine. They'd gone to Napa Valley for their honeymoon. *Maybe someday we can get back there for a second honeymoon. Right now, I can only hope.*

After they got back to the house, they said their good-byes to Sophie and went in to check on Lucy. Mark took the Viagra while Kyle was in the bathroom. It worked. *It seemed like old times again.*

Mark was up early making breakfast. Kyle walked into the kitchen and put his arms around him. "Last night was great," he said. Kyle poured himself a cup of coffee and Lucy wandered in. She said she had a dream that her daddies let her have a puppy. Now she was on a mission. Kyle looked over at Mark and smiled. Maybe there was a puppy in their future.

Mark dropped Lucy off at school and later ran into Mario at Starbucks. He said that Ruby was doing well. He showed Mark pictures of the twins. Mark was relieved about the good news concerning Ruby. He had been praying for her. Life was good this morning. Maybe everything was going to be okay after all.

He headed over to Dr. Lamb's clinic to pick up his methadone. Mark had planned on talking to Dr. Lamb or his primary care doctor about his problem with impotence, but he decided against it. A, it was a difficult and embarrassing problem to talk about, and B, both men were straight. It was just easier to talk to his buddy George.

Now he just had to figure out how to get more Viagra. That wasn't too difficult. He'd learned that you could buy just about anything on the street if you had the money and you knew the right people.

Chapter 38

Six weeks after implanting the LVAD, Ruby was finally coming home. It was such a happy day. They kids were excited that their mother was finally coming home. A woman had been hired to help care for Ruby and the babies. She wasn't actually a nurse. She was a nurse's aide. Emma was a middle-aged woman who attended Ruby and Mario's church. Of course, she was African-American. Sarah and Mario knew that was best. Reverend Washington wouldn't have it any other way. She had started a few weeks ago and was working out well. Her schedule was flexible so that she could stay on in the evening when Mario had school. She had hospital experience and also knew how to care for children since she had raised six children of her own. As promised, Beverly had stayed on, helping out with the twins until Emma was hired. Beverly continued to come over after Emma started to help her get accustomed to caring for the babies. She thought Emma was a sweet woman and very capable. Beverly was beginning to feel better about things.

Beverly and Martina were planning on going over to Ruby and Mario's for the homecoming. The kids were all staying home from school to welcome their mother home. Martina had missed Ruby so much. She hadn't been able to visit Grandma Ruby in the hospital. There had been a lot of visitor restrictions during flu season. Children were especially restricted. Mario didn't want to overwhelm his wife with too much fanfare about her homecoming, but he knew Ruby would want to see her granddaughter.

Beverly had prepared dinner to leave with them for that night. She had even consulted the nutritionist at the hospital to see what special dietary restrictions Ruby would have. It was mostly a sodium restriction. She prepared a chicken dish that was flavored with lemon and lots of fresh herbs. She also brought sweet potatoes to roast and fresh asparagus to steam. There was a banana cream pie for dessert. Sweet potatoes and bananas are high in potassium which made them good choices for Ruby's diet. Beverly was sure that Ruby was tired of the hospital's bland food and would be grateful for some fresh vegetables. Martina was bursting with excitement. She was busy working on a welcome home picture. Beverly wanted to give Ruby some time to settle in before she headed over. They stopped at Wegmans for flowers and arrived at Ruby and Mario's after lunch.

Beverly thought Ruby looked much better. Her color was good and she was less puffy-looking. She didn't look so tired. She was beautiful. After her surgery and the stay in the ICU, she'd spent every day regaining her strength in the cardiac rehab unit. It was such a blessing to see her. She was holding a baby in each arm when they got there.

"Grandma Ruby! I've missed you so much!" Martina squealed.

"Oh, honey, I've missed you, too. Let's put the babies down and then you can tell me all about you." Martina presented her with the flowers and her card. She climbed up on Ruby's lap and chatted away. She even sang her the new song that she'd learned in preschool.

Ruby was delighted. Beverly could tell she was fighting back tears. "Oh, Lord, it's so good to be home." Although Mario had done his best to keep her homecoming low-key, it wasn't really working out that way. Everyone was overjoyed to see her. It was obvious how much her family loved her. Beverly didn't want to overstay their welcome. She gave Emma instructions about heating up dinner and convinced Martina that they needed to go.

Beverly appeased Martina by promising a stop at Sugar Plum for a frosted sugar cookie on the way home. Mark wasn't too busy, so he took a break to have coffee with Beverly. He was anxious to hear about Ruby. Beverly knew that Mark was having problems of his own. She was glad that he seemed to be okay. They arranged a playdate for the girls that weekend. Beverly bought some cannoli for dessert. She gave Mark a hug and they headed home.

Now that she wasn't caring for the twins anymore, she was back to everything that she had been involved in before. She was on the board at the cancer center, and she volunteered at Martina's school. Dr. Martino had convinced her that she needed to find healthy outlets for her stress. Beverly loved to paint and play her violin. She was back to doing both. She was almost done with her watercolor painting of the Parisian café that she was working on as a surprise for Brad. She had even bought a violin for Martina and had started giving her lessons. Martina loved it and she seemed to have a natural musical talent. *At least maybe I have passed something on to my granddaughter.*

It had taken her awhile to get past the slight of being replaced caring for the twins, but she finally got over it. It took a long discussion with Dr. Martino. They talked about racial differences and racism. It was good to talk about it all in a safe and completely nonjudgmental setting. She'd had some of these same conversations with Dr. Martino when Erica first started dating Dwight. Her feelings about the Reverend Tobias Washington were hard to reconcile. She had never met anyone like him before. Her WASPy upbringing had never prepared her for someone like him. Dr. Martino asked her about her parents. She told him that she'd had an affluent upbringing in Greenwich, Connecticut. Her parents had never approved of her marrying a lower-middle-class boy from an Irish-American family in Brooklyn. Beverly said that their relationship was strained. Her parents were never involved in the lives of their grandchildren. They'd come to Rochester for her son's funeral, but not for her husband's or even Erica's. They'd been in Europe when Erica died and hadn't come back for her funeral. They'd sent flowers, and that was their only gesture of sympathy.

She couldn't even imagine what they would think of her raising her biracial granddaughter. Her parents' lives revolved around golf and tennis at their country club, sailing in Newport, and international travel. Beverly was an only child. She often felt sad and guilty about her relationship with her parents but, over the years, cared less and less.

"That generation was very different. People were caught up in their racial, ethnic, and religious identities. The civil rights movement was only beginning. Feelings in the South ran deep. Reverend Washington has experienced hatred and bigotry. He is protective of his African-American identity. He is also a Baptist minister. He preaches for a living. I can only imagine that he has a very powerful influence over his family. It is your relationship with Mario and Ruby that matters most. Loving Martina is learning to love and respect this part of her heritage. I'm sure as she gets older, it will be more and more important to her."

The thought of it overwhelmed Beverly. She knew how difficult it could be raising a teenager. She couldn't even imagine the challenge of helping Martina find her own identity.

"Beverly, concentrate on your immediate family... Martina and Brad. Ruby and Mario know you are there to support them in any way you can. Ruby's heart condition is now a fact of their life. They need to figure it out and ask for help when they need it. Maybe taking a step back for now is a good idea."

She was trying hard to take that step back. The night after she had the long session with Dr. Martino talking about racism and Reverend Washington, she'd had a horrible dream, which made her realize that she was too consumed with Ruby and Mario's situation. In her dream, she was over at their house caring for the twins. Reverend Washington came into the nursery. He was handling a snake. In her dream, she grabbed Martina by the hand, ran down the stairs, and out the door. "*Run!*" she screamed. It woke Brad. He had to stay awake with her the rest of the night.

Still, she thought about Ruby all the time. Her life, too, had changed so drastically. Ruby was used to caring for others. Now she needed to rely on others for help. Ruby was the strongest and most determined woman she had ever known. She knew that some of that tenacity was instilled in her by her father. She also knew about Ruby's steadfast faith in God. After the deaths of Dwight and Erica, she would often talk to Beverly about the healing power of God. Beverly wanted God to find a heart for Ruby, but she was afraid to ask. She couldn't bear it if her prayers weren't answered and Ruby just became more ill and died. Sometimes Beverly wished she had a time machine. She wanted to go back four years in time. Ruby would be a healthy nursing assistant who knew her husband from the hospital because she helped to take care of some of his patients. Tom and Erica would be alive. Her life was happy and not so complicated. Beverly thought that Ruby probably wished she had that time machine, too. But then she wouldn't have Mario and those beautiful new babies. Then she thought, I wouldn't have Brad, and there'd be no Martina. These thoughts went round and round in her head much of the time these days. It was exhausting.

Beverly decided to work on her painting for a while and maybe call Pam to see if she could meet up for lunch. She knew that Helen would look after Martina.

* * *

Ruby finished feeding Little Mario. She and Emma had a system where they alternated who would feed which twin. When Ruby saw her son's face, she didn't see Mario. She saw Dwight. He looked so much like his brother, likely because Dwight had resembled her. Lillie Mae looked more like Mario. Caring for the babies was what kept Ruby going. She really missed being a nurse and working at the hospital. She'd started working at the hospital when she was only seventeen years old and still in high school. She'd worked part time on the weekend. At the time, her family was living in Rochester. Her father had been offered his own congregation in Atlanta. Ruby had wanted to stay in Rochester. She would be graduating high school in less than a year. Her sister, Sarah, was a year older than she. Sarah had been dating Henry. They were planning on getting married. Sarah had wanted to remain in Rochester, too. Ruby and Sarah had lived at the YWCA until they could afford their own apartment. Their father wasn't all that happy about them staying on in Rochester but had said they were adults now and could make their own decisions. He'd said that a poor congregation in Atlanta needed him, and the Lord was calling him to go.

Sarah had married Henry, and Ruby had been on her own. She'd finished high school and continued working at the hospital. She'd taken all the overtime hours she could. Money had been tight but she'd gotten assistance from the Department of Social Services. Then she'd met Jerome Taylor. He was older, good-looking, and charming. He always seemed to have money, but Ruby didn't know where he got it. He didn't have a job. She'd succumbed to his charm and attention and had sex with him whenever he came around. Then she was pregnant. He'd still come around to see his son, but not all that often. After Ruby had his son, he'd become controlling and abusive. The abuse had started in her pregnancy. Ruby remembered her feelings of shame. She had become a battered woman. Jerome had always managed to manipulate her feelings, express his remorse, and end up back in her bed. He'd had a nasty cocaine habit and drank too much. That's when most of the abuse had happened. Jerome's behavior had become more criminal. When Dwight was just four years old, Jerome had planned and executed an armed robbery. The victim had ended up in a wheelchair for life. Jerome had entered the store and held the owner at gunpoint. His accomplice had grown impatient with the victim when he couldn't open the safe and shot him. They'd both been convicted and sent to state prison. Eight years later, he was out on parole. Ruby let him back into her life when he'd come back to see his son. He had convinced her that he was a changed man. Then Ruby had found out she was pregnant again... this time with twins. Jerome had ended up back in prison before the twins were even born. He'd continued to write to her from prison, always claiming that he had found the Lord and was a changed man. Every time he was up for parole, it was denied. Ruby thought it was probably because he got into fights in prison or was involved in prison drug trafficking.

Ruby worked hard to be the best mother she could be and provide for her children. Sarah and Henry were always supportive. Her father was a forgiving man. He'd told Ruby she had to forgive herself for her errors in judgement and pray for the strength to be the best possible person she could be. He'd said that God had blessed Ruby with a nurturing heart and that she was smart. He'd encouraged her to pursue her degree in nursing. He'd even sent her money from time to time. Now, after all her hard work, study, and sacrifice, she had only worked as a registered nurse barely three years. Ruby wondered if she would ever be well enough to work again. Right now she was just grateful to be home and able to help care for her babies. She had Mario and her children. Her job now was to regain her health. She also wanted for Mario to concentrate on his studies to become a nurse anesthetist. Her girls needed her. It was hard to believe that they would be in high school in the fall.

Easter was right around the corner. Easter was all about rising up and new beginnings. Ruby knew she had to accept that this was the beginning of her new life. She thanked God every day that the surgery to implant the LVAD was successful and that she was alive and home again. Her father had always said she was blessed with a nurturing heart, but it had become a weaken heart. Now she prayed for a new heart, but that meant tragedy for someone else. Praying for her life was praying for someone else's death. Ruby didn't know if she could ever reconcile that in her mind. She had checked organ donor on the application to renew her driver's license last year. She now wished that she had considered donating Dwight's organs after he'd been shot. His death had been so senseless. Maybe it would have given her some comfort. Dwight was on her mind a lot lately. He had always been a tremendous support to her. She could just hear him say, "It will be all right, Ma." A mother could not ask for a finer son. He'd been sweet and kind and gentle. Oftentimes she thought that if she did die, at least she could see Dwight again, but she didn't want her mind to go there. She knew she had five other children, including Anthony, and a granddaughter to live for. She had to stay strong, and she was feeling a little stronger every day.

Chapter 39

The work week started out as usual for Spencer. Lizzie was always on time. Today she was even a little early. She already had the coffee made when Spencer came down to the kitchen. Lizzie handed him a mug of coffee. She dropped his eggs in a pot of simmering water to poach. The girls were already up and having their breakfast. Ivy was always a happy little girl on Mondays because Lizzie was back. The weekends when Lizzie didn't babysit, the girls really missed her. Lizzie told them of a special project that she had planned for them after school. Spring was right around the corner. They would make some decorations to dress up the house for spring. Ivy even allowed Lizzie to braid her hair today. Lizzie reached into her purse and pulled out some new hair ribbons. Haley wanted her hair braided, too. Lizzie told Spencer to have a good day and gave him a kiss on the cheek. Spencer was getting used to the kiss. It was fairly harmless, or so he thought. He took off for the hospital. Monday was always a busy clinic day. Lizzie and Ivy walked Haley to the end of the driveway and watched as she got on the school bus. Lizzie buckled Ivy into her car seat, and they took off for preschool. She noticed that Scarlett's grandmother dropped her off today. Her mother must be working.

Lizzie had become obsessed with learning everything she could about Bridget. *There was something about her.* Lizzie didn't think she was right for Spencer. Lizzie did not find her very friendly. Lizzie had asked the girls about her. They just said, "She's okay," or "She's nice." They talked more about Scarlett and said that she was so much fun. Lizzie could see that Scarlett was a delightful little girl. She for sure did not let her disability get in her way. Lizzie knew that Spencer and the girls spent a lot of time with Scarlett and her mother. Lizzie would not give up on her dream about someday having her own relationship with Spencer. She fantasized about Spencer all the time. She had a dream about Spencer. In her dream he was making love to her and telling her how much he needed her.

Lizzie could feel a headache coming on. Lately she had been having a lot of headaches. She thought it was probably stress. She'd just broken up with her boyfriend, and this was her hardest semester in school so far. She was almost done. She couldn't wait until the semester was over and she graduated, but then the prospect of looking for a job overwhelmed her. She had so much debt in school loans. If she did find a job, she would have to stop working for Spencer and the girls. She knew her life would probably be changing soon, and she hated the uncertainty. Lizzie took some Motrin and decided to lie down before she hit the books. She set an alarm on her phone so that she would wake up in time to pick Ivy up at school.

Bridget went to the peds clinic to say hello to Spencer on her lunch break. He was in his office. His office was pretty small. There was his desk, a small credenza, and two chairs. His diplomas were on the wall. He had a picture that Haley had drawn for him framed, which was also on the wall. He had photographs of his kids in frames on the credenza. There was also a photo of himself and his wife. It looked like it had been taken on the beach. Spencer looked happy. His wife was beautiful. She was smiling, and her long brown hair was wind-blown.

"Well, this is a nice surprise." Spencer walked out from behind the desk and kissed her. Bridget tugged at his belt buckle. She locked the door. Spencer had her sprawled out on the desk and had her scrub pants down in no time. "God, you've got to love a naughty nurse!" After their quickie, he buckled up his pants and tucked in his shirt. He kissed her. "You had better go before I get fired. I'll call you tonight." He smiled at her, and she took off.

Spencer had never known a woman like Bridget before. He couldn't believe that he'd just had sex with her in his office. He couldn't help smiling. He knew that her visit was just a booty call. He just happened to look over at his credenza and saw the familiar photo of himself and Anna. He took it and put it in the bottom drawer of his desk. He was sorry that Anna had to see what had just gone on. It was something that Anna wouldn't have ever done. It was so hard to sort out his feelings. He loved Bridget for the exciting woman that she was, but his love for Anna ran deep. She would always be the true love of his life. He was pretty unglued when he went back out to the clinic to start the afternoon schedule of patients. It was hard to deal with colic, sore throats, and pooping problems after what had just happened in his office. His residents seemed especially needy. It seemed like they needed more than the usual amount of direction today. He went to the break room and got some coffee. He needed to focus.

As Bridget walked backed to the NICU, she wondered if she'd just gone too far. Spencer was pretty conservative. Maybe sex in the workplace was a little too much for him, although he'd seemed to be a willing participant. There was still so much unsaid between her and Spencer. She didn't feel at all confident in their relationship, although he often told her that he loved her. She wasn't sure about her future with Spencer.

When Spencer got home that evening, his house was decorated with spring tulips and bunnies. The kids were happy. Lizzie had made a pot of homemade chicken noodle soup. It smelled delicious. She was becoming quite a cook. She and the girls were making biscuits. The girls wanted her to stay for dinner. It appeared that she and the girls were having such a good day. How could he say no? They all enjoyed dinner together. It was calm and the girls were chatting away about school and their friends. Lizzie looked over at Spencer and smiled. She was such a blessing in his life. She gave the girls so much stability. Lizzie told the girls that she wished she could stay longer, but she needed to get home to study. What she didn't say was that her headache had come back. Spencer put his girls to bed. Lizzie must have really tired them out. They went right to sleep after only one story. He went downstairs, finished cleaning up the kitchen, and poured himself a Scotch. He had a lot on his mind. It was mostly about Bridget. *A normal guy would be pretty happy if he had gotten lucky in his office. So what's my problem?*

The week passed by fairly quickly. Ruby and Mario brought the twins in for their three-month checkup. The twins were great. Spencer thought that Ruby looked well, considering her current status. Her color was good, and she didn't appear short of breath. It was so nice to see them. Spencer thought they were a remarkable family.

He hadn't seen Bridget at the hospital the rest of that week and hadn't spoken to her since she had paid him that visit to his office. He wasn't sure why that was. He knew that he should call her tonight. He did, and the call went to voice mail. She called him back on Saturday morning. She was working that weekend. Spencer thought she seemed a little reserved on the phone. She wasn't quite herself. They made plans to take the kids out for pizza on Saturday night.

It turned out to be just dinner...nothing more. Bridget had to work on Sunday, and Spencer needed to work on drafting the research study he wanted to do in the clinic. He told her all about it, and she listened, giving him her full attention. She had questions. It was a study focused on the link of poor school performance and obesity in school-age children. He was coordinating the study with a nutritionist and school psychologist in the Rochester City School District. He had definitely seen his share of obese children in the clinic. Childhood obesity was reaching epidemic proportions. He thought that he might even extend the study beyond the clinic to private pediatric practices in the Rochester suburbs. There was a lot of work to do. Bridget said she was impressed, and that she sometimes wished that her scope of nursing practice went beyond caring for infants. After a platonic kiss in front of the kids, they said good night. He promised Bridget that he would call her the following week.

Spencer knew that he hadn't challenged himself to do anything beyond what was required of him since Anna had died. It felt good to feel excited and motivated to do more. He wanted to make a name for himself at the university, and he wanted to set a good example for his residents.

Early on Sunday morning, Spencer got a call from Lizzie's father. He was frantic. He said that Lizzie woke up with a headache and complained of nausea. Her speech was slow, and she wasn't acting like herself. She'd then had a full-blown seizure. He'd called 911 for an ambulance, and he was in the emergency room with her now. Mr. Snow went on to say that the reason he called was to inform him that Lizzie wouldn't be able to work tomorrow. He also said, "Could you please look out for Lizzie and make sure she gets the best care possible?" Spencer couldn't believe it. Lizzie had seemed fine all week. Spencer was very concerned.

"Mr. Snow, I'll be there as soon as I can. Thank you for calling." Spencer called the neighborhood girl he used for babysitting to see if she could come and stay with the girls. He explained that it was urgent, so she came right over. Spencer had never met Lizzie's father, but he knew they were close. She lived with her dad. Her mom had died when she was eleven. She had a brother who was married and lived in New York City. Spencer often thought the reason Lizzie was such a good nanny was that she understood what it was like to grow up without a mother. Spencer found Mr. Snow and introduced himself. He said that Lizzie had continued to seize in the ambulance, and they'd told him it was best that they put her in a medically induced coma. They had already done a lumbar puncture and were planning on taking her for a CT scan. Mr. Snow told the ED attending physician that it was okay if Dr. Harris was involved in discussions regarding his daughter's condition. Spencer spoke with the neurology resident who came down to do a consult. Spencer learned that Lizzie had significantly increased intracranial pressure. She had no fever and a normal white blood cell count. They didn't think it was an infectious process. First on the differential diagnosis list was a probable brain tumor, which was not uncommon in young adults. *Oh, my God, poor Lizzie.*

Mr. Snow had not yet been told about the possibility of a brain tumor. He only knew that keeping Lizzie in a coma would rest her brain, and they would learn more after her CT scan. Mr. Snow sat in a chair with his head in his hands. If it was a brain tumor, Spencer knew that the university had one of the best neurosurgeons in the East. His specialty was brain surgery. It was Brad Williams. It was the only thing that was giving him comfort right now. He was quite fond of Lizzie. His children loved her. This was going to be a hardship for everyone.

"Mr. Snow, I think you should call your son in New York City. Maybe it would be comforting to you to have him here. The days and weeks ahead may be rough. I will for sure do everything I can to make sure your daughter gets only the best. My girls and I love Lizzie. She is like family." Spencer hugged him. Mr. Snow was now crying. Spencer convinced him to go to the cafeteria with him to have lunch while Lizzie was at her CT scan. When they got back, they were informed that they were moving Lizzie to the ICU. Preliminary results showed a mass. They would do an MRI tomorrow to get a clearer picture.

Lizzie's father asked Spencer to call him Ben. "Ben," Spencer said, "a mass means that this might be a brain tumor. That sounds awful, but the location of the mass appears to be in a very operable area. We will know more tomorrow. If your daughter does need surgery, my friend Brad Williams is one of the best brain surgeons in the country. We must stay positive and pray for the best."

Spencer stepped out to call Brad. Ben sat at Lizzie's bedside and held her hand. It was clear that he wasn't leaving. Spencer filled Brad in on everything that was happening. Brad said that he would look in on her in the morning. Spencer explained that he had to leave to get back to his kids. Ben's sister was with him now. He said good-bye and promised to be back in the morning. He told Ben he could call him at any time until then.

It was dinnertime when he finally got home. He thanked the babysitter and paid her generously. He heated up the soup that Lizzie had made earlier in the week and made grilled cheese sandwiches. The girls thought he went to the hospital to see a patient. They didn't know it was Lizzie. He didn't know how to tell them. He got a call from Brad. Beverly offered to help out with the girls tomorrow. She would come over first thing in the morning with Martina. They would see Haley off to the bus, and she would take the girls to preschool and pick them up. Helen would stay with Ivy and Martina when Beverly went back to meet Haley when she got off the bus. Spencer could pick up the girls after work and stay for dinner. Brad assured Spencer that Beverly was happy to help out. He only had to remember to leave their car seats. Spencer was grateful for the offer. The next morning, he told the girls that Lizzie wasn't feeling well, so Martina's mother would be watching them today. They were fine with it.

Spencer realized that this would be a problem for a while. He needed to figure out a solution. He didn't want to impose on Beverly. Tomorrow, after he found out more about Lizzie, he would give his father a call to see if he could come to Rochester and help him out.

Beverly helped Spencer with the girls again on Tuesday. Beverly assured him that it was no trouble and Martina loved it. She said it was like having sisters. Spencer's father was coming up the next day. By Wednesday, Lizzie was out of her coma and they had moved her out of the ICU. Another MRI was scheduled for today. She cried when she saw Spencer. "I'm so sorry," she said. "I've really let you and the girls down. Are they okay?"

Spencer held her hand. "They're fine, but they're worried about you." He gave her the cards that the girls had made for her. He also bought her some yellow roses. "You've just got to concentrate on getting past this. We are all here for you."

"But this all came at such a bad time. Now I won't be able to graduate on time, and you have no one to help you with the girls."

"You can finish your degree when you're well again. My father is coming to Rochester to help with the girls. He gets lonely sometimes and loves spending time with his grandchildren. Haley and Ivy adore him. He has a special way with Ivy… always has." Lizzie was crying again. Her emotions were very labile.

"Oh, Spencer, I love your girls. I love you. I just hate that this has happened."

He did his best to soothe her. He was beginning to realize the depth of her feelings and commitment to him and the girls. Her father and her brother walked in. They all tried to calm her down. The transport person came to take Lizzie for her MRI.

Chapter 40

Things seemed to be back on track for Kyle and Mark. Methadone was fairly effective in controlling Mark's pain, but he hated the side effects and his trips to the methadone clinic. He was required to attend group therapy. He couldn't find much common ground with the addicts in group. He kept to his word, though, and was staying clean. The only drug he bought now on the street was Viagra. He always bought from the same dealer, who would come to the bakery when Mark called him. The guy had a sweet tooth.

Mark and Kyle had an appointment to see the neurosurgeon that Brad Williams recommended. If this doctor recommended surgery, Mark was now willing to give it a try. He was only fifty-two. He was tired of feeling like an old man. Mark had been paying regular visits to Ruby. He was inspired by her. She was so brave. She had rallied to have the surgery to implant the LVAD, and she was willing to undergo a heart transplant to save her life. She knew that Mario and her children needed her. She wanted her health back. Mark thought he should do the same for Kyle and Lucy. Business was good. He wanted even better control over his pain so that he could be more productive. He loved being a pastry chef, but it required long hours on his feet. Maybe surgery was the answer.

Kyle was feeling better about things, too. This was good, because he was in the heat of tax season and putting in some long hours. He didn't need stress right now. One night after working particularly late, he decided to stop by the bar close to his office to have a drink before heading home. He had already called Mark to tell him that he would be late. Mark was used to Kyle's long hours at this time of year. He ran into Austin. He hadn't had any contact with Austin since he'd met him at Starbucks to tell him he couldn't see him anymore. He looked as handsome as ever. Austin flashed him his big, sexy smile as soon as he walked in. Kyle knew he was still very attracted to him. Austin wanted to buy him a drink and sat down next to him at the bar. *It's just a drink*, Kyle thought, but he really didn't trust himself.

"I've missed you," Austin said. "I've never met anyone like you. I wish that you would have given us a chance."

"Austin, you know I'm married. We are trying to work things out. Things are better now."

"Are you really happy, Kyle?"

"I'm trying to be happy," he said.

"As I said before, I'm willing to be the other man in your life."

"I can't do that," Kyle said. He told him about the private investigator and the pictures taken of them together...the especially incriminating picture of them kissing in the back of the cab.

"I'm really sorry that happened, but isn't that all over now? Didn't you say that the petition for visitation rights was denied? You said that you were 'trying to be happy'. I don't know what that means."

"It means that I am committed to working things out with Mark."

Now Austin had his hand on Kyle's knee. "I know that I could make you happy. We have chemistry. I know you can feel it."

Kyle could feel it. He knew it was true. Once again, Kyle gave in to temptation. He agreed to meet up with Austin back at his apartment. He didn't want to be seen leaving with him, so he waited twenty minutes after Austin left before heading over to his apartment. It was already getting pretty late. He knew he couldn't stay too long, but he knew Mark was a sound sleeper, more so now on methadone. He would already be in bed when he got home. Mark probably wouldn't even hear him come in. Kyle knew it was wrong, but he couldn't help himself.

He saw the red lights flashing in his rearview mirror. *Oh, fuck! You had better be cool.* Kyle knew he had had two martinis. He was chewing gum, mostly because he wanted his breath fresh for Austin. He hoped that he wasn't stopped for suspicion of DWI. He hoped that the cop wouldn't lean in and smell alcohol on him.

"Sir, are you aware that you were traveling fifteen miles per hour over the speed limit? What's your hurry? Where are you going?"

"I was just going to a friend's house to drop off his taxes. I'm an accountant. I guess I was distracted. I'm sorry."

He gave the cop his license and registration, and the cop went back to his patrol car to run his license through. Kyle knew his license was clean.

He gave Kyle back his license along with a speeding ticket. "It looks like you are usually a law-abiding citizen. Just slow it down some. You've got some time before April fifteenth. Good night, sir."

Kyle breathed a sigh of relief. He didn't want to take the chance of blowing into the breathalyzer. He was always careful about drinking and driving. Now, however, he was having second thoughts about hooking up with Austin. It was wrong... period. He couldn't believe that he'd almost let it happen again. He didn't even bother to call Austin. He went straight home.

The next morning Kyle sat with Lucy while she was eating her breakfast. Mark was in the shower. "Poppy said we could have all my friends over for an Easter egg hunt!" She was bubbling over with excitement. Easter was late in April this year.

"Oh, really, that sounds like fun!" Mark walked in and poured himself a cup of coffee.

"What do you think, Kyle? The daffodils and forsythia will be in bloom. The yard will look beautiful. We can have a brunch for the parents. We've worked so hard on the house. I think we should show it off."

Kyle knew that when Mark had an idea like this, it was hard to talk him down. Besides, tax season would be over. It would be fun. Kyle kissed Mark and Lucy good-bye and headed off to the office. "We'll talk about it more tonight. I'll try to make it home in time for dinner." He was feeling a little guilty about last night. When he turned on his phone, he saw that he had several text messages and a voice mail from Austin. He didn't listen to the voice mail. He had work to do and couldn't be thinking about Austin.

That night Kyle did make it home for dinner, and the planning for the Easter egg hunt began. They decided it would be the Saturday before Easter. Lucy would invite her best friends from school... of course Martina, Scarlett, Ella, Ashley, and Ivy. She wanted Ivy's sister, Haley, to come and a few neighborhood kids, too. They would invite ten children in all. Mark and Kyle thought that it would be a manageable crowd. They knew all the parents. It would be a great party. Pam and Sam would come, as well as Sophie and Jimmy. Of course, they would include Mario and Ruby, and Helen, too. Mark later told Kyle that he thought he could talk his buddy, George, into wearing an Easter Bunny costume and coming for a surprise visit. Mark had plans to make an incredible cake. This was the Mark that Kyle had fallen in love with.

Mark called Beverly to tell her about the party. She, of course, insisted upon making a few dishes for the brunch. Ruby insisted on bringing a pan of macaroni and cheese. "Let me do this, Mark. It won't be any trouble and it makes me feel normal... like I can still do things that I used to enjoy. I would never dream of coming empty-handed." *Oh, Ruby, I just love you.* Sometimes just thinking about Ruby made him cry.

God was smiling down on them, and the Saturday before Easter turned out to be an absolutely beautiful day. It was sunny and about sixty-four degrees. Everything was set up outside. Mark and Kyle had dyed six dozen hard-boiled eggs and had them hidden all around the backyard. All the parents sipped Bloody Marys or mimosas as they watched the kids hunt for their eggs. There was for sure lots of excitement.

Bridget and Spencer were happy to see each other there. They hadn't seen each other much in the past few weeks since Lizzie had fallen ill. Spencer seemed to be tied up supporting everyone through the crisis.

"I've missed you," he said to Bridget. "Lizzie's illness has been hard on all of us. Supporting her and her family has made some demands on my time, but it's what I need to do. We've grown very dependent on her. She's like family. My kids are heartbroken. Her father is devastated." He filled Bridget in on all the details. Spencer was happy that he had such a fun event to bring the girls to. They had been so sad lately.

"Dinner tonight?" he asked.

"I've got to work at three," she said. "Maybe you could come over when I get out of work for a drink."

"I'll look forward to it," he said. He had missed her.

Those who knew Ruby were so happy to see her. She seemed to be doing well. She looked beautiful. If you didn't know it, it was hard to tell that she was ill. She stowed the battery pack for the LVAD in a fashionable bag that looked like a purse. Aside from the cords and a few lumps under her clothing, there wasn't much to see.

When the kids were finished hunting for eggs, Mark sent George a text that he was up next. He rode into the driveway in his vintage yellow Thunderbird convertible. The Easter Bunny's entrance into the party was a sight to behold. All the parents had their phones set to video. The kids all ran up to the car. The Easter Bunny had a gift bag for each child. Next they served the food. Mark and Kyle set up tables on the wraparound porch and out on the back deck. George changed into his normal clothes, and his partner stopped in to join them all for brunch. There was quite a spread. Mark's cake was a show-stopper. He'd even made frosted bunny and chick cut-out cookies. It has been a great party. Of course, none of the kids wanted to leave. Everyone was encouraged to go home with leftovers.

Mark thanked George for his starring role as the Easter Bunny.

"You know I loved it," he said. He slipped something into Mark's hand as he shook it. "Have a happy Easter, my friend." Mark smiled. It would for sure be a good night.

Pam hugged Mark and her son. "You guys sure know how to throw a party. That was so much fun!" It was nice to see Kyle and Mark happy again. Things seemed so much better. She and Sam stayed to help clean up. They offered to take Lucy for the night. Mark and Kyle were exhausted and grateful for the offer. They promised to bring her back in the morning so that she could find her Easter basket. They could have breakfast and all go to church together.

Mark and Kyle took a long walk and sat on the porch for a while and talked. It has been such a good day. The party was a huge success. When it started getting dark, they called for their Chinese takeout and found a movie to watch on TV. After the movie, Mark said that he wanted to take a hot bath. His back was bothering him a little from all the work he'd done for the party and the long walk that they'd taken. He thought some Motrin and a hot soak in the tub would help. Kyle took the opportunity to have another glass of wine. He brought it into the bedroom and got undressed for bed. He relaxed with his wine while he was waiting for Mark. When Mark finally came in from the bathroom, he didn't look so good. "Mark, are you okay?"

He said he was just a little dizzy, but then he passed out. Kyle was panicked. Mark's color was quite pale. He put his ear down on Mark's chest. His heart beat didn't sound regular. Kyle immediately called 911. He feared that Mark was having a heart attack. *Thank God Lucy is with my mother.* The paramedics got there pretty quickly. They said Mark's blood pressure was very low and that he was having a mild heart arrhythmia. They asked Kyle about Mark's current medical condition and medications that he was taking. Kyle told them that he was on methadone and had also taken some Motrin before taking a bath. They started an IV and gave him some oxygen. Mark started coming around. The paramedics first suspected an overdose and reached for the Narcan. Then they thought it was probably just a hypotensive episode. They continued to monitor Mark's heart when he got settled into his cubicle in the emergency room.

The ED doctor came in to evaluate Mark. She asked him how long he had been on methadone, and if he had ever experienced this kind of dizziness before. Mark said that he had not. "Mr. Fazio, are you being completely honest? Did you take anything else tonight?" The doctor was a young Asian woman, probably in her late thirties. She was definitely on her game. She was all business.

Kyle just looked at him. "Mark, what's going on?"

"Okay, I also took Viagra." Kyle said nothing. Now he realized why Mark's problems with impotence were gone.

The doctor shook her head. "It was probably the combination of methadone, Viagra, and the hot bath that caused your blood pressure to drop. It was the perfect storm. We will continue to monitor your heart and give you hydration. If your vital signs are stable in a few hours, you can go home."

"Mark, you scared the shit out of me. Who gave you the prescription for Viagra?"

"There's no prescription. George gave it to me." There was no way that Mark was going to say that sometimes he bought it on the street. "Kyle, I wanted to satisfy you. I was having problems. It was for us, and for a while it worked. I think I probably just stayed in the tub too long. You know I'm not very good about staying hydrated."

"I can't believe you would take something without checking it out with a doctor first. George makes a good Easter Bunny but not such a great doctor."

Now Mark had tears in his eyes. "I can't risk losing you to another man… a younger man. I love you." Kyle saw the pain and remorse in Mark's eyes. *How angry with Mark could he be? It was just a few weeks ago that he'd almost had sex with Austin again.*

"I love you, Mark. Please, just talk to Dr. Lamb about the Viagra." When the doctor came back, she said the same thing. She also said that Mark was stable and okay to go. Mark and Kyle took a cab home and went to bed. They were both exhausted. It had been a long day.

Chapter 41

Lizzie was home from the hospital. She was going to continue to have some outpatient testing in preparation for her craniotomy in three weeks. She was taking medication to keep her seizures under control. Her tumor was in the temporal lobe. Brad was now involved in her care because he would be doing the surgery. Spencer admired his skill in counseling and teaching his patients. Spencer was with him when he talked to Lizzie about her surgery. He reassured her that the tumor was in a very operable area and removing it should not have any significant change in her functioning. Since she was right-handed, he thought that her speech and memory centers were probably on the left side of her brain, but he wanted to make sure. She would need a procedure called a Wada test.

They would insert a catheter into her femoral artery and feed it up through the right carotid artery. They would then inject medication that would sedate the right side of her brain. The test would be performed when she was awake. If she could still speak and answer questions that tested her memory, they would know that her speech and memory were on the left side of her brain. Removing a tumor on the right side would probably not significantly affect her memory or speech. Lizzie had the Wada test and it concluded that her speech and memory centers were on the left side of her brain. She was good to go. She also had an appointment with a neuropsychologist. They wanted to do some cognitive testing before her surgery. They would repeat the testing after surgery to see if the surgery had caused any cognitive impairment. The neuropsychologist also prepared her for what she would face in the recovery period after surgery. He said it would take awhile to get used to her "new brain."

Lizzie was accepting of her condition but continued to be quite emotionally labile. She asked to see the girls. She knew that it would be awhile before she could see them again and still look like herself. She didn't want them to see her with a shaved head. Ivy would be too frightened. Ben brought his daughter over to Spencer's house one night for dinner, about a week before the surgery. Spencer's father made a nice meal. He and Ben seemed to strike up an easy conversation. Maybe it was because they were both widowers, or maybe it was because they were both teachers, but it was clear they established an easy rapport.

Haley and Ivy were so happy to see her. They told her all about school and their friends, and of course all about the Easter egg hunt. Lizzie was a little teary from time to time but, for the most part, did pretty well. The girls wanted her to put them to bed, and she wanted to do it. She had even brought her guitar and took it upstairs to play for the girls. Ben said that she had seemed to find a lot of comfort in her music. He asked Spencer about Brad. Spencer was able to reassure him about his ability as a surgeon. He told Ben that pediatric brain tumors were common, and Brad had done surgery on many of his patients. Some of them were as young as two years old. He was highly skilled. Ben said that he had a good feeling about Brad, and he felt that he could trust him with his daughter's care.

The visit had gone well, but Spencer knew that his daughters did not understand the full extent of Lizzie's condition. Lizzie said that Ivy had cried when she kissed her good night. Lizzie came back downstairs and packed up her guitar. "Thank you,

Spencer, for having us over tonight. She kissed him on the cheek and then hugged him. She was really crying now.

"Lizzie, we love you and think about you all the time. We are praying for you. I think that you are going to be okay. Stay strong. I will always be here for you." Spencer was relieved when she and Ben finally left. He poured a glass of Scotch for himself and his dad.

"Son, that girl has feelings for you."

"I know, Dad. I just don't know what to do about it. I think it just started out as a crush, but the more she got involved in our lives, the stronger her feelings got. She's never said anything or acted on those feelings, aside from the kiss on the cheek. Ivy has said a number of times that she wished that I would marry her."

"Lizzie seems like a mother to her. She was only two when Anna died. She barely knew her mother before she died. Your Ivy is a very sensitive little girl. This is going to be devastating for her. Your girls are longing for a mother. Have you thought about getting married again? Tell me how things are going with Bridget."

"I love her, Dad, but it all happened so quickly. Do I love her because I need her? I don't love her like I loved Anna. I'm still so confused. I don't want to rush into marriage." Spencer poured himself another two fingers of Scotch.

"Son, of course you don't love her like you loved Anna. She's not Anna. Do you love her for the woman that she is? How do Haley and Ivy feel about her?"

"I think they like her, but not the same as Lizzie. They love Lizzie."

"They see Lizzie almost every day, and Lizzie is in your home. She is involved with them at a very personal level."

"What about you, Dad? Didn't you ever come close? Was there ever a woman you thought you might be able to spend the rest of your life with... to be happy again?"

"No, I didn't." Now his Dad got up to pour more Scotch. "It was different for me. You boys were well on your way to independence when Mom died. I was lucky enough to find the finest woman on earth, and I had her for twenty-five years. I never found anyone else who even came close. I have accepted that. I think *you* have found someone and you love her. Don't be afraid."

After his father went to bed, Spencer was alone with his thoughts. He hoped that he hadn't made his father too sad tonight. He knew how much his father cherished his mother. He and his brothers were not surprised that their father never found someone else. *Twenty-five years is a long time. I only had Anna for eight.*

Spencer's father assured him that he was happy to be here to help out with the girls. Spencer sensed that it would be a long time before Lizzie could come back and work as a nanny. She might never come back. Brad told him that her tumor was probably a glioma... a malignant tumor. She would probably need, at the very least, radiation. The road back might be a long one. He couldn't rely on his father for childcare forever. His home was in Philadelphia, and he had commitments there. His father was active in doing volunteer work and had his other grandchildren in the area. Spencer knew that he needed to interview for a new nanny. He dreaded the process.

Brad had wanted Spencer and Bridget to get together with him and Beverly. Beverly said that she wanted to get to know Bridget better. Spencer hadn't even seen Bridget since the Easter egg hunt, which was a few weeks ago. He'd never ended up getting over there to see her that night because Ivy had ended up getting sick. He had been up with her most of that night because she was vomiting. He hadn't wanted to leave her. He'd sent Bridget a text. He'd thought she understood.

When he called Bridget about dinner, she seemed a little distant but wanted to go. Scarlett was already planning to sleep over at her grandparents' house. Brad asked Spencer to play golf, and they could then meet up with the ladies in the clubhouse afterwards for dinner. Spencer still wanted to pick Bridget up. He didn't feel right asking her to meet him there. Spencer's father and the girls had plans for a late-afternoon movie and dining out for pizza. Spencer had missed Bridget. He was looking forward to the evening. Spencer's dad gave him a wink. He told him to have a good time and that he wouldn't wait up for him.

It was a beautiful day. Spencer and Brad played nine holes in the afternoon. Brad was a superb golfer with a five handicap. The course was awesome. Brad told Spencer that Beverly was a pretty good golfer, too. He asked if Bridget played. Spencer said, "I don't know. I guess there's a lot I don't know about Bridget." That led to a conversation about how his relationship was going. Brad was always a good listener.

After Spencer showered, he went to pick up Bridget. She looked beautiful. She wore a straight black skirt and a white silk blouse. The skirt was fairly short and showed off her cute little body and great legs. Spencer noticed that she wore the earrings that he had given her for her birthday. She kissed him when she answered the door. "I've missed you," he said.

"Have you?" she said. Spencer noticed a little edge to her voice. He had been preoccupied with Lizzie's situation. Maybe Bridget was feeling a little neglected. This was a side to Bridget he had never seen.

"What's wrong, Bridget? Are you angry with me? You don't seem like yourself."

"Spencer, I haven't heard from you in over two weeks... not a phone call or even a text."

"You know that I have been caught up in this situation with Lizzie. I'm sorry. I should have called you. I really am sorry. Can we just set it aside for now and enjoy the evening? We can talk about it later when I take you home."

"Okay," she said.

Beverly had met Bridget before at preschool, so introductions didn't need to be made. Bridget seemed to loosen up a little after she had a glass of wine. Beverly was good at bringing Bridget into the conversation. She asked Bridget about her family and growing up in Rochester. She also wanted to know about her career in nursing and working in the NICU. Beverly told her that she admired her for pursuing such an important career and being such a good single parent. Beverly went on to say that her Martina adored Scarlett and always said, "My friend Scarlett is so special. She is determined, and that makes her good at everything she does." That brought up a discussion about how Martina had learned what the word *determined* meant. Beverly explained that her great-grandmother had taught her the meaning of the word when

Martina had told her about how her friend Scarlett could do anything that she set her mind to, even if she had only one good arm. She now used the word all the time. She would say something like, "I'm determined to finish this puzzle." She told Ruby every time that she saw her that she had to be determined to get well. There was a little awkward silence in the conversation. Ruby's condition had touched so many people. They all shared the same concerns for Ruby's future. The conversation was getting a little heavy.

Beverly asked Spencer how he was managing with the girls since Lizzie had become ill. She said that she had always been impressed with Lizzie when she saw her with Ivy at preschool. She had to be an excellent nanny. Spencer sensed that Bridget did not want to talk about Lizzie. He reached for Bridget's hand under the table, but she withdrew her hand and reached for her water glass. Then it dawned on him that maybe Bridget was feeling a little jealousy toward Lizzie. He saw Lizzie more than he saw her. Lizzie was important in his life. She was young and pretty, too. She wasn't that much younger than Bridget. Maybe it was making her feel insecure, or maybe she wondered if there was ever any more to his relationship with Lizzie. Spencer chastised himself for not thinking about this before. He knew he needed to talk about it with her. Spencer quickly changed the conversation over to talking about his dad and how supportive he had been.

They ordered dessert and after-dinner drinks. Beverly told Bridget that she was on the board of the cancer center at the medical center. She was vice-chairman of the fund-raising committee. They were having a spring fashion show and luncheon. They still needed one more model. She asked Bridget if she would be willing to do it. Bridget said that she was flattered and would be happy to do it. Beverly told her that she would call her with the details.

Spencer ordered crème brulee for dessert. He announced that Bridget was a fabulous cook, and that she had made him chocolate crème brulee for Valentine's Day. She looked at Spencer and smiled. It was the first time she smiled at him the entire night, but he didn't see warmth in her beautiful blue eyes. Tonight they were an icy blue. Usually she was so relaxed and easy-going. She clearly wasn't herself tonight.

After finishing up their drinks, they all said good night. Bridget said almost nothing on the drive home.

Spencer was anxious to be alone with her. Normally, as soon as they were alone, they would start undressing each other. Most times they weren't even fully undressed before sex began. Spencer wanted to talk to her first, so when she went for his belt buckle, he took her hand and brought it up to his mouth. He kissed her fingers. "I want to talk first," he said. The look in her eyes told Spencer she wasn't expecting his reaction. Spencer was confused. She was sending him mixed signals.

"Bridget, I said I am sorry for not calling you in the past few weeks, and I meant it. I love you. I'm sorry if I hurt you or made you think that I take your love for granted. Bridget, I want all of you... not just your body. I want your heart and your soul. You are a wonderful lover, but you hold back when it comes to real intimacy. It's like you don't trust my feelings for you."

"That's because I don't. I've learned not to trust men. Once you've been burned by a hot pan, you learn to use a pot holder. Spencer, I love you, too, but I think that you're still in love with your wife. I'm afraid that you will change your mind about me and move on to someone else. I was just here when you needed someone. You were lonely. I was a port in the storm. I need to be cautious. I don't want to be hurt again, and I cannot let someone into my life that will leave me and Scarlett again. We've had times that we've acted like a family. Scarlett loves it. I love it." Bridget was getting a little teary now. "I guess you are a family when you are with Lizzie, too. Are you sleeping with her, too?"

"I can't believe that you would think that!" he said. The anger in his voice was unmistakable. "Do you really think that I would do that? If you do, you don't know me at all."

"I want to trust you, but I guess I'm just not there yet."

"Bridget, you are the woman in my life. I do love you. A part of me will always love my wife. She's the mother of my children. What kind of man would I be if I didn't support Lizzie and her family through this crisis? It's the right thing to do."

"Maybe we've moved into this relationship too fast," Bridget said. "Maybe we should just take a break."

"Is that what you want?" Spencer asked, still angry.

"I think so. Help Lizzie and your girls through all of this. It sounds like it is what you need to do."

He took a deep breath and then kissed her. "I don't think we're through, Bridget. I love you." He kissed her again and took off. Spencer felt stung. This was not at all what he'd expected. It seemed like a lot of unnecessary drama. He hadn't realized Bridget's insecurities ran so deep. Maybe taking a break was the right thing to do. After all, she had been the only woman after Anna. He had never really met *this* Bridget before and tonight he was unsure of how her felt about her.

Now Bridget felt awful. She really didn't think Spencer was sleeping with Lizzie. *Why did I say that? Maybe he does love me. I was just worried because I hadn't heard from him. Now what if I've lost him? I think I've been trying too hard.* Now she was really upset. Bridget knew that she would never find another man like Spencer. Yes, he did have a little baggage, but then again, so did she.

The following Friday night, Bridget had plans to go out with her girlfriends. One of them had just gotten engaged, and they were all going out to celebrate. The friend who was getting married had been one of her friends since grammar school. They didn't see that much of each other anymore, but she was the kind of friend that when you did catch up with her, it seemed like you'd just seen her yesterday. She was so happy, and Bridget was happy for her. Although Bridget wasn't much in the mood for going out, she didn't want to disappoint Mandy. She got a babysitter. Fortunately, the girl who was babysitting was a college student. She had her own car. Bridget didn't have to worry about how she would get her home. Even though she charged a little more, it would be worth it. The girls all chipped in and rented a limo. After she thought about it, she decided she needed a night out. It might take her mind off of Spencer, and it would probably be fun. She went way back with these girls.

And it turned out, she was having fun. There was a band at the last bar that they went to. She was up at the bar ordering a drink, and she couldn't believe who'd just walked in... Kurt! One of her friends told her that he had been traded back to the Rochester Red Wings, and he was pitching. Baseball season had already started. He saw her right away. "Well, hello, Blue Eyes." She had to admit he was pretty hot... definite eye candy. He always had been. He handed over money to the bartender and said, "I'll get that for the little lady, and I'll have a Heineken." He gave her his most winning smile.

"I heard you were back playing for the Red Wings," she said.

"It's good to be home. Look, Bridget, I wish you would consider giving me another chance. I've been thinking about you a lot lately. I know how wrong I was to take off on you when you were pregnant. I wish you could believe how sorry I am about that. I'm very ashamed. We were always good together. I've never stopped loving you."

"I stopped loving you the day you walked out on Scarlett and me." Bridget wondered what had caused Kurt's sudden epiphany. She almost kind of felt sorry for him. Kurt was like that sad, mournful guy in a country-western song. He even wore cowboy boots. When she looked in his eyes, it seemed like he was tearing up. She had never known him to be so emotional. The band was back from their break. They started their next set with a slow song. It was an old Rolling Stones song, "Wild Horses."

Kurt took her hand. "Will you dance with me?" Bridget followed him out onto the dance floor. He held her closely. Bridget could feel him smelling her hair, and he gave her ear a gentle nibble.

Bridget broke away a little. "Kurt, what are you doing?"

"I can't help myself, babe. I'm begging you for another chance. I'll try to be more like the man you want me to be. Doesn't our little girl deserve a daddy? I want to try." He was holding her close again. Then he did it. The song ended, and he kissed her. Bridget didn't pull away this time. She had to admit it felt good. He took her hand and walked her back to the bar. They sat down. He held her hand at the bar. He bought them each a shot.

"Here's to second chances," Kurt said. They downed their shots. Kurt looked deeply into Bridget's eyes. He took his finger and traced it along her lips and down her neck to between her breasts. He kissed her again. Bridget couldn't believe she was letting this happen. A part of her had never stopped loving Kurt, despite her hurt and anger. She thought he seemed sincerely remorseful. They danced again.

She told Kurt she was going to the ladies' room, and on the way back, she checked in with her girlfriends. They knew about her history with Kurt, and most of them encouraged her to see where things would go with him. Bridget hugged Mandy, the bride-to-be, and went back to the bar. After that shot, she was feeling a little drunk. Kurt said he wanted to take a cab and get out of there. They went back to her place. Kurt paid the cab driver. Bridget told him that he had to wait outside until the babysitter left. She told him to take a walk around the block.

Bridget just let it happen. She had sex with Kurt. *Oh, my God, he was always so good in bed!* He had such an athletic body... he was a pitcher, after all. He had muscular arms and these big, strong hands, but Kurt was gentle. As self-centered as Kurt could be, he wasn't in bed. He knew how to bring pleasure to a woman. He knew how to make her crazy, and he did. After a few hours, Bridget made him leave. She certainly didn't want him there in the morning. She didn't want Scarlett to see him. "Kurt, just because we hooked up tonight doesn't mean that we're back. I have a lot of thinking to do."

He got dressed and kissed her. "Okay, babe, I understand, but remember I love you." He kissed her and took off.

The next day, Bridget had a wicked hangover and some drinker's remorse. She was glad that she didn't have to work. She wanted to keep busy. It was going to be a nice day. She took Scarlett to the zoo. Bridget couldn't get Kurt off her mind. After she thought about it more, she realized that she didn't feel all that bad about sleeping with Kurt. She obviously had some unresolved feelings for him. She knew she needed to sort them out before she went any further in her relationship with Spencer. He was Scarlett's father. Maybe Kurt had changed and grown up a little. She and Spencer were on a break. Spencer had his own unresolved feelings to reconcile. Back when they were together, loving Kurt had been easy. He was a simple, uncomplicated guy. Her relationship with Spencer was much harder to navigate. She was never quite sure that she could be herself when she was with him. She was never really sure want he wanted. She never knew what he was thinking. His past was too much of his present. Bridget knew she had a lot of thinking to do.

Chapter 42

Ruby had just gotten home from her appointment with her cardiologist. Sarah had taken her, and since it was at the hospital, Mario had met her there. The babies were sleeping and the kids weren't home from school yet. "Stay and have a glass of iced tea with me." Sarah was happy to join her. She still worried about losing her sister. She tried to spend as much time as she could with her. Ruby's checkup had gone well. Everything was stable.

"Do you ever think that maybe you should forget about the transplant and just go on living with your LVAD?" Sarah asked. "A transplant sounds so risky. You seem to be doing well."

"I'm doing okay, Sarah, but this is not what I want. I want my old life back. My family deserves more than I can give them now. I want to be a better wife and mother. I want to get back to nursing. I want to live long enough to see Little Mario and Lillie Mae graduate from high school. I want to dance at the girls' weddings. I won't live that long with an LVAD. I'm too young to settle for this kind of life. Don't get me wrong, Sarah, I thank sweet Jesus every day that I survived surgery and was able to come home. Now I want more. I just have to pray that somewhere and sometime soon there will be a new heart for me.

Someone was knocking at the door. Sarah got up and went to the door. It was the Fed Ex man. She signed for the letter addressed to Ruby. A bad feeling came over Ruby when her sister handed her the letter. It was from the chaplain at Attica. Ruby was listed as Jerome's next of kin. He was writing to inform her of Jerome's death. "Oh, my God," Ruby said. She was trembling. The letter went on to say that if she wanted more details, she could call him. Ruby had met the chaplain and spoken to him before because he had arranged for Jerome to come to Dwight's funeral. He'd been able to convince the warden to allow it. She thought that he was notifying her personally, rather than the warden, as a courtesy. "Sarah, I've got to call the chaplain and find out how it happened. He is the father of three of my children." Ruby was crying and upset now. Sarah got her a glass of water. Ruby made the call. Sarah was afraid to see her so upset.

The chaplain told Ruby that it was fairly certain that Jerome had died of a heart attack. He had developed problems with hypertension and was on blood pressure medication. His blood pressure still was not under control, and he had an upcoming appointment to be taken to the hospital for more testing. He was found with cocaine on his fingers and up his nose. He had suffered a cardiac arrest, and they were unable to resuscitate him. He went on to tell Ruby how shocked he was to hear that it had happened. He had thought that Jerome was a rehabilitated man and might even have been granted parole this year. Jerome was never without his Bible and had become very spiritual. He had earned his GED and was taking college-level classes. The death of his son had really changed him. He added that, unfortunately, drugs did find their way into prisons.

Ruby was trying to process everything. She didn't know what to say. The chaplain explained that the family could claim his body and make funeral and burial arrangements. If they could not afford to do so, his body could be turned over to the state board of corrections, and it would be buried, cremated, or donated to medical science at the discretion of the county.

"I was never married to Jerome," Ruby said. "I have never met his family."

"I'm sorry this is difficult for you, Ms. Washington, but as his next of kin, it is up to you to decide. Please take some time to think about it and call me back."

Sarah hugged Ruby. "That man is still causing you pain even though he is dead."

"Mario and I can't afford to pay for his funeral, but doesn't even Jerome deserve a Christian burial? I don't know where to even begin looking for his family. Jerome never talked about them. Maybe there is no family to be found, and that's why I was listed as his next of kin." Ruby vaguely remembered him mentioning growing up in foster care.

"Ruby, you don't need this now. This stress is not good for you. Let's go out for dinner tonight. You, Mario, Henry, and me... We'll talk about it. We'll figure it out."

Mario was angry that this situation had been dumped on his wife's lap and was causing her so much stress. Henry was furious. He had seen the pain Jerome had caused Ruby over the years. He remembered a battered Ruby, several times with a black eye and once, a broken arm. "Let the scum burn," Henry said. That just made Ruby cry. Everyone got quiet. It was an interesting comment coming from Henry. He was a firefighter.

"Ruby, I'm sorry I said that, but it's hard for me to forget the horror he inflicted on you."

"That's okay, Henry. You and Sarah were the ones always there to put me back together again. You were always more than an uncle to my children. Dwight would have never become the person he was without your love and support. He worshipped you. You can say what you need to say."

"Sarah, do you think Daddy would pay for a funeral? He's always preaching about a loving and forgiving God. Wouldn't he want the father of his grandchildren to have a Christian burial?"

"Ruby, how can you ask that of Daddy? I'm sure God has forgiven Jerome, but I'm not sure Daddy ever has. Who would go to this funeral? Would you really want Danielle and Denise to meet their father for the first time in his casket?"

Mario held Ruby's hand. "Ruby, your father is already helping us out as it is. We certainly can't afford to pay for a funeral right now. Maybe turning his body over to the board of corrections is the best thing to do. You could request that his body be turned over to medical science. At least his death could be of some good."

"I guess maybe that's the best solution." Ruby hadn't touched any of her food. This whole situation had put a bad taste in her mouth and made her so very sad. The others were able to move on and talk about other things. Mario and Henry had another beer and talked about baseball. Sarah sat and drank her wine. She knew her sister was in a lot of emotional pain.

That night Mario held her, and they talked some more. "Ruby, I think this is best," he said. "A funeral is much too stressful for you right now. Let him go. Think of the girls. It would be awful for them." Ruby had a restless night. There was so much on her mind. When she did finally fall asleep, she dreamt that the house was on fire. Everyone got out except for her. Finally Henry came in to get her.

The next day Beverly came over with Martina to visit. Beverly knew how much Ruby loved lemon meringue pie and had made one to bring over to her. Beverly could sense that something wasn't right. Ruby told her all about it. Beverly couldn't believe that this was happening to Ruby right now, and that she actually wanted to have a funeral for the man who had tortured her. She didn't understand it, but she could see the emotional pain it was causing her. She remembered that when Dwight died, Jerome had been escorted into the funeral home in shackles. Erica had been horrified. Beverly could still remember Ruby embracing a sobbing Jerome.

Beverly knew that paying for a simple funeral would be something she and Brad could easily afford. After all, it was for Martina's grandfather. If it gave Ruby some sense of peace, it would be well worth it. She knew that Brad would agree. She made the offer.

"Beverly, I can't believe that you would do this for me. You are so kind. Mario, Sarah, and Henry think it is too stressful for me, and it would be too hard on the girls. The twins have never met him or even seen a picture of him. I've just told them that he took off before they were born and that he wasn't ready to be a father. They never asked any more. Dwight never wanted to talk about Jerome, either. Dwight knew that his father was in prison. The twins have never been told. They don't know that Dwight's father was also their father."

"They're older now, Ruby. Maybe you could tell them. They might want to know. What they fantasize about their father might be worse than the truth. Perhaps if you do have this funeral, it might give you closure, and in the end, it may be less stressful than turning over his body to the prison. It could just be a graveside service. They wouldn't have to view the body.

You could tell them the simplest version of the story. He was in prison for armed robbery but was working hard in prison to become a better man. He was taking classes, meeting with the chaplain, and reading the Bible every day. The chaplain said he was rehabilitated. You can just tell them that he died of a heart attack, which is true. They don't need to know about the cocaine. Ruby, we're family. Let me help. You, Jerome, Tom, and me…we are Martina's biological grandparents. Let's put him to rest and in the past, but in a good way.

Ruby thought that this was a solution that she could live with. She was not sure how Mario would feel about it. She did think that Beverly was right. If Jerome had a Christian burial, it would relieve some of her stress about his death, give her closure, and resolve a painful part of her past. The girls were older now. They would probably at some point start to ask more about their father. Now she only had to convince Mario that having the funeral was the right thing to do. He didn't always understand how deep her connection was with Beverly. He probably wouldn't like taking that kind of help from her, especially because it involved money. It was about pride… not only about his pride as a man and his ability to take care of his wife, but it was also about black pride.

It was Brad who finally convinced Mario to let Ruby accept Beverly's offer. Mario held Brad in high regard. He respected his opinion. Brad helped him to realize that it was Ruby's decision to make, and a funeral would probably give her closure. He told Mario that, in his career, he had treated many battered women. Their mental scars ran deep. Domestic violence was all about control. If Ruby felt guilt about how Jerome was put to rest, he would continue to control her even after his death. She needed to feel right about her decision.

Ruby had a close personal relationship with the pastor from her church. She had sought out guidance from him in the past. Reverend Brown and her father had co-presided over Dwight's funeral. He knew about Jerome and her past with him. He said he would do the service. He even called the prison chaplain at Attica to learn more about Jerome and his efforts toward rehabilitation.

Beverly drove Ruby to Attica to sign the necessary papers. It was only about an hour away. Ruby had visited Jerome in Attica a few times in the early years of their relationship. She seemed unfazed about going. Beverly had never been to a prison before. She had no idea what to expect. After going through the metal detectors, they were escorted to the warden's office. The prison chaplain was also there. Beverly was proud of Ruby. She remained unemotional and took care of business. The chaplain remarked that he was happy that the family found a way to give Jerome a funeral. Ruby reached for Beverly's hand and held it. After the meeting they found a place to have lunch before heading back to Rochester.

"Beverly, I can't thank you enough for doing this for me. Mario, Sarah, and Henry haven't been all that supportive of this plan, so I'm glad that you came with me today. They said that they would come to the funeral, though. I hope you and Brad will come, too." She went on to tell Beverly that she had already talked to Danielle and Denise. Apparently they'd known that their father was in prison. Dwight had told them. She had a few pictures of Jerome, which she'd shared with the girls. Ruby said their talk went well.

When they got back to Rochester, Ruby insisted on going to the funeral home to make arrangements. She just wanted to get it done. Beverly thought it was too much for one day, but she took her anyway. Maybe if she got all of this done, she could get a good night's rest. It didn't take too long. They chose a very simple casket. Ruby planned to cover it with a spray of red roses. She said that she could call the florist when she got home. The funeral would be the day after tomorrow. Beverly had already talked to Ruby about where she wanted Jerome buried. Beverly priced out a plot in the same cemetery where Dwight had been buried. It wasn't in the same section, but it wasn't far. Ruby was pleased with it. They were done. Ruby insisted on paying for the flowers and Reverend Brown's fee. She said that in time, she would purchase a marker for the grave. The mortuary fees and cemetery plot were reasonable. For Beverly and Brad it was a modest expense, and they were happy to help.

The funeral was a short, simple affair. It was a lovely day in early May. Helen took Martina for the day. Mario took the day off, and the kids all stayed home from school to go. Brad was able to arrange his schedule so that he could be there. Reverend Brown gave a few remarks. He said that Jerome was a flawed man but had found refuge in the love of Jesus. "Our Lord is a loving and forgiving God and will grant Jerome eternal rest."

He recited the twenty-third Psalm.

The Lord is my shepherd; I shall not want. He maketh me to lie down in green pastures: he leadeth me beside the still waters. He restoreth my soul: he leadeth me in the paths of righteousness for his name's sake.

Yea, though I walk in the valley of the shadow of death, I will fear no evil: for thou art with me; thy rod and thy staff they comfort me. Thou preparest a table before me in the presence of mine enemies: thou anointest my head with oil; my cup runneth over. Surely goodness and mercy shall follow me all the days of my life: and I will dwell in the house of the Lord forever.

And finally, a woman from Ruby's church sang "Amazing Grace". The service took less than twenty minutes, but it was beautiful in its simplicity. Beverly couldn't help but wonder if everyone was thinking the same thing that she was: *Did someone like Jerome really deserve this respect?* This was for Ruby. She did deserve the respect. Beverly was glad they'd had the funeral. After the service, everyone left and got on with their day.

That night Brad said, "That was a wonderful thing that you did for Ruby. You are quite a woman. Do you know how much I love you?"

"Oh, Brad, I hope that is the last funeral I have to ever attend with that family. Did I ever tell you that Ruby and Dwight came to my husband's funeral? Then, of course, there were Dwight's and Erica's funerals. Will it ever end?" She was crying now. "I'm so afraid that we will lose Ruby, too. I just couldn't bear it."

"Whatever happens, I will always be here for you." He kissed her.

"Make love to me, Brad." Beverly always felt peace and security in his arms. After she and Brad were married, she'd realized that she was the luckiest unlucky woman on earth. *What would I do if I lost Brad?* She was afraid to even think about it.

Chapter 43

Just when Mark thought his life was getting better again, it clearly wasn't. He was having more pain. It now radiated down to one of his legs. He knew that Kyle was still a little angry about the Viagra incident, and now Mark was nervous about taking it. He'd never discussed taking Viagra with Dr. Lamb as promised. He had little interest in sex anyway. It was something that had been discussed by others in group before. Decreased libido was a common problem on methadone. No one said anything about trying Viagra, and he wasn't about to bring up his own experience. He hated going to group and the drug testing and having to go clinic every day for one single dose of methadone. He had hoped that he could transition to Subutex or Suboxone and just see a therapist for weekly sessions. He couldn't even go out of town on a vacation. He wanted to take Lucy on a vacation to the beach. Dr. Lamb didn't think that Subutex or Suboxone would relieve his pain like the methadone and might put him at risk for relapse. "Mark, it's too early in your recovery to change therapy. What's really going on?" He finally told Dr. Lamb about the problems in his marriage.

"I'm married to a man fifteen years younger than me. How can I keep him happy? The methadone is taking a real toll on our sex life." Mark took a big sip of water. *This man is so attractive and I'm sure he's straight. I can't believe I'm telling him this, but I'm sure he's heard it before.* Mark finally told him about the Viagra incident. Dr. Lamb was clearly not pleased that he'd taken someone else's prescribed medication.

"Don't even think about buying Viagra on the street. Mark, haven't you learned anything here? Viagra and methadone are not always a good combination, but I guess you've learned that. I'm sure the methadone is taking a toll on your libido, but maybe you should see a urologist about your problems with erectile dysfunction. I think that maybe you and your partner could benefit from some counseling." Mark left his session with Dr. Lamb just as frustrated as before.

When he was feeling down, it was Lucy who could bring him back up. He had no weddings booked this weekend, so he was not under any pressure at the bakery. His assistant could finish up any of the smaller orders. It was such a beautiful day. He decided to take the afternoon off and spend it with Lucy. He picked her up at school. They stopped to pick up a pizza and took it to a park along the canal for a lunchtime picnic. Afterwards, Lucy fed little pieces of her pizza crust to the ducks. Mark took some great pictures with his phone. He took her to a bookstore and let her pick out a book. She found a book about a little girl and her puppy.

"Poppy, can we go get a mani-pedi?" It was their special thing to do. Kyle always did more of the activities that involved physical activity... Sea Breeze which was the local amusement park, bike rides with her in the back riding in her bike trailer, the play gym, and sledding in the winter. Mark was usually just a spectator. Mark would bake with Lucy or do craft projects with her. He was creative. Lucy would become an avid reader because Mark made sure he read to Lucy every day. He and Kyle were a good team, but Mark often wished he could engage in more physical play with Lucy. He and Lucy were in their chairs soaking their feet and in walked Melanie. *Oh, my God, I can't believe this.* Mark wasn't sure how to handle it. He couldn't just ignore her.

She was escorted to a chair right next to Lucy. He was certain that she hadn't requested that chair. It was the only one remaining. Melanie looked at Mark and raised her eyebrows. She shrugged her shoulders. Mark wanted to be the bigger person here, so he smiled and said hello. It was really hard to forget what had happened in court and the trouble she had instigated, but after all, if it weren't for Melanie, Lucy would not even be here right now. Then he remembered about her ovarian cancer. "Lucy, this is a friend of mine. Her name is Miss Melanie." Lucy smiled at her sweetly and said, "Hello, Miss Melanie, do you like getting a mani-pedi, too?"

"Oh, I do, Lucy." Lucy, being Lucy, chatted away. She told Melanie all about their picnic and feeding the ducks. She said that she'd even seen a mama duck with her babies. "Poppy says they're called ducklings. Poppy is a baker, you know. One time he made this cake in the shape of a duck for a baby shower party. You wouldn't believe the Easter Bunny cake that he made!" Lucy went on to tell her all about the Easter egg hunt. Thanks to Lucy, this whole situation was not as awkward as Mark had feared. Lucy continued chattering away the entire time. Mark would join the conversation when he could. Finally, they were done and were sitting under the dryers. "Miss Melanie, Poppy promised me ice cream when we're done. Do you want to come? "

Mark was being so nice. Melanie didn't want to push it. "Thank you, honey, but I can't today. There is somewhere I have to be." She would have loved to spend more time with her daughter. She got up and gave her credit card to the salon owner. "This is for the three of us," she said. She handed over some additional cash for the tip. She hugged Lucy. "It was so nice to meet you, Lucy. I really enjoyed talking to you." She hugged Mark, too. "Thank you for this, Mark."

He simply said, "You're welcome. Thank you, too."

"She was a very nice lady, Poppy."

Mark took Lucy home. He got comfortable in his favorite recliner and watched TV with Lucy. Kyle would be home soon. It had been quite a day. He was exhausted, both emotionally and physically. He decided to have a glass of wine before Kyle got home. It was still pretty early. He found that if it was just a small glass, and if he had it early, it would clear before he got to clinic for testing the next day. He rarely took the chance, but he was a little unglued today.

It was Friday. Kyle used to look forward to Friday nights. He and Mark would either make plans to go out or spend some quality time together at home. They would give Lucy her dinner early and, together, put her to bed. Kyle would cook something fabulous for just the two of them. He loved to cook. They would open up a good bottle of wine. Then there was afterwards...it was always their night. Lately, Friday nights weren't so great. Mark was usually tired.

Late that afternoon, Kyle got a text from Austin. "Meet me for a drink?" It was still pretty early. Kyle was tempted. He knew that Austin sensed how unhappy he was in his marriage and was persistent in pursuing him. He wasn't giving up. Mark had called Kyle to tell him about taking the afternoon off to spend it with Lucy. Kyle knew that Mark would for sure be tired tonight. He thought he could have a quick drink with Austin and go home. He knew that he shouldn't, but he did. As long as nothing happened, he didn't see the harm in it.

They talked. "Kyle, have you ever thought about leaving Mark? I know you're not happy, because if you were, you wouldn't be here with me. You're a young man. Sometimes marriages can't be fixed, and the best thing to do is to move on... for everyone's sake. Divorce doesn't have to be a dirty word. It doesn't mean you have to give up Lucy. I wish you would give us a chance."

"Austin, we can only be friends for now. I've really got to get going."

Austin looked at him with a hopeful, longing look in his eyes and a subtle, seductive smile. He said nothing, but his look said everything.

"Okay," Kyle said, "but this has got to be quick." He followed Austin back to his apartment. It was quick… very quick, but immensely satisfying. Kyle got home a little later than expected but not really all that late. It was just before seven o'clock. Both Mark and Lucy were asleep in front of the TV. He saw the empty wineglass next to Mark. Lucy awoke when Kyle kissed her.

"You and Poppy must have had so much fun this afternoon." Kyle made them grilled ham and cheese sandwiches and cut up an apple and some carrot sticks.

She told him all about her adventures that afternoon… even about the new friend that she'd met at the salon, Miss Melanie. Kyle couldn't believe it. *God, what was Mark thinking!* He had to read to Lucy quite awhile before she finally settled down and fell asleep. He had a little trouble waking Mark up to get him to bed. He knew it was probably the wine, and he wasn't pleased about that, either. He suspected that Mark would sneak a glass of wine from time to time, but he never did it in front of him.

Mark kissed Kyle good night. "Sorry, man, our little Lucy really tired me out."

Kyle went back to the living room and finished off the bottle of wine that Mark had opened. He got a text from Austin. His text said, "It could work for us. Give it a chance." Kyle started thinking about what Austin had said about marriages that couldn't be fixed. He was young. Maybe he should move on. He didn't see Mark's problems resolving anytime soon. It was hard to envision his future with Mark. Then he thought about Lucy. Being only Lucy's adoptive parent, he didn't know if Mark would have more leverage in court when negotiating a custody agreement. He hated that he needed to worry about that. It was bad enough that he had to worry about Melanie.

They didn't have much time to talk the next morning. Mark had to head off to clinic and then on to the bakery. Lucy had a playdate with Martina. Kyle and Mark agreed to meet up for lunch. Kyle was feeling all kinds of negative emotions. He was ashamed, angry, frustrated, and sad. He'd once thought that Mark was the love of his life; now he wasn't sure. Kyle took a deep breath when he saw Mark walk into the diner. He was limping a little. His leg was bothering him again. The problems with his back were now affecting the nerves to his legs.

The waitress took their order, and Kyle jumped right in. "Mark, I can't believe you let Lucy spend time with Melanie. How could you let that happen? What the fuck were you thinking?" Kyle took another deep breath. He knew he needed to lower his voice and calm down.

"Take it easy. I'm telling you it was unavoidable." Mark explained exactly how it had happened. "I told Lucy that she was a friend of mine. Lucy and I were sitting in a foot bath. It was hard to just get up and leave. I handled it the best way that I could. You know Lucy. She has quite a personality. She likes to talk, and Melanie soaked it up. Melanie wasn't pushy at all. She mostly just listened. I couldn't help but think about the ovarian cancer. She might never have kids of her own. It seemed harmless to let her enjoy that brief time with Lucy.

"How do you know that she didn't follow you there?"

"That's a little paranoid, Kyle, don't you think?

"I just don't like it. I noticed that you were limping today. Did you make that appointment for the surgical consult?"

"I know... it's time. I will make it on Monday. Dr. Lamb said he thinks that I should see a urologist about the ED. I am planning on making that appointment, too. God, Kyle, I want to go back to being us."

"Mark, you've been promising me for months that you would talk to the surgeon. Why do you keep putting it off? It's just a consult."

"It's all so overwhelming. I don't think you understand how frustrating these problems are for me."

"Mark, your problems have become my problems, too. They are destroying our marriage. I miss us being us, too. You are not the same man that I married. I'm worried about our future together. I'm not happy. I'm worried about you, me, and Lucy as a family."

Mark was deeply wounded by Kyle's last comments. He had never been quite that blunt before.

"Dr. Lamb suggested that maybe we should get counseling. I think our marriage is worth saving."

"Mark, let's start out by talking to the surgeon. Make the appointment. We'll go together."

Chapter 44

It was the morning of Lizzie's surgery. The first thing to happen was for her to have her head shaved. She insisted that she was okay with it. Her father wanted to be there to hold her hand, but she wanted to be alone. One of the nurses first cut her pretty, honey-brown hair and then took clippers and did the rest. She gave Lizzie a hand mirror when she was finished. "See, Lizzie, you're a beautiful girl, even with a shaved head." Ben fought back the tears when he saw his daughter. Spencer was with Ben and Lizzie's brother. Spencer had taken the day off. He wanted to be there, and he felt like it was the right thing to do. After all, he was the medical director of the clinic. No one was about to give him a hard time about it. He had only taken a few days off since he'd started his position. Lizzie had taken such wonderful care of his children; now he wanted to make sure the same was being done for her. He also knew that Lizzie would like it that he was there for her dad.

Spencer spoke to Brad briefly before he went in to scrub. Brad seemed confident. He reassured Spencer. "I think it will go well. We will keep you and Lizzie's family updated during her case." Brad had requested that Mario be his scrub nurse. Mario was efficient and very intuitive in the OR. He and Mario made a good team. Brad had asked Spencer if he knew what kind of music Lizzie enjoyed. He knew that she sometimes played classic rock songs on her guitar. He remembered her singing the Joni Mitchell song to the girls. Brad decided to play Joni Mitchell when she was brought into the OR and would switch over to a little James Taylor after she was under anesthesia. Mario knew Brad's favorite tunes, and he knew that Brad was adamant about keeping the music soft and low.

A lot of surgeons liked to play music in the OR. It lifted some of the tension in the room, relaxed the patients, and helped the surgeons to concentrate. Brad had told Mario that this case was special. She was the nanny for Spencer's children. There was really no need to say that, because Mario knew that, for Brad, every case was special. He was an extraordinary physician.

They called out to the waiting room. They had excised a sample of tissue and were waiting for the preliminary report from pathology before proceeding any further. Lizzie was stable and so far everything was going well. The next report was that the mass was a tumor…a glioma, which was a malignant tumor. They would go ahead and remove the tumor, obtaining good margins around it, without disrupting too much normal brain tissue.

After the surgery was completed, they moved Lizzie to the recovery room, and Brad went to the family waiting room to speak to Lizzie's father. "Mr. Snow, I think the surgery went well. The tumor was modest in size. It was about the size of a gum ball. It was not difficult to remove. I don't anticipate that Lizzie will have much of a loss in function after she makes her full recovery. However, recovery from brain surgery can be a slow process. She will need a lot of support before she returns to her former self. It may be frustrating for her. The brain is a remarkable organ in its ability to recover and adapt." He went on to explain that it would take a few days for the final pathology report to come back. "I have a high regard for the pathology department here." He shook hands with Ben and his son. "Please feel free to have the staff page me if you have any concerns. I think Lizzie will be okay." He shook Spencer's hand. "Spencer, I'll talk to you soon."

Spencer's father insisted on making a meal for Ben and his son that night. Spencer told Ben that they could see Lizzie when she awoke from anesthesia, but she would be pretty sedated most of the night. He could take a break and have dinner. He convinced him that it would be good for him to do so. Finally, Lizzie was awake and moved to a special neuro intensive care unit. Her head was bandaged and her right eye was swollen shut. Brad was there when Spencer, Ben, and Lizzie's brother walked in. He was holding Lizzie's hand. He explained that the swelling in her eye was expected. It was because of the surgery. Her eye would be fine. She had about a four-inch incision behind her right ear. Her hair would easily cover it. Lizzie was groggy, but she was smiling. Then she was crying. Brad explained that she might be emotionally labile for a while.

The nurse came in to give Lizzie some pain medication. Spencer told Ben to come to his house about six o'clock. He caught up with Brad outside in the hall.

"Really, there were no surprises today. I think she will do well. It looked like a tumor I've seen many times before in patients that are in their early adulthood. I suspect it's an oligodendroglioma...a slow-growing tumor, not very aggressive. She will probably need radiation but not necessarily chemotherapy."

Spencer went up to the clinic to see how the day had gone. They were just winding down. Everything was fine there, so he headed home. The girls were happy to see him, and whatever his father was cooking smelled absolutely delicious. Spencer had explained to the girls as simply as he could that Lizzie needed an operation to help her get better. He didn't want to scare the girls. They didn't ask too many questions. Haley held her sister's hand and told her about a boy in her class that had an operation on his tummy. He had come back to school already and was fine. They really just wanted to know if she would be okay. They knew that the operation was today. He reassured them that Lizzie was fine. Spencer's dad said that the girls had talked about Lizzie all day. He'd kept them busy by making cards for her. Spencer honestly didn't know what he would do without his father. Spencer set the table and opened up a bottle of wine. "Dad, I can't believe you made beef stroganoff. This is all so thoughtful. I'm sure the Snows are grateful that they won't be eating in the hospital cafeteria tonight."

"It was my pleasure, son. I'm sure it was a stressful day for all of you."

It was a heavy evening. After the Snows left, Spencer put the girls to bed, and his dad cleaned up the kitchen. He came downstairs and poured a Scotch for himself and his dad. It had gotten to be a habit, and something they both looked forward to. Spencer finally confided in his father about his taking a break with Bridget. He seemed surprised but said he understood. "I know it's difficult moving on, son." Then his father told him something that surprised him. He had met a woman whom he was becoming interested in. When Spencer was at the hospital, and the girls were at school, he would go to the local Starbucks to have coffee and read for a while. That's where he'd met her. She was a regular, too. She had also been widowed for many years, and they shared many of the same interests. They had met up several times for coffee and sometimes took walks along the canal. He was planning on taking her to dinner Saturday night.

"Good for you, Dad."

"I'm not in a big rush to get back to Philadelphia. I've been enjoying my time here. I love spending time with you and the girls. I have really found a connection with this woman, and I want to give it a chance. Her name is Mary. Summer is right around the corner, and I'm sure you could use the help with the girls, especially once school is out. Is it okay if I stay for a while?"

"Well, of course, Dad. We love having you here." Spencer was relieved, because he wasn't sure what he would do with the girls once school was out. He had set up a couple of interviews to hire a new nanny. His father staying on for a while would take the pressure off. He couldn't believe that after all these years, his father had found someone he was actually interested in pursuing. This woman must be very special.

The final pathology report was back. As Brad had suspected, Lizzie's tumor was an oligodendroglioma, grade two. The radiation oncologist recommended a six-week course of radiation to treat any remaining tumor that Brad had been unable to resect. She would need time to recover from surgery before they could begin radiation, which would probably start in June or July. They had her on medication to control the swelling in her brain and also medication to prevent seizures. She seemed to be making a good recovery from the surgery. Ben would be able to take her home at the end of the week. Her aunt, Ben's sister, would be staying with them while Lizzie was recovering.

Spencer had to go to the NICU to check on a newborn patient of his who had just been transferred there. He ran into Bridget. He spoke first. "Hello, Bridget. How are you? I've been thinking a lot about you. I've missed you."

He could tell by the look on her face that she wasn't ready to see him yet. "I've missed you, too," she said, "but we've needed this time. I think I still need more time."

"Okay, you know where to find me." Spencer felt a little brushed off. This separation wasn't really working for him. He was more confused than ever. He had thought that he and Bridget were building a solid relationship. Apparently, it wasn't so. Maybe it was all about the kids and the sex.

* * *

Kurt wanted back into Bridget's life, and she wasn't sure how she felt about it. If her father found out, he would be furious. Kurt was trying so hard. He came over to the house with tickets for a baseball game. It was a Saturday afternoon game. He really wanted her to come and bring Scarlett. Kurt seemed different. It was like he had been put in a rock tumbler and shined up. He was sincere. He called one night and asked if it was okay if he came over. He said that from now on, he would ask and not just show up at her door. Scarlett was already in bed when Kurt came over. They had a long talk. Kurt told her over and over again that he was ashamed that he had walked out on her. He said that he'd been afraid and had doubted that he could be a good father, or any kind of a father. Then he finally told Bridget his story.

Kurt hated his own father. His father was a stern man who always demanded perfection, and there was no pleasing him. He favored Kurt's older brother, Karl. His brother had died from leukemia at the age of twelve. The summer before he died, his brother had been the captain of his Little League team and led them to the state championships. After Karl died, his father would take all his anger and frustration out on Kurt. He became more critical of him, especially when it came to baseball. He always told Kurt he could never measure up to his brother, saying he wasn't as smart and definitely not as athletic as Karl. He would punish Kurt if he didn't play well in a game. Once he'd gotten into an argument with his father after a game he played in high school. His father had punched him, breaking his nose. His mother would often try to intervene on Kurt's behalf, but that enraged his father even more. Kurt got a full baseball scholarship to SUNY Albany. It was a Division One school for college baseball. Kurt's father had said their baseball program was a joke. A real accomplishment would have been a scholarship to Vanderbilt or the University of Miami, or a contract to play professional baseball. His mother ended up leaving his father after Kurt took off for college. Kurt didn't think that his father had ever physically abused his mother, but he knew that his father had definitely verbally and psychologically abused her. Kurt hadn't seen his father since. His mother told him that his father had recently moved out of state.

Bridget knew that Kurt had never finished college. He ended up playing baseball for different minor league teams. She knew that he kept in touch with his mother. She still lived in Rochester.

Kurt said that he was happy to get traded back to the Rochester Red Wings, and Rochester was a much better place without his father living there. He was happy that Bridget still lived in Rochester. He wanted to make things right with her and have the opportunity to be a father to the daughter that he had abandoned. His mother needed him and he wanted to be a better son. She didn't even know that she had a grandchild. He was also hoping to finish up his college degree.

Kurt wept when he admitted that he'd been afraid of what their baby would look like, and if maybe there would be other things wrong with her. He had been afraid that she might die. "I can see now that there was nothing to be afraid of. She's a smart and beautiful little girl. I'm not the same man who left you four years ago. I think that I've finally grown up and resolved some of my issues concerning my father and my brother's death. I think we could be a family. Please Bridget, forgive me."

Bridget just looked at him. He was breaking her heart all over again. She realized that she didn't hate him anymore. The entire time they'd been together, Kurt had never shared his story with her. He'd never told her that he had an abusive father or even a brother who had died. Bridget had thought he was an only child. He'd only said that his parents were divorced, and the only family he kept in touch with was his mother. She had sensed that he didn't like talking about his family, so she'd never pushed it. She'd never met his mother. Kurt did say that he didn't know of many happy marriages, and he didn't think marriage was for him. She had always hoped that he would change his mind once their baby was born.

Now Bridget saw the pain and sorrow on Kurt's face when he told her his story...the story she'd never known. Bridget hated to see anyone in pain. She held Kurt as the tears streamed down his face. She kissed him and took him into the bedroom. They made love. She couldn't believe that she still had this much love for the man who had so deeply disappointed her and then abandoned her. He'd abandoned their child. But know she was starting to understand.

"Bridget, will you let me get to know my daughter? I have so much to make up for."

"I don't know if I can make her understand. She's heard some not-so-nice things my father has said about you."

"Your dad... I'm sure he detests me even more than my own father. At least he has a reason."

"Kurt, you know I've been seeing someone. Our relationship is pretty serious. I can't believe you've come back to me now."

"Then why did you just make love to me? I know the other night after seeing each other in the bar, you were a little wasted, but you're not tonight. I'm hoping you still have feelings for me. I still love you. I never stopped loving you. Whoever it is that you are seeing, he isn't Scarlett's father. He can't love you the way I do."

"Kurt, I haven't heard from you in four years. I don't know what I'm feeling."

"Babe, I'm telling you, I've got my shit together now. Let's give it a go. Please, let's be a family... you, me, and our Scarlett."

"Kurt, I'll bring Scarlett to that game on Saturday. I'll try to talk to her. We'll see how it goes. Slow, Kurt... we need to take it slow." She couldn't believe she was letting this happen.

Chapter 45

Beverly couldn't believe that it was almost Memorial Day. Preschool would be over in a few weeks, and they would be heading into summer. Beverly was trying to figure out how she would keep Martina busy all summer. She knew that once school was over, Ruby's nurse wouldn't be working for them anymore. The girls would be home to help out with the twins. Ruby was much stronger now. She really didn't need a nurse anymore, and Beverly knew that Ruby would be happy to see her go. Ruby just wanted to get back to being Ruby. She was recovering her strength. Beverly knew how much she loved spending time with Martina. Maybe she and Ruby and Martina could have a standing date each week to spend the day together. Mario was busy putting in time to fulfill his clinical hours required for his nurse anesthetist program. He would be finished soon.

Beverly was hoping she and Brad and Martina could take a vacation. Beverly loved when she and Erica had gone to the Jersey shore with her friend Christy and her mother before Martina was born. Cape May, New Jersey, was charming and beautiful. She loved it. Maybe they could go there. She remembered Spencer Harris telling her that he and his wife were married in Cape May. She thought that maybe Pam and Sam could join them and bring Lucy along to play with Martina. They could rent a house. If she really wanted to do it, she knew she had better look into it right away. She stopped at the boutique to see Pam. Pam loved the idea and said she would talk to Kyle and Mark about bringing Lucy. She confided in Beverly about her fears concerning the state of Kyle and Mark's marriage. She sensed something was very wrong. "Maybe they need some time alone together," Pam said. "They might like that I take Lucy for a week." Beverly planned to talk to Brad about Cape May that night.

There was a beautiful cream-colored silk blouse in the shop that Beverly wanted to buy. She was feeling good today and wanted to have a special evening with Brad. Today's session with Dr. Martino had gone well. He thought she was finally ready to come off her antidepressant medication. She had finished the watercolor she had been working on for Brad and was picking it up from the framer that afternoon. She wanted to give it to him tonight. She was planning on making an especially nice dinner. She would grill salmon and make a spring risotto with spinach, asparagus, and peas. For dessert she planning to bake a key lime pie. Martina was at Helen's. She stopped by to pick her up. Martina and Helen were in the middle of cookie baking. Martina didn't want to go home. "Can she stay here with me tonight, Beverly? I would love to have her." Beverly was fine with that. She could for sure have a special night with Brad. Martina already had pajamas and a toothbrush that she left at Helen's. Beverly said that she would be by in the morning with a change of clothes and take her to school. Beverly hugged them both and headed for home. Just like Erica, Martina adored Helen and loved their special time spent together.

Beverly did her dinner prep when she got home and then decided to take a long, relaxing bubble bath. She poured herself a glass of Chardonnay to sip when she was in the tub. She dressed in her new blouse, which she paired with some black Capri pants. She pinned her hair up and put on her favorite gold earrings. They were a Christmas present from Brad, which he'd given to her that very first Christmas they were together. She still remembered him making love to her and taking the wrapped present out of the drawer of his nightstand. Brad had romanced her since the day they met. He still did. He was chivalrous. He was her knight in shining armor. She couldn't imagine life without Tom and Erica if Brad hadn't been there for her.

It was a beautiful evening, and warm. She thought that they could eat out on the patio by candlelight. She set the table and had Brad's martini chilling for him. She put on some jazz...Diana Krall. She was one of Brad's favorite singers. Brad walked in the door and put his arms around her as she was working at the counter. He kissed the back of her neck. She turned around, and he kissed her again. He told her how beautiful she looked. He eased her down onto the floor and grabbed a cushion from a kitchen chair to put under her head. He continued kissing her, unbuttoning her blouse and moving down to her breasts. He slid down her Capri pants and panties, and then made her one very happy woman, in her own kitchen, at five-thirty in the afternoon. "Oh, my God, Brad, that was good!"

"Okay, my love. Whatever it is you're cooking smells delicious, and I'm starved. I'm going to take a shower." He smiled. "It might have to be a cold one. I'll be back down soon."

Beverly put on her pants and pinned her hair back up. She couldn't stop smiling. *How lucky am I?* She put the salmon on the grill. Brad came back down and sipped his martini while he watched Beverly grill the salmon. They talked. He loved the idea about going to Cape May for a beach vacation.

It was a beautiful night. The moon was full, but it was getting cool outside. They went back to the den. Beverly poured herself another glass of wine and got a Scotch for Brad. They had dessert, and then she presented him with the painting. At first, he was speechless. She could tell how much he loved it.

She told him she could come to his office tomorrow to hang it for him. They reminisced about their honeymoon in Paris. Of course, they had to take advantage of an evening to themselves. They went upstairs to bed. Brad made love to her tenderly. He took his time. Sometimes the depth of his passion overwhelmed Beverly to the point of tears. He held her until she fell asleep. That night Beverly had a dream that she and Brad had a baby. It was a little girl. They named her Joy. She was beautiful. She looked just like Erica. The next morning she couldn't get the dream out of her head. It was such a sweet and happy dream, but the next morning, it just left her sad. She knew that there would be no baby.

A few weeks later, Beverly and Brad got a call from Mario. Ruby's last EKG had shown that she was having some episodes of non-sustained ventricular tachycardia. Her cardiology team was concerned. It was possible that Ruby could develop a more malignant arrhythmia, or even have a sudden cardiac death. They wanted to implant a defibrillator as soon as possible. This meant more surgery for Ruby. It wouldn't be as big a procedure as implanting the LVAD. This new development would move Ruby up on the transplant list. Beverly was extremely upset. Brad did his best to explain the situation to her and alleviate some of her fears, but every day he prayed that there would be a heart for Ruby soon. He was worried about Ruby's worsening prognosis. Brad went to early mass the next morning on his way to the hospital. He would often find Helen there. Hopefully their prayers would be answered.

They were wasting no time. Ruby would have the surgery later in the week. It was expected that she would only have to remain in the hospital a few days. Brad reassured Beverly that the defibrillator was a good thing. It was extra insurance and could possibly save Ruby's life. Beverly met up with

Sarah. They could at least be honest with each other and verbalize their fears. They were both worried that something might happen, and Ruby would die before she got her new heart. Beverly and Sarah cried together. They wanted to do all their crying before the day of the surgery.

The surgery went well, without complications. Everyone was relieved. Ruby smiled as they brought her back to the room. "I'm okay," she said. "This was a good thing. The good Lord is watching out for me." The nurse ended up staying on at Mario and Ruby's after all.

Chapter 46

Mark was becoming more depressed. He sensed that he was losing Kyle. He did see the urologist as Dr. Lamb had suggested. The urologist said that he didn't think that Mark's erectile dysfunction was caused by either a cardiovascular problem or an enlarged prostate. His hormone levels and all his other bloodwork were within normal limits. He thought that in Mark's case, the ED was related to decreased libido from the methadone and psychological problems... stress in his marriage, depression, and performance anxiety. He said that if his partner wouldn't agree to couples therapy, he might benefit from seeing a therapist himself. He handed Mark a card. He said that this particular therapist specialized in treating men's anxiety and depression. He was the preferred therapist among his gay patients. He was hesitant to offer Mark a prescription for Viagra because of the hypotensive episode he had experienced before. He shook Mark's hand. "Try the psychotherapy, Mark."

The appointment with the neurosurgeon went somewhat better. Dr. Thomas was also a trained orthopedic surgeon. Kyle went with Mark for the consult. They both liked him. Dr. Thomas studied Mark's most recent MRI and explained the surgery to remove the bones spurs in his back, especially where they were impinging on the nerves to his leg. He was fairly confident that he could restore Mark's gait and hopefully give him some relief from his chronic back pain. He outlined the risks and benefits of the surgery. He described the surgery and recovery. "Of course, there are no guarantees. I think the surgery will improve the quality of your life, but it probably won't relieve your pain entirely." Dr. Thomas went on to explain how they would control his postoperative pain. He would have to be closely monitored because of his problems with opiate addiction.

Mark told him about his father's death after routine hip replacement surgery. "Infection can complicate any surgery. It sounds like your father died from sepsis. There may have been contributing factors. I really can't say for sure, Mark. For your surgery, the overall mortality rate is about 1.8 per 1000 patients. Take some time to think about it. I would be happy to perform your surgery if you decide to go forward with it. Please contact me if you have any further questions."

Mark still felt discouraged. *What's the point in having the surgery if I still might be dealing with chronic pain?* Kyle perceived the information differently. "Mark, he said that he thought the surgery would improve the quality of your life. Isn't that what you want? I want that for you, and I want that for us."

"Kyle, I need some time to think about it." Mark had never told Kyle about his appointment with the urologist. "Kyle, whether I decide to have the surgery or not, I think we need to get some counseling together. I know our marriage is in trouble. Won't you do this for me?"

Kyle's answer was clipped. "I'll think about it." After the appointment, Kyle went to his office. Mark headed for the bakery. They agreed to talk more that night.

Kyle loved Mark, but his love, like his patience, was wearing thin. He was tired of dealing with Mark's problems. He couldn't imagine what benefit would come from counseling. He felt that he had been supportive to Mark. He didn't know what more he could do. He knew that if it weren't for Lucy, he probably would just move on and file for divorce. He couldn't bear to break Lucy's heart. He hoped that Mark would have the surgery, and maybe he could return to his former self. Kyle had been dealing with his frustrations by seeing Austin. They were, indeed, having an affair now. He knew it was wrong, but he couldn't help himself. Mark wasn't much of a husband anymore. Mark had his own secrets.

Mark knew that Kyle was a private person. He didn't think he would agree to the counseling. It wasn't his thing. Kyle had become hard and bitter. He was no longer the easy-going, gentle man whom he had married. Mark was becoming desperate. He hated methadone clinic and his marriage was a mess. He knew how he could make himself feel instantly better. *Heroin... I just need to feel good... even if it's for one day.* He was tempted to find his favorite dealer, and he almost did but knew that it would just complicate his life more. Now in times of weakness, it wasn't Kyle that he would think about; it was Lucy. She was his reason for living. He decided to stop at the bookstore on the way to the bakery instead. He bought a book for Lucy. Then he went to a children's store and bought her a pretty new dress. He knew that she would love it.

Mark heard the bell jingle over the door of the bakery. He looked up from the cake he was working on and saw Melanie standing there. She wanted to order a cake for her husband's birthday. He wrote down her order. "Mark, I want to thank you again for that day at the salon. Could I take you and Lucy out for lunch sometime soon? You don't have to tell her I'm her mother. I just want to see her again." Kyle had been such a prick about Lucy seeing Melanie the last time, he didn't know if he should chance it. Melanie had such a hopeful and kind look on her face. "Okay," he said. They set up a time for the following week. Lucy would be out of school by then. Mark reasoned that if he let Melanie occasionally see Lucy, she wouldn't make trouble for them. If Kyle found out, he would have to explain his reasoning to him. Melanie had given him and Kyle a very precious gift. He felt like it was the right thing to do. *This was their daughter... his and Melanie's. Shouldn't they be the ones to make the decision? These weren't formal visitation rights. It was just lunch, and he would be right there.*

Mark picked Lucy up at day care and met Melanie, as planned. Mark only told Lucy that they were meeting up with a special friend for lunch. Lucy was delighted to see Melanie again. Early on at lunch, of course, most of the conversation was directed to Lucy. When she was finished eating, she wanted to color her placemat so she could give it to Kyle that night. "Oh, Lucy," Mark said, "Daddy will love it." Melanie raised her eyebrows. "I'm Poppy and Kyle is Daddy. It works for us." Mark knew that Melanie was never told the results of the DNA testing.

"Melanie, I heard about the cancer. I'm so sorry." He placed his hand over hers. "Will you be okay?"

"Mark, it's sweet of you to ask after what I put you and Kyle through. I'm cured."

"Will you be able to have children?"

"I have a uterus but would need in vitro fertilization. Both of my ovaries were removed. I would have to use a donor egg."

They both thought that Lucy wasn't paying attention, but as soon as she heard the word *egg*, she said, "Poppy always lets me break the eggs when we're baking together." She took her butter knife and demonstrated how she had to lightly tap the center of the egg to make it crack.

Melanie smiled. "Lucy, you are too precious. I bet Poppy loves to bake with you." Lucy went back to coloring.

Melanie shook her head and spoke quietly. "I have no eggs. I chose not to freeze any eggs before surgery. I didn't want to delay treatment by taking time to plan egg retrieval. It's complicated and I didn't want to take all the hormones. The cancer was stage one. I didn't want to chance it spreading."

Lucy continued coloring and didn't appear to be paying much attention to Mark and Melanie's conversation anymore. When she was finished with her picture, she wanted to talk about the puppy she was hoping to get. Both Mark and Melanie were glad to change the subject and direct attention back to Lucy. Mark knew they shouldn't have even been talking about it at all. Lucy was smart. Hopefully it had gone over her head. He just felt like he needed to know Melanie's situation.

On the way home, he talked to Lucy. "Do you know anyone at school that you like and want to be your friend, but maybe Martina doesn't?"

"Oh, Martina isn't friends with Ella like I am. Sometimes she doesn't like it when I play with her."

"Well, Daddy doesn't want to be friends with Miss Melanie, so maybe we better not tell him we had lunch with her."

"Okay, Poppy. I won't tell, but I think she's nice."

Mark couldn't believe it was the same Melanie he and Kyle and been battling in court. She was more like the Melanie they had chosen to be the mother of their child. Maybe spending that little time with Lucy proved to her that Lucy was happy and that he and Kyle had been good parents to her. That night he planned on telling Kyle that he had decided to have the surgery. He wanted to do it mostly for Lucy. She deserved a father in better physical   condition. He wanted off opiates.

Mark knew what his mother's alcoholism had done to him and Sophie. He didn't want that for Lucy. Mark would start seeing the therapist, too. He needed to take control of his life again. He was ready.

Chapter 47

"Wherever you go, go with all your heart."

-Confusius

Lizzie was starting her radiation treatments. She was doing well. Her father would bring her over from time to time to visit with Haley and Ivy. Spencer had signed the girls up for several sessions of day camp. Day camp would start after the Fourth of July. His dad continued to spend a lot of time with the girls. His relationship with Mary was moving forward, and Spencer was happy for his father. He had finally found that special woman after all these years. Mary didn't have grandchildren of her own, and she adored Bill's granddaughters. Together they helped ease Spencer's childcare problems, but he couldn't depend on his father and Mary forever. He knew he would have to hire a new nanny soon. Summer loomed ahead, and he was trying to figure everything out. He still wasn't seeing Bridget. He missed her. The girls frequently asked if they could get together with Scarlett and her mother. Spencer and Bridget were cordial when they ran into each other at the hospital, but Spencer didn't push it. She still seemed a little frosty.

He wanted to take the girls for a vacation at the end of June before they got busy with camp. It was a good time for him at the hospital, because the new crop of residents wouldn't start until July. His in-laws wanted him and the girls to come to Cape May and spend a few weeks at their beach house. He knew the girls would love it. Ivy was too young to remember spending time at her grandparents' beach house, but Haley remembered and was excited about the plans. He decided to spend a week there with the girls, and then he would come back to Rochester. Harry and Irene wanted the girls to stay a second week. They said that they would be happy to drive them back to Rochester. They wanted to finally see Spencer's new home. Spencer liked the plan. He loved Harry and Irene's place. It was only a few blocks from the beach. He and Anna had spent a lot of time there.

Spencer had played golf a few more times at Brad's country club. He decided to ask Brad to sponsor him for his own membership. He thought he would meet some new people there, and he knew that his father would also like joining him on the golf course. The girls would love going to the pool. They were excited about everything that was planned for the summer. Mary wanted to take the girls shopping for summer clothes. Spencer was grateful for the offer. She would keep all the receipts and Spencer would reimburse her.

Shopping with the girls was something Lizzie had always done in the past. Lizzie wanted to help out with the girls over the summer, after her radiation had been completed. Although her radiation treatments took less than a half hour each day, for now, radiation made her completely exhausted. Lizzie couldn't drive for at least a year because of her seizure disorder. Spencer knew she was frustrated about the driving. For now she had to settle for visits with the girls when someone could bring her over. Maybe, between his father, Mary, and occasionally Lizzie, he could wait until September for a new nanny to start. He still, however, had to find a new nanny. Lizzie being unable to drive just wouldn't work.

Every morning Haley and Ivy asked if they were leaving for vacation today. Spencer showed them pictures of the house and pictures of them at beach when they had been there as a family before Anna had died. Anna held Ivy, who was just a little baby in a sunbonnet. Spencer was making a sand castle with Haley. He told the girls that he had married their mommy in Cape May. Haley asked if he would get married again. He just said, "Maybe, honey." The girls were good on the long drive there. As soon as Spencer took Exit 0 off of the Garden State Parkway and entered Cape May, he couldn't get Anna off his mind. He crossed the bridge and could feel her spirit all over town... places they had walked to, streets they had biked, outdoor cafes where they had dined. He hadn't been back in two years. It was hitting him hard. Cape May would always be their Camelot. He knew that he had to pull it together before they got to Harry and Irene's house. Anna's parents were thrilled to see them.

Irene got the girls unpacked, and Harry made Spencer a drink. The vodka gimlet was Harry's signature Cape May cocktail. It was vodka and sweetened lime juice. He served it up, chilled in a martini glass with a wedge of lime. Spencer and Anna had probably conceived Ivy after an evening of sipping gimlets on the porch. "Thanks, I could use that."

"I imagine you can, son." Harry was such a kind man. They sat on the front porch. Irene put a big bowl of shrimp out. The fresh seafood from the local market was incredible in Cape May. She had some snacks for the girls. They talked. Everyone was much more relaxed than at Christmas. Harry grilled steaks and corn on the cob. It was a pleasant first night. Despite the long ride and Harry's gimlets, Spencer still couldn't sleep. He had too much on his mind.

Spencer got up early every morning to bring his coffee down to the beach and watch the sunrise. He found it peaceful. He would then take a run. It was when he did his best thinking. He was still very much in love with his wife, but he was excited about the new love he had found. He did love Bridget. She was smart and caring and beautiful. He thought about her all the time. He thought she might be the one. He missed her. He wanted his girls to have a mother again. It had been unintentional, but he was sorry he had hurt her.

Still he knew he needed more time. *Will I lose her? Will she wait for me? But she's holding back, too. I just can't figure her out.* His love for Anna had been so uncomplicated. Spencer finally decided that he would know when it was right. He would know when, and if, he should ask Bridget to marry him. At least he was feeling stability in his life. Unfortunately, Lizzie's illness had upset that stability. He had come a long way in the past year, but now he needed to hire a new nanny and figure out things with Bridget. The week in Cape May flew by. The weather was terrific. He got some sun, lots of exercise, spent quality time with his girls, and enjoyed some much-needed relaxation. Spencer hated to go, because he knew he had some important decisions to make when he got back. He was relieved that Irene hadn't asked him too many questions. He was sure the girls would fill her in after he had gone. The night before he left, he had a drink with Harry on the porch after the others and gone to bed. "Son, Irene and I want you to be happy. Anna would want you to be happy. Whatever your future plans may be, we won't stand in your way. We know how much you love the girls and you are an exceptional father. You're a young man. Let yourself live again."

"Thanks, Harry. Whatever the future holds for me, you and Irene and your family, will always be a part of it." Later in bed, he got to thinking. *How could I ever bring Bridget here?*

* * *

Bridget and Scarlett had gone to a few of Kurt's games. Kurt came over one night for dinner. He bought Scarlett a baseball glove. Bridget looked out her kitchen window and watched Kurt teach Scarlett how to catch the ball in her glove. It brought tears to her eyes. He was so patient with her, and she was catching on quickly. She never let her disability get in the way. Bridget knew that he was starting to win Scarlett over. She was succumbing to Kurt's charms. He could be so sweet. Bridget didn't know what to make of it.

Scarlett asked him to read her a book before she went to bed. He read her four books. Bridget could hear him singing a lullaby to her. She let him kiss her good night, but she still called him Kurt.

"That's quite a little girl we have there. You've done a wonderful job with her. She astounds me. I can't believe how she caught on to catching that ball." He kissed Bridget. "Babe, I've got a present for you, too." He took a little box out of his backpack. It was a ring box. He opened it up. "Bridget, will you accept my grandmother's ring? Will you marry me?"

Bridget gasped and put a hand over her mouth. She couldn't believe what was happening. The ring was beautiful. It was a fairly large emerald-cut diamond, in an antique platinum setting. Now she was crying. "Kurt, this is all too soon! I don't know if I can marry you! I can forgive you for the past, but I just don't know if I can forget the past. I don't know if I can ever trust you again. You broke my heart. I can't let you do it again, and I for sure won't let you break Scarlett's heart." She was trembling.

He held her as the tears rolled down her cheeks. "Bridget, I swear to you. I'll never hurt you again. I want to be a good husband and father. I love you. Please take me back. Let us be the family we were meant to be."

"Kurt, I can't possibly give you an answer tonight. I need time to think. Can you please go now?"

"Okay, babe, take all the time you need, as long as your answer is yes." He kissed her and started unbuttoning her blouse.

"No, Kurt, we can't do this tonight. It will just complicate my feelings." She kissed him. "Please go."

He put the ring box down on the coffee table and left. Bridget opened the box and looked at the incredibly gorgeous ring that was obviously a family heirloom. She tried it on, and as fate would have it, the ring fit perfectly. She left it on and went to pour herself a glass of merlot. *I can't believe any of this! I don't know what to do. I know that Spencer will soon ask me to marry him. Marriage to Spencer would be a good, stable life. I love him. But my Kurt's come back, and he's better than ever. He's Scarlett's father, and all the love I once had for him is coming back. I don't really trust him, but I'm not sure if I trust Spencer, either. Maybe he would leave me if I don't measure up to his Anna.* Bridget was on her third glass of wine before she was finally able to close her eyes and go to sleep.

The next morning Bridget woke up and gasped as she looked down at her hand. She was still wearing the ring. She took it off, put it back in the box, and put the box in the drawer of her nightstand. *Oh, my God, what the hell am I going to do now?*

Chapter 48

It was Mario's fortieth birthday.   Ruby wanted to do something to celebrate. His birthday fell on a Sunday. The night before, on Saturday, she and Mario would have a date night and go someplace special for dinner. She wanted to have a barbeque on Sunday to celebrate. He had been so good to her through all her health problems and had been working so hard in school. He was almost done with his nurse anesthetist program. It had been such a crazy year, but they were getting through it. Ruby couldn't believe it was already August. The twins were now mobile. They had just started to crawl. Their prematurity had not set them back at all. It had been such a hot summer, which had been a little hard on her. She didn't tolerate the heat and humidity very well with her heart condition. Thank God their house was air-conditioned. It looked like they were in for a break in the weather. Sunday was forecasted to be seventy-five and sunny. It would be perfect weather for the party. She would even be able to sit outside.

It would be mostly family coming, but Ruby wanted Kyle and Mark to join them, too. They could bring Lucy, and the girls could play. Henry would be in charge of the grill. Sarah would help her with the side dishes. Beverly was anxious to help. She wanted to take care of appetizers. Everyone, especially Mario, loved her crab cakes. Helen insisted on bringing potato salad. Of course, Mark was making the cake. Kyle was bringing the beer. Ruby was looking forward to the party. She had a good feeling about it. The kids were excited. Mario was worried about her overdoing it. It was something he worried about all the time.

It was about four o'clock. The party was in full swing. Henry was putting the final basting on the chicken and ribs. Ruby's and Mario's cell phones rang at the same time. It was someone from the Finger Lakes Donor Recovery Network. Mario was the first to answer. There was a heart for Ruby! Mario grabbed his wife and kissed her. "Oh, baby, if this is the right heart for you, it will be the best birthday present ever." Mario stood up on one of the benches of the picnic table and asked for everyone's attention. "We just got the call! There's a heart for my Ruby." Everyone cheered. There were lots of tears. "The heart will be coming from Buffalo. Ruby's doctors will have to approve it, but they think that it is a good match. Thank you everyone for coming to my party. Please stay and celebrate and keep the good feelings going. Ruby and I have to go now." Mario went inside to grab the bag that been packed for months. Ruby kissed her children and gave as many hugs as time allowed. They were off. Everyone stayed on to party. They felt a power in their togetherness.

Chapter 49

Joshua

Joshua had been a cop for ten years. Crime was always up during the long, hot days of summer, especially in Buffalo. There was more drug activity, domestic violence, and shootings. They were in the middle of a full moon. He knew it might be a crazy day. Joshua's wife turned over and went back to sleep after his alarm went off. He showered and got dressed for his shift. He gently kissed his wife as she peacefully slept. He knew she wanted to sleep until the baby awoke. Joshua looked in on his baby girl... curled up, thumb in her mouth. He was a lucky man. He went through the drive-up window at McDonald's and bought breakfast. It was Sunday. He hoped it would be a quiet day.

His work day had not started off well. The 911 dispatcher sent him to a car wash. The attendant was hysterical and vomiting into a garbage can. There was a car stopped at the exit of the car wash. There was blood and brain matter spattered all over the inside of the windshield. Joshua called for another officer to assist him. When he got there, they were able to push the car out and open the car door. It was quite ugly. The victim had apparently entered the car wash and fired a single shot through his temple midway through the wash cycle. The attendant said he hadn't seen that the man had a gun when he was hosing off the car preparing it for entry. It was noisy during the wash cycle. He hadn't heard the shot. He'd seen that the car was stalled and the owner hadn't put it back in drive to exit. Joshua put on a pair of gloves and reached into the victim's pocket in search of identification. He now wished that he hadn't had that second Egg McMuffin. He called the coroner so that the victim could be officially declared dead, however obvious that it was. He now had the unfortunate task of notifying the next of kin.

He and the other officer went to the address on the victim's license. It was still pretty early. It was only eight o'clock. The victim was fifty-eight. His wife answered the door. Joshua felt so sorry for the poor woman. Her husband had told her that he was leaving for golf, as he did every Sunday morning in good weather. She said that her husband had a history of depression. Once a very successful investment banker, he had been let go. He had been out of work for almost a year now. They were having some financial difficulties and problems in their marriage. He had been drinking more. She hadn't even known that he owned a gun. Their only child was married and lived on her own out of state. The woman sobbed in Joshua's arms. He asked the woman who he could call for her. He called her sister and left after she arrived. Joshua hated suicide calls, especially after the act had been completed. There was nothing you could do. Joshua thought suicide was a misguided, selfish, and cowardly act. It was always devastating for the family. Besides grief, the family had to deal with guilt, thinking there was something they could have done to prevent it. *Thank God, that woman didn't have to see her husband with his brains spattered all over the beautiful leather interior of his Mercedes.* When Joshua had looked through the man's wallet for his identification, he'd seen a photo of a baby girl. He wondered if it was his daughter or maybe his granddaughter. It saddened him, but it also angered him. He thought about his own baby girl.

The rest of the morning was uneventful, just some routine traffic stops. Joshua called his wife to see what her plans were for the day. She said that she was planning on taking the baby for a walk in the park, then lunch at her mother's. "I love

you, Tiffany. Give baby girl a kiss for me. See you tonight."
He was working a twelve-hour shift.

"I love you, too, Josh. Come home to me; be safe." That was
Tiffany's classic line to him. *Come home to me; be safe.*

A domestic violence call came in. Two officers were
dispatched to the scene. The upstairs neighbors had called it
in. They heard a woman screaming and a baby crying in the
downstairs apartment. Joshua was the first to arrive. The
screen door was unlocked. He heard the screaming coming
from the back of the apartment. He could tell the situation
was escalating quickly, and he didn't want to wait for his
backup. The victim was in the kitchen. She held a baby in her
arms. She looked terrified and was screaming hysterically.
There was a glowing crack pipe on the kitchen counter. The
perpetrator was enraged. He was obviously high, on crack
cocaine and maybe alcohol. He held a knife to her throat.
"Give me my baby, bitch!" As soon as he spotted Joshua, he
fled out the back door. He jumped into a car parked on the
street and took off. Thank God, he hadn't grabbed the baby.
Joshua followed him in his squad car. He radioed in a
description of the car and license plate number. As soon as the
perp saw that he was being followed, a high-speed chase
ensued. It went on through several blocks in the city, then
onto the expressway. The driver of a truck failed to yield to
Joshua's car as it merged onto the expressway, despite the
blaring siren and flashing lights. He never moved over to the
left lane. He hit Joshua's car going eighty-five miles per hour,
the impact causing Joshua's car to flip over the guard rail and
down an embankment. An ambulance was dispatched to the
scene, and Joshua was taken to the hospital. The driver of the
truck suffered only minor injuries but was taken into custody.
The perpetrator that Joshua had been chasing had gotten
away.

They were able to stabilize Joshua, but he was on life support. He had serious internal injuries and head trauma. Tiffany arrived at the emergency room with her parents. She was inconsolable. The doctors tried to explain the critical nature of Joshua's head injury. Now that they had his internal bleeding under control, they would do an EEG. He was transferred to the burn/trauma unit.

She was told that it was possible that her husband had irreparable brain damage or, in other words, might be brain-dead. Her father held her as she sobbed uncontrollably. Her mother held the baby, who was crying, too. By now, there were several police officers in the waiting area. Joshua was well liked and highly regarded in the department. He was a good cop. One of the officers told Tiffany's father that the driver of the truck had been texting seconds before the crash occurred. He'd been speeding and failed to yield to an emergency vehicle. He could be charged with aggravated criminally negligent homicide if he had caused the death of a police officer in the course of performing his duty.

It wasn't long before the doctors told Tiffany that, as they'd suspected, Joshua's EEG confirmed that he had suffered brain death. They explained that when there is no longer brain activity, a person has died. Now it was the respirator delivering oxygen that was keeping his heart beating. She and Josh had talked about end of life wishes before. She was his health care proxy. She knew that he had wanted to be an organ donor. She needed to tell this to the medical team caring for Josh.

Tiffany called Josh's mother. His immediate family lived in Buffalo. She wanted to give them the opportunity to say their final good-byes. More police officers had arrived, as well as the news media. Tiffany was trying hard to keep it together, but it was all so overwhelming. A kind, soft-spoken gentleman approached her and asked to speak with her privately. He took her into a small conference room. He said he was a representative from the United Network for Organ Sharing, or ONOS. He apologized for having to speak to her so soon after finding out about her husband's current condition but also explained it was necessary. He went on to explain the organ donation process. They discussed which of Josh's organs she wanted to donate. While they were having this discussion, his fellow officers filed into Josh's room, a few at a time, to say farewell. Josh's mother and sisters arrived. Tiffany's parents tried to console them and filled them in on what was going on. Tiffany was nervous about what his mother would say about the decision to donate Josh's organs. She only said, "That's sounds like something my Josh would want to do. Just let me have some time with him while his precious heart is still beating." Tiffany gave his mother and sisters their time with Joshua.

Tiffany went outside and sat on a bench under a tree, where it was shady and cool. She tried to collect her thoughts. It was all so hard to process. Just last night they'd watched their baby girl take her first steps. They'd made love and talked about the trip they were taking to Italy in October for their tenth wedding anniversary. She'd always feared that someday something would happen to Josh while performing his duties. She'd always thought it would be a gunshot. He would be shot somewhere not protected by his bulletproof vest. She knew inner-city Buffalo could be dangerous. She'd never thought her husband would be killed in a car wreck out on the expressway. She wondered about the call that had taken him there. She dreaded the upcoming days and Josh's funeral. Tiffany went back into the hospital and told the nurse she needed a few minutes alone with her husband, and then she would be ready for the end.

She went in and pulled up a chair close to his bed. She took his hand. It was still warm. She took her other hand and placed it on his heart. She could feel it beating. The monitor said it was beating at seventy-two beats per minute. It was difficult for her to accept the fact that he was dead because his heart was still beating. The doctors had explained that the heart had the ability to beat independently as long as it had oxygen. They needed the respirator to deliver oxygen to Josh's organs to keep them viable for recovery. She wasn't sure that his mother really understood this.

Tiffany looked at her husband. He was a man with a big heart. She couldn't imagine life without him. They had been together since high school. He was like no other boy she had ever known. He was strong and smart, but modest and kind and gentle. After high school graduation, he'd gone to Syracuse University on a basketball scholarship. He was only five feet, seven inches tall, but like in high school, he'd been a fearless point guard. He'd majored in political science and joined the police academy in Buffalo after graduation. He had missed her. Josh had asked Tiffany to marry him right out of college. He'd wanted to work and save enough money to buy a house before they started a family. He'd wanted his wife to be able to stay home with their baby and not have to work. She liked that. Her husband was the man who was first to volunteer to support some community event. He mowed his elderly neighbor's lawn and took his mother to all her doctor's appointments. He knew that he had type O negative blood…the universal donor. He gave blood faithfully every eight weeks. Josh took care of everyone. He was an extraordinary man.

Tiffany knew it was time to let him go. "Good-bye, Josh, you will always be the love of my life." She kissed him one last time and walked out to tell his medical team that she was ready for them to move forward with the surgery to harvest his organs. Her parents took her and the baby to their house. The police officers remained to console one another.

The week following Josh's death was just too much. Tiffany was heartbroken, devastated, and truly overwhelmed. She had to deal with her own shock and grief, care for her baby girl...an active toddler, and plan a funeral. She felt that she had to support Josh's mother and his sisters through their grief, and also comfort his fellow officers. The news media was requesting interviews. Tiffany felt that she needed to project an image of strength and composure for the other wives of police officers who would be watching her. She had to accept the simple fact that she was a widow at the age of thirty-three. She was now a single mother. The rest of her life loomed ahead of her. She couldn't begin to imagine life without her Josh.

The outpouring of support and sympathy from the community gave her comfort. It was a beautiful tribute to her husband. Well over a thousand people came to calling hours. Mounted police stood at the entrance of the funeral home. Players from the Buffalo Bills came to pay their respects. Joshua had gotten to know several players from working with them on community events. Sometimes he had been assigned to Ralph Wilson Stadium on game days.

People lined the streets in respect as the police escorted the hearse carrying Joshua's body through the streets of downtown Buffalo to St. Joseph's Cathedral. The funeral was standing room only. Many watched the funeral on closed-circuit television in the auditorium of another church building.

Tiffany asked the ONOS representative if the recipient of her husband's heart would give permission for her to know a little bit about who received his heart. She didn't want a name or to contact the recipient; she only wanted some basic information. Consent was granted, and she learned that Josh's heart went to the mother of newborn twins whose heart had become weakened and damaged during her pregnancy. She was also told that she was African-American and a nurse. Knowing this gave Tiffany some solace. Maybe someday they would agree to meet.

Chapter 50

September, *the following year*

Beverly wanted to have a big party to celebrate Martina's fifth birthday and also her entrance into kindergarten. It was hard to believe that she was already starting kindergarten. Beverly was planning for a lot of people; it wasn't just a children's birthday party. It was a much bigger celebration. It was a celebration of life. Of course, Martina's besties would be there... Lucy, Scarlett, and Ivy, but there would be neighbors, family, and other friends there as well. Beverly decided it would be a pig roast, and she would have the party catered. That way she would be free to enjoy it, too. She planned on adding some of her own dishes to give the party her personal touch. She rented a bounce house for the kids and also hired a set of clowns, Charlie and Chuckles. Mark made the cake, which was a big yellow school bus. It promised to be a great party. Martina was so excited about the party, and she was captivated by the pig turning on the spit. "I'm going to have to explain all of this to my friends," she giggled. "Why does that piggy have an apple in his mouth?"

Mario and Ruby were there with their kids. Little Mario and Lillie Mae were twenty-one months old now and were crazy little animated toddlers. Ruby had been living with her new heart for a little over a year now, and she seemed to be back to her former self. The transplant surgery had gone smoothly with no complications, partly because the heart was an ideal match for her. Her donor was a man small in stature, making his heart a good size for her. Both donor and recipient were African-American and close in age. They both had type O negative blood, which was the least common type for African-

Americans. Ruby was told that only seven percent of people in the U.S. had type O negative blood. Only four percent of African-Americans had type O negative. The odds hadn't been in her favor. It seemed like a miracle. People of the same ethnic background usually had the best blood compatibility. Geographically, the heart had been close. It only had to come from Buffalo. The transplant team had been excited about the match. She was hoping that someday the donor's family would agree to communicate. She wanted to know more about the man who gave her the gift of life. For now she could only pray for his soul and ask God to watch over his family.

Ruby was back to work, but only part time. That was perfect for her, because it enabled her to spend more time with the twins. Ruby and Mario's financial status had improved, as Mario was now working as a nurse anesthetist. All the surgeons loved working with him and often requested him for their cases. She was very proud of him. Ruby looked around at those at the party today. There were so many people there who had supported her through the challenges of the past year. Yes, she had endured some bad times in her life, but God was surely smiling down on her today. She had her health and the love of so many family and friends.

Kyle, Mark, and Lucy were there. Mark looked great... younger somehow. He did end up having the laminectomy, and it was successful in relieving most of his pain. He was no longer tied to the methadone clinic. He was able to transition to Suboxone, and he was even weaning from that. His doctor thought that they would be able to manage any residual pain with non-narcotic medications. His and Kyle's marriage seemed to be back on track. They had just returned from a second honeymoon in Napa Valley. Kyle had ended his sordid little affair with Austin. It was actually Austin who had ended it. Big surprise... he'd grown tired of being the other man in Kyle's life. He'd realized that Kyle would never ask Mark for a divorce. Austin had found someone else when he had been vacationing in Cape Cod over the summer. His new partner had moved to Rochester and they were living together. Kyle was happy for Austin. He was also happy to have his husband back...the Mark he'd fallen in love with. Mark eventually found out that Kyle had been involved with Austin again. It was then that Kyle had agreed to go to counseling with Mark. They knew that the secrets and deceptions had to stop if their marriage was to be saved. Mark finally confessed to Kyle about meeting up with Melanie. Melanie never pushed it. Sometimes Kyle would join them when they got together. Someday Lucy would probably need to be told about the role Miss Melanie had played in her life. For now, they just let it be.

Melanie only asked to see Lucy from time to time to see how she was doing. She had promised Kyle and Mark and even herself that she would never ask for more. She said that she never regretted her decision to be a surrogate. She had good news of her own. She and her husband were adopting a baby. The baby was soon to be born to a teenaged rape victim. They were thrilled to be getting a newborn. Melanie had met the mother through the court system. It was to be a private adoption. The arrangements had been made.

 Mark had called Beverly to ask if Melanie could come to the party, too. He explained who she was without getting into too much detail. He also told Beverly that Lucy didn't know that Melanie was her biological mother. Pam and Sam were at the party as well. Kyle introduced his mother to Melanie for the first time. A lot had changed since their ugly court case.

Scarlett came to the party holding the hand of her father. Bridget had married Kurt just that summer, a year after they had become engaged. It'd taken him a year, but he had convinced Bridget that he loved her and Scarlett, and he could be a good husband and father. Bridget couldn't deny that she had found her love for Kurt again, and now it was so much more. Scarlett loved having a daddy, and Kurt did everything possible to make up for lost time. Bridget's father was initially furious about Kurt's return to his daughter's life but eventually accepted it when he saw how happy the three of them were together. Bridget had a beautiful church wedding. Her only attendants were her sister, Megan, and Scarlett, who, of course, was her flower girl. Bridget was finally content with her life. She had thought it would be wonderful to be a doctor's wife, but she realized she only wanted to be Kurt's wife. Scarlett was thrilled to meet Kurt's mother and devoured the attention from both of her grandmothers.

Spencer wasn't surprised that Bridget had broken up with him, but he was shocked that she'd gone back to Kurt. That made the breakup so much worse. He couldn't deny his hurt. He had loved her. He licked his wounds and then realized that he wasn't ready to get married again, and also that Bridget probably wasn't the right woman for him. He was able to admit to himself that most of their relationship had been about sex and the connection they'd had as single parents. He had loved her, but not like a man should love a woman to take as his wife. He and Bridget were still friends, but even a year later, their encounters were awkward. Spencer had been seeing someone else for almost a year now. She was with him today at the party. Bridget checked her out.

Carley had been Haley's first grade teacher. Spencer had always thought that she was a warm and genuine woman, also beautiful in a *girl next door* kind of way. She was more Anna than Bridget, but really very different than either of them. He could imagine the little boys in her class having a crush on her. She had always been friendly towards Spencer but never flirtatious. Once Haley was in second grade, he thought it was okay to ask her out. Carley was only a few years younger than Spencer. She was completely single. She had never been married and had no children. Initially she was a little shy and very reserved. His relationship with Carley was developing over time. At first, she was like a fine red wine that needed to open up and breathe. Then, like a good red wine, he found her to be smooth and balanced with a long finish. Their relationship was uncomplicated. He tried to not look too far into the future. It had taken his father twenty years to find the next true love of his life. He did hope that it wouldn't take *him* that long. Spencer's father had taken his new love to Cape May just a few weeks ago and married her. It was a small but lovely ceremony. Spencer served as best man. He brought the girls to the wedding, and his brothers and their families were there as well. He even invited Carley to come along. Taking another woman to Cape May was a big step for him. The girls stayed at their grandparents' house. Spencer and Carley stayed at a hotel. Spencer introduced Carley to Harry and Irene and it was okay. It had been three years now and everyone's pain had eased a bit. Spencer's father kept his home in Philadelphia, and Mary kept her home in Rochester. They split their time between their two homes. They were very happy.

Spencer was able to find just the right nanny to replace Lizzie. She had been working for him a year now. It was a long road back, but Lizzie had made a full recovery and was finally able to complete her master's degree. She had just started her first teaching job. She got together with Spencer and the girls on a regular basis. Beverly and Brad had invited Lizzie to the party. It was, after all, a celebration of life.

Joshua had left Tiffany with a precious gift. Tiffany had found out she was pregnant a few weeks after her husband had died. She had given birth to a son on May twelfth of that year. The pregnancy was totally unexpected. They had just started thinking about another baby. Of course she named the baby Joshua. Tiffany had hope for the future and could once again feel the warmth of the sunshine. She knew that Josh was smiling down on her. Although he was gone from this earth, he lived on in so many ways.

About the author

Michele Piraino attended Alfred University and has a B. S. in Nursing. With a background in pediatrics and obstetrics/gynecology, she currently works as a registered nurse at the University of Rochester Medical Center. Her home is in Pittsford, N. Y. She has three daughters and four grandchildren.

She enjoys her vacation home in Cape May, N. J.

Her writing is a mosaic inspired by her life experiences. Hearts broken is a sequel to her premiere novel, *What We Need To Survive.*

www.michelepiraino.com

Acknowledgements

Mary K. Dougherty, Bootstrap Publishing, my coach and consultant

Amy Knupp, Blue Otter Editing

Monica Piraino and Bryan Ingram, Brand&Butter LLC, cover design

Denise Hartung, author's photo

James R. Woods, MD, who taught me to appreciate the miracle of maternal-fetal medicine

Gordon Whitbeck, MD, for his medical expertise Stacie Whitbeck, his wife, for her undying enthusiasm

My family, friends, and colleagues who encouraged me to keep writing

Made in the USA
Middletown, DE
30 July 2017